TRANSNATIONALISM

Transnationalism

Canada–United States History into the Twenty-first Century

Edited by

MICHAEL D. BEHIELS
AND REGINALD C. STUART

McGill-Queen's University Press
Montreal & Kingston • London • Ithaca

© McGill-Queen's University Press 2010
ISBN 978-0-7735-3762-0 (cloth)
ISBN 978-0-7735-3763-7 (paper)

Legal deposit fourth quarter 2010
Bibliothèque nationale du Québec

Printed in Canada on acid-free paper that is 100% ancient forest free
(100% post-consumer recycled), processed chlorine free

McGill-Queen's University Press acknowledges the support
of the Canada Council for the Arts for our publishing program.
We also acknowledge the financial support of the Government of
Canada through the Canada Book Fund for our publishing activities.

Library and Archives Canada Cataloguing in Publication

Transnationalism: Canada-United States history into the twenty-first
century / edited by Michael D. Behiels and Reginald C. Stuart.

An anthology of papers presented at the Organization for the History
of Canada conference, Spring 2004, Ottawa, Ont.

Includes bibliographical references and index.
ISBN 978-0-7735-3762-0 (bound). – ISBN 978-0-7735-3763-7 (pbk.)

1. Canada – Boundaries – United States – Congresses. 2. United States –
Boundaries – Canada – Congresses. 3. Canada – Relations – United States –
Congresses. 4. United States – Relations – Canada – Congresses.
5. Transnationalism – Congresses. 6. National characteristics – Congresses.
7. National security – Congresses. 8. Indians of North America – Congresses.
I. Behiels, Michael D. (Michael Derek), 1946– II. Stuart, Reginald C.
III. Organization for the History of Canada. Conference (2004: Ottawa, Ont.)

FC249.T73 2010   303.48'271073   C2010-903380-9

This book was typeset by Interscript in 10.5/13 Sabon.

Contents

Acknowledgments

The editors wish to acknowledge all those who contributed in a variety of ways to the writing, the editing, and the final production of *Transnationalism: Canada–United States History into the Twenty-first Century.*

Most importantly, the authors kept faith with us throughout a very lengthy process. They all responded to our entreaties in a timely manner as they provided us with successive drafts with the goal of transforming a series of discrete conference papers into well-honed thematic chapters. Unfortunately, many excellent papers could not be included in the final selection as the editorial process developed through its various stages. The editors would like to thank all the evaluators whose constructive critiques, during two rounds, assisted the authors and the editors in improving the final product. The authors and the editors are very grateful that the Organization for the History of Canada – which organized the Conference on Canada-United States Relations: Do Borders Matter? – agreed to provide a crucial and timely subvention that ensured publication. From that point the editors had assistance from MQUP's editorial staff.

The editors salute the support of MQUP's excellent professional staff, and we offer fulsome praise for Ron Curtis, our expert copyeditor. Finally, the editors would be remiss in our duty if we did not thank our spouses, Linda Behiels and Penni Stuart, who assisted with copyediting, technical advice, and much of the work that transformed the manuscript into a book. A hearty thank you to everyone for bringing this project to fruition. Read and enjoy – and be enlightened on a topic that will be central to Canadian-American relations as both societies move forward together into the twenty-first century.

TRANSNATIONALISM

1

Introduction

Forging a New American Continent; Transnational Theories and Studies

MICHAEL D. BEHIELS AND REGINALD C. STUART

To borrow a felicitous term coined by an American journalist, have scholars of Canada–United States relations contributed to the "imaginative forging" of a new American continent over the past two centuries?[1] Is this new perception of the two neighbours reflected in the analytical approaches to Canadian-American studies? The expression "Canadian-American" has, since the scholarly field emerged in the 1930s, been the default framework for studies of the relationship between Canada and the United States. The accumulated scholarly literature has become extensive and sprawls across time, space, and a welter of academic disciplines. Political scientists, sociologists, demographers, geographers, literary scholars, creative writers, pollsters, and historians have contributed and continue to contribute to the wide range of literature in the field. This growing body of work on Canadian-American affairs is increasingly difficult to master and digest, let alone integrate. For example, this corpus of work has altered in myriad ways our sense of the Canada–United States border. Scholars used to treat the border as a concrete line between two sovereign countries. They now understand that, although the border has separated the countries and their policies, it has had far less impact on cultural values, ideas, ways of life, human relationships, economic enterprises, and even perspectives on international affairs. Several authors in this anthology in effect, if not directly, have adopted a transnational perspective on the complex patterns of the relationship between Canada and the United States and Canadians and Americans.[2]

However, if the North American experience has been transnational, this surely implies convergence. The prevailing demographic and economic asymmetries convince many Canadians that US values and even policies will smother Canada's identity and independence. Many of the authors in this anthology recall George Grant's lament for a Canada that could never be because its leaders failed to resist economic linkage with the United States. Once again, however, location and geography supplied the stage on which the asymmetrical Canadian-American relationship emerged and evolved through time. Pierre Elliot Trudeau's "elephant and mouse" analogy captured that image for modern nationalists and implied circumstances where Canada was a perpetual prey to American moods and interests.[3] At the same time, ideological and partisan metaphors and slogans, however appealing on an emotional level, have obscured the realities of the past and formed roadblocks for understanding. And the question remains: do borders matter?

For example, how has the border shaped Canada–United States external affairs beginning with the conflicts of the transatlantic imperial era and ending with the current "Global War on Terror?" How did the border matter for migration and settlement patterns, for cultural conceptions and expressions, the evolution of economic activity from agrarian-commercial to industrial-technological times? Most recently, the dust and political fallout from September 11, 2001 (9/11) has begun to shape all aspects of North American life, as well as cross-border affairs and relations. At the moment, it appears that 9/11 has resurrected the border's significance as a divider, not to serve Canadian nationalist aspirations but American security fears. Ironically, a wide range of Canadians have resisted Washington's policy of making the border a barrier and resetting the ground rules for how we see Canadian-American affairs. "Do Borders Matter?" was therefore a timely and natural theme for the Organization for the History of Canada's planning group to ask and establish as the central theme for its spring 2004 conference. Over three days at Ottawa's National Conference Center analysts and scholars from a wide range of disciplines presented nearly seventy papers to probe if, and how, the Canada–United States border mattered. This anthology offers the best of those presentations.

The papers probe and explore, but do not offer a consensus. They also suggest that the Canada–United States relationship has been simultaneously bilateral and transnational. Moreover, they provide a variety of insights into specific issues that sorted into five central themes that form the organizational scheme for this book and reflect how innovative this scholarship has become: "First Nations," "Identities and Culture," "Conflict and Cooperation," "Security in North America," and "Future Imperfect." Combined, these themes suggest that borders matter in some ways, but not in others. It depends on what is being discussed and the period under discussion. The variety and depth in recent scholarship of the Canada – United States experience in North America embraces bilateral, binational, and transnational perspectives. This rich and lively scholarship reveals that while the border has mattered in political terms, it has mattered far less in economic, social, and cultural terms. Transnationalism allows us to better perceive and understand less-appreciated dimensions of the shared Canadian and American experience in North America since the late eighteenth century beneath and beside the political relationship.[4]

James T. Shotwell and the "Carnegie" scholars created the field of Canadian-American relations in the 1920s. Their books, published over the next few decades, defined both structural and historical themes that their successors picked up and expanded upon. The Carnegie scholars included historians, political scientists, demographers, journalists, geographers, and economists. They were as concerned with cross-border business and investment, migration patterns, and social mingling as they were with political affairs, whether in a triangular or a bilateral framework.[5] More recently, with the appearance of the Association for Canadian Studies in the United States (ACSUS), its popular scholarly conferences and its periodical, *American Review of Canadian Studies*, have dealt increasingly with Canadian-American themes and issues, as well as Canadian studies. The *Canadian Review of American Studies* embarked upon a similar mission from a Canadian perspective, but failed to flourish. The bibliography on Canadian-American relations and affairs, meanwhile, grew exponentially through the 1960s.

Moreover, after a slow start two of the few general texts on Canadian-American history have gone into several revised editions and US Canadian studies centers (which always deal with Canadian-American affairs) have found a footing in Canada with help from the Canadian-American Fulbright Foundation and other funding sources.[6] Much of the work from these periodicals and centers has contributed to the growing sense that in North America, the United

States and Canada, and Canadians and Americans, have engaged more in a transnational than in a bi-national relationship from the late eighteenth century onward.[7] "Transnational" accepts political sovereignties but argues that cultural, social, economic, and even many political themes transcend borders. So the idea of a greater North America has the same validity as that of a greater Europe, which led to the European Union.

The question of Canadian and American commonalities, similarities, and differences has shaped the research and writing on North American affairs. Sociologist Seymour Martin Lipset, for example, devoted much of his career to Canadian-American studies. He concluded that while Canadians always saw themselves in a comparative context, that was not true of Americans. At the same time, each resembled the other more than they did any other people. In the end, Lipset devised an analogy of two trains with separate historical starting points that steamed toward each other but avoided a collision. They ran instead along parallel tracks that Lipset believed would never meet.[8] For him, borders certainly did matter.

Geographers have also shaped our understanding of whether borders matter. The emergence of historical geography in the 1950s and 1960s offered fresh perspectives on well-known historical events and trends. D.W. Meinig, in particular, understood that people saw landscapes in multiple ways through different "beholding" eyes and usually thought in cultural, social, and economic ways, more than in political ways. Through his own "beholding eye," Meinig reinterpreted the American experience in ways in which the border did not matter, and so saw transnational North American rather than just US patterns.[9] Other historical geographers have taken the same perspective. The Canadian-American Center of the University of Maine at Orono has developed a "Borderlands" project and a series of conferences and publications that developed a transnational sense of the Canadian-American relationship. Overall, the authors have concluded that borders mattered as political boundaries, but not in cultural, social, or economic ways in a transcontinental Canadian-American borderland superimposed over the border from the Atlantic Northeast to the Pacific Northwest.[10]

Sociologists and historians have defined North Americans in other than "national" ways, have borrowed the borderlands concept, and have used historical-cultural evidence to shape parts of North America that ignore political borders. Edward Grabb and James

Curtis, for example, have argued that four societies emerged. The American South had an agrarian and slave-based history, with a racial duality that had more in common with Caribbean societies than other parts of the United States. English Canada and the Northeastern US states comprised a separate social group. French Canada was unique, albeit with historical traces in northern New England. The Great Plains and the Pacific North West constituted two more cultural and social North American regions. Choose a different theme, and a fresh region emerges, for example for Canadian writers who moved to US urban centers such as New York and Chicago from 1890 to form literary communities with Americans and to work in centers with greater opportunities to be published. They often developed North American perspectives and largely eschewed the Protestant British Canadian elite's insistence on the British heritage. Methodist circuit riders in search of converts ignored borders in the early nineteenth century and held camp meetings in western Upper Canada to the consternation of Anglican clerics, but not to the consternation of people who found personal salvation. The same proved true later, in the era of urban revivalism. Fire-and-brimstone American preachers such as D.L. Moody, Sam Jones, and J. Wilbur Chapman came to Toronto and Montreal to help local evangelicals gain converts and cash to keep their causes going. American philanthropic organizations in the early twentieth century saw Canada as a similar, next-door society and as part of their field of activity. The Carnegie and Rockefeller Foundations extended their programs into Canadian intellectual and professional life and helped to develop libraries and universities. The Carnegie Foundation Library at Main and Hastings Streets in Vancouver became a heritage building.[11] Even members of North America's Anglo-elite wrote and spoke of themselves as members of a common family with shared blood. They admired Great Britain's prestige in the era before World War I, and that spirit of transnational values and fellow feeling contributed to an Anglo-American rapprochement that included Canada.[12]

In one sense we already have a large bibliography on North American transnationalism, although the term has not been much used in the analysis of and writing on Canadian-American affairs. Historians of the major borderland regions – the Atlantic Northeast, the St Lawrence and Great Lakes basin, the Great Plains, and the Pacific Northwest – have transnational rather than national outlooks, as studies of the late colonial era in the North Atlantic region show.[13] Our understanding of the transnational commercial and industrial region in western Ontario and Michigan (indeed of the entire Lake Erie and Detroit River littoral) is well developed and became clear well before the Free Trade Agreement of 1988.[14] Moreover, many scholars and writers have interpreted Great Plains history as a transnational experience.[15]

The essays in this anthology grow out of and expand on the historiography of Canadian-American affairs and relations and contribute to our understanding of how a transnational approach helps us to understand the past, present, and future of Canada and the United States in North America. Part 1 offers perspectives on the experience and interaction of First Nations peoples after the formal jurisdictional division of upper North America in the 1783 Treaty of Paris. No one knew for decades where the line diplomats had agreed upon was until survey parties began their work after the War of 1812–15. The frontier regions were mostly unpopulated, and where British provincials and Americans did intermingle, as in the Passamaquoddy Bay region and along the St Lawrence River valley, locals largely intermingled as their interests and relationships dictated. These local patterns remained even when the border had been marked to the Lake of the Woods area by 1845.

The essays in the First Nations section (part 1) explore the impact of these themes on Native-White affairs. Roger Nichols shows (chapter 2) how rare Native-White interaction was in either jurisdiction. Natives in the United States near the border used what the Sioux on the Great Plains referred to as the "Medicine Line" to their advantage, as when they fled US military forces to find sanctuary after Sitting Bull and the Sioux had wiped out George Armstrong Custer's command at the Battle of the Little Big Horn. Nichols notes a reverse example when the Cree fled south from Saskatchewan after the Northwest Rebellion of 1885. The Medicine Line's power stopped the Whites, but not the Natives. He also notes Chief Joseph's belief in the Medicine Line, but Chief Joseph failed to reach it for sanctuary with his Nez Percé. Whichever way they headed, Indians suffered the same cultural, social, and economic hardships and domination under insensitive governments. In that sense, the border made little difference. It did not matter for Indian experience at White hands in North America.[16]

Robin Fisher (chapter 3) explores these themes in the Pacific Northwest of the 1840s, when a massive influx of Whites into the Oregon Territory in the United States contrasted to the slow trickle of British settlers. The Oregon Treaty of 1846 established the border, but the political line mattered little for the Natives or for miners. It was merely a jurisdictional marker. Meanwhile, officials in British North America associated violence to the south with popular sovereignty and had the luxury of time to shape policies, because they had no exploding White population to manage. The relative lack of settlers in British Columbia shaped Indian policy and the divergence of the Indian-White experience in the two jurisdictions. The border did not much matter, Fisher suggests, but he calls for more study to probe how such issues as time, local conditions, and the two political jurisdictions might allow us to compare Indian-White relations in the Pacific Northwest.

The chapters in part 2, on identities and culture, grapple with how transnationalism gives us perspective on the limitations of the border as a barrier to the development of interwoven identities and culture in North America. If cultural distinctions between Canada and the United States blur, Canadian nationalists contend, then surely Canada's national identity will whither. And without a distinct culture from that of the United States, Canada is surely doomed as a sovereign nation. Reginald C. Stuart demurs. He demonstrates (chapter 4) that North American mass entertainment's development was transnational from the outset but did not smother Canadians' evolving sense of political and institutional identity. Definitions of culture as sensibilities or eternal verities aside, mass entertainment (often termed "popular culture") emerged as a facet of modernization when democratic free-market countries moved into the consumer age and treated forms of entertainment as commercial ventures. Proximity, asymmetry, geography, a shared language, and evolving technology drew Canadians (French Canadians, Acadians, and Québécois included) into a North American free market mass entertainment system. Moreover, although British and French Canadian elites insisted that Ottawa must protect and nurture a national "culture" to preserve a national identity, for the mass of Canadians identity included the interrelated streams of ideas and forms in a transnational North American mass entertainment system that evolved from the late nineteenth century onward. So, did the border matter for a Canadian culture? Yes and no, because it depends upon what we are talking about.

Jennifer MacLennan (chapter 5) probes how an anti-American "discourse" has shaped Canadian images of Americans, as well as Canadians sense of national identity. But how has the border shaped Canada's national self-image? She argues that Canadian anti-Americanism is focused on the United States rather than on Americans as a people. The border therefore matters for Canadians as a line between their country and a global superpower, but not for how neighbours interact or think about one another. Furthermore, MacLennan believes that anti-Americanism helps Canadians to define what they are not and therefore reassures them about who and what they are. Finally, she reminds us to maintain a sense of balance and perspective in such views and affirms that the separate identity many Canadians believe in is vital.

Ruth Compton Brouwer (chapter 6) examines Canadian-American links in the overseas missionary work from the late nineteenth century to the Cold War era. Canadians and Americans mingled and intermarried within the Protestant churches' foreign missions, especially in Korea. Canada-United States asymmetry, proximity, and shared church organizations drew Canadian Presbyterians, Methodists, and even Anglicans into working with Americans because Canada lacked the population and resources the United States possessed. As a result, missionaries often shed their national outlooks. Brouwer deftly weaves in how little the border mattered for these missionaries because their common cause transcended national divisions. As a result, these Americans and Canadians lobbied both Ottawa and Washington to intercede after Japan's invasion of Manchuria in 1931. Did the border matter? For missionaries, it was a jurisdictional but not a spiritual or cultural line.

Part 3, on border conflict and cooperation, explores how the border mattered almost above all else when diplomacy and international affairs were involved. Often, however, national differences receded as discussion developed and Ottawa and Washington reached an accord or a modus operandi over shared problems and policies. The border affirmed distinct jurisdictions and sovereignties, but issues and their solutions often proved transnational rather than merely bilateral. Philip Scarpino (chapter 7) notes how the borderline drawn through the Great Lakes has mattered in the Ottawa-Washington relationship, but far less for local authorities that share management of such issues as navigation or pollution. Perhaps upwards of one hundred political organizations claim jurisdiction in these waters, which has meant a highly complex political environment for policy development and application. Scarpino traces these themes through the Boundary Waters Treaty and International Joint Commission (1909) and other working groups in the 1960s and 1970s. The potential for conflict was ever present, not just between Ottawa and Washington but also between Ottawa and Ontario, and Washington and Michigan, Minnesota, Ohio, New York, and Pennsylvania. All must concur that a problem exists before any other steps can be taken. Then comes debate about what to do, and if a consensus emerges, about who will pay and how any agreement will be managed. Borders mattered a good deal, but not as national lines. Scarpino's thorough, detailed, and clear analysis suggests the daunting complexity of transnational forces in the shared and separate histories.

Bruce Muirhead (chapter 8) deals with the political and cross-border conflict that developed from the transnational automobile industry operating in a continental market that emerged in the 1920s. Muirhead examines Canada's economic-nationalist opposition to accelerating trade with the United States in the 1960s and concludes that the nationalists were out of step with their times, which emphasized shared interests within and beyond North America. Ideological arguments for Canada's national economic development failed to take account of transnational realities. Negotiations over the Auto Pact revealed that Canadian and American officials in government and industry had a shared sense of their respective interests at stake. Public and private sector leaders, including industry and union officials and senior politicians from the state and provincial levels, worked toward an agreement that all pledged to live with. The border mattered a great deal for all involved, but once the Auto Pact was in force, the border diminished as a divider for this transnational North American industrial sector.

Tammy Nemeth (chapter 9) traces Ottawa-Washington relations over energy policies from the 1960s to the 1990s. The border mattered very much indeed but so did domestic politics. Nemeth focuses on the uncertainty and discontinuities that partisan and electoral politics generate when governments change in Washington and Ottawa but issues sail on. Private interests wanted to reduce or eliminate the border for the development and marketing of energy in a North American market. Canadian partisanship and political ideology, especially in Pierre Trudeau's National Energy Policy, complicated all negotiations. When a Conservative government took power, however, it negotiated the Canada-US Free Trade Agreement. After that the border's significance faded for what soon became a bi-nationally managed, integrated transnational energy system.

Part 4 of this book is devoted to the omnipresent issue of security, which, after the events of September 11, 2001, has come to trump even trade relations. The studies deal with the strategic and ideological background for the security and defence relationship Ottawa and Washington developed in the twentieth century. Stéphane Roussel (chapter 10) lays the interpretive foundation with his consideration of the North American "democratic peace." He explains in theoretical and empirical terms why the long peace developed, arguably from 1815 on, but certainly after 1867. Although it is problematic to talk about a sovereign "Canada" until 1931, because London retained final authority in foreign policy, Roussel's analysis is persuasive. Canadian politicians understood asymmetry and noted the gradual British withdrawal from North America through the later nineteenth century. They managed and resolved issues when they arose, as John A. Macdonald did during the US Civil War and as Ulysses S. Grant's administration did over the Fenian raids. Roussel's exploration of divergences and shared interests highlights the Canadian-American interdependence that evolved in transnational cultural, social, economic, and even political affairs from the late nineteenth century onward. Neither disagreement nor bruised feelings generated even a contemplation of the use of force to pursue national policy goals in either Ottawa or Washington. When US and British differences over the Venezuela boundary dispute in 1893 produced "war" headlines, for example, policy-makers in both countries drew back at once. Roussel's detailed review of cases where the border seemed to matter and points of contention offers important insight into the pragmatic substance beneath the historical cliché of the "undefended border."

In chapter 11 Galen Roger Perras explores the ever-enigmatic character of William Lyon Mackenzie King and his management of Canada's increasingly complex relations with the United States. Perras argues that after 1932 King's security policy involved cautious discussions with President Franklin Delano Roosevelt. FDR, especially after 1936, became increasingly concerned about North

American cooperation for hemispheric defence that included Atlantic and Pacific waters. This goes beyond what we usually associate with the president's pre-1939 policies. Perras explores discussions between US and Canadian officers and officials that gained urgency after France fell in May of 1940 and Britain seemed to face defeat. Ottawa-Washington talks quickened, and King sought to balance Canadian sovereignty with US protection.

Rachel Lea Heide's chapter (12) explores the Clayton Knight Committee (CKC), established in the United States to recruit Americans into the British Commonwealth Air Training Plan. Isolationists argued that the CKC violated US neutrality laws, but FDR's administration (especially the State Department) and members of Congress protected the organization. Heide reinforces Perras' picture of Mackenzie King's willingness to integrate when necessary, but not necessarily to integrate with Washington. Greg Donaghy (chapter 13) examines Canadian-American security issues in the Cold War era through the lens of intelligence sharing and consultation in the 1950s. He shows that Canada was a *sotto voce* active partner in the US nuclear deterrence. Public statements and commentary contrasted with decision making and policy. Security integration extended beyond the tier of early-warning lines, and even NORAD's integrated continental air defence systems. Canada was even a de facto nuclear power for a time, because it stored atomic weapons at the US Goose Bay base. Donaghy takes readers inside Lester Pearson's relationships with US presidents and officials and explores themes of conflict and cooperation that preoccupied high Washington-Ottawa policy circles in the 1950s. His evidence and analysis reveal a far more equal cross-border political relationship than those critical of Canada's alleged complicity in US foreign and defence policies during the Cold War have allowed.

Part 5 is titled "Future Imperfect" because forecasting evolution in the overall Canadian-American relationship is a perilous venture once generalities and clichés such as convergence and divergence are discarded. The future always proved not what it had been cracked up to be, as Yogi Berra once quipped.

Norman Hillmer (chapter 14) shows us, for example, that O.D. Skelton had a clear-eyed sense of how Canada-United States relations should, and likely would unfold in the 1920s and 1930s. Skelton, an early North American Liberal nationalist, was far more

North American in his outlook than we might expect of a senior policy-maker for a prime minister who cherished the British connection. Yet Skelton clearly and effectively discriminated among the various threads of the relationship. For him and the prime minister, economic interests should dictate neither political nor cultural policies. Nor did Canadian-American social similarities determine Canada's sense of national identity. A visionary Skelton viewed Canada as a North American nation. He understood that he was in advance of most Canadians in this respect, including King, although not those in private groups, among them editors, some academics, and those who worked with American officials and their institutions.

In chapter 15 Stephen J. Randall explores the American approach to Canada since World War II and finds considerable consistency in US policy and practice. He reminds us of the complexity of the US government and the multiple political and policy linkages across the border between Washington and Ottawa. US policy-makers have on the whole assumed that Canadian officials on most occasions view major international issues as they do, but they have also accepted disagreement from time to time. Randall surveys (with one foot in each capital) the evolution of recent US policy and concludes that Washington officials now see Canada as a minor international actor. At the same time, the events of September 11, 2001 and subsequent events have forged a shared outlook on North American security, and Randall predicts that collaboration and integration will continue at both policy and operational levels.

Transnationalism: Canada-United States History into the Twenty-first Century suggests that to determine if "borders matter," we have to decide on what we are talking about, and when and where. Cultural, social, economic, and political themes have interwoven between the two peoples and countries from the late eighteenth century to modern times. Geographic location and asymmetry have made it impossible to separate these North American Siamese twins. The border matters in many ways, but not in many others. We can know when the border matters or does not matter only once we define clearly what aspect or aspects of Canada-United States relations are being analyzed. This is because our simultaneously shared transnational and separate national histories remain in constant flux.

NOTES

1 Anthony DePalma, *Here: A Biography of the New American Continent* (New York : Public Affairs 2001). DePalma emphasizes the divergences as much as the convergences.

2 Examples are John W. Bennett and Seena B. Kohl, *Settling the Canadian-American West, 1890–1915: Pioneer Adaptation and Community Building* (Lincoln: University of Nebraska Press 1995); Sheila McManus, *The Line Which Separates: Race Gender, and the Making of the Alberta-Montana Borderlands* (Lincoln: University of Nebraska Press 2005); John C. Bukowcyk, Nora Faires, David R. Smith, and Randy William Widdis, *Permeable Borders: The Great Lakes Basin as a Transnational Region, 1650–1990* (Calgary and Pittsburgh: University of Calgary and University of Pittsburgh Press 2005); Stephen T. Moore, "Creating a Smuggler's Paradise; or, the Creation of the Canadian-American Northwest as a Transnational Region, 1846–1914," paper presented at the Association for Canadian Studies in the United States (ACSUS) biannual conference, November 2007.

3 George Grant, *Lament for a Nation: The Defeat of Canadian Nationalism* (Toronto: McClelland & Stewart 1965); Philip Resnick, *The European Roots of Canadian Identity* (Peterborough: Broadview Press 2005), and see Stephen Brooks' review, "An Essay for its Times," *American Review of Canadian Studies* 36 (2006): 131–6.

4 See David Thalen, "The Nation and Beyond: Transnational Perspectives on United States History," *Journal of American History* 86 (1999), one essay in a theme issue on transnationalism as a concept for historical interpretation and its implications for United States history.

5 Carl Berger, "Internationalism, Continentalism, and the Writing of History," in Richard Preston, ed., *The Influence of the United States on Canadian Development: Eleven Case Studies* (Durham: Duke University Press 1972), 32–54; see also Reginald C. Stuart, "Continentalism Revisited: Recent Narratives on the History of Canadian-American Relations," *Diplomatic History* 18 (summer 1994): 405–14. The first major study remains John Bartlett Brebner, *North Atlantic Triangle: The Interplay of Canada, the United States, and Great Britain* (New Haven: Yale University Press 1945).

6 Stephen J. Randall and John Herd Thompson, *Canada and the United States: Ambivalent Allies*, 4th ed., rev. (Montreal: McGill-Queen's University Press 2008); J.L. Granatstein and Norman Hillmer, *For Better or For Worse: Canada and the United States into the Twenty-first Century,*

2d ed., rev. (Toronto: Thomson Nelson 2007); see www.acsus.com. Major
centres are at the Universities of Calgary, Montreal, Western Ontario,
and Windsor. For the Canadian Association of American Studies, see
www.umanitoba.ca/outreach/canamstudies.

7 Herbert Eugene Bolton, "The Epic of Greater North America," *American
Historical Review* 38 (1993): 448–74, reprinted in Lewis Hanke, ed.,
*Do the Americas Have a Common History? A Critique of the Bolton
Theory* (New York: Alfred A. Knopf 1964), 67–100. See also Reginald C.
Stuart, *Dispersed Relations: Americans and Canadians in Upper North
America* (Washington, DC, and Baltimore: The Woodrow Wilson and
Johns Hopkins Presses 2008); David M. Thomas and Barbara Boyle
Torrey, eds., *Canada and the United States: Differences that Count*,
3d ed., rev. (Peterborough: Broadview Press 2008).

8 Seymour Martin Lipset, *Continental Divide: Values and Institutions of
the United States and Canada* (Toronto and Washington, DC: C.D. Howe
Institute and National Planning Association 1989).

9 D.W. Meinig, "The Beholding Eye: Ten Versions of the Same Scene,"
in D.W. Meinig and John Brinckhoff Jackson, eds., *The Interpretation
of Ordinary Landscapes: Geographical Essays* (New York: Oxford
University Press 1979), 32–48, and *The Shaping of America: A
Geographical Perspective on 500 Years of History* (New Haven:
Yale University Press 1993–2006): *Atlantic America, 1492–1800*
(1993); *Continental America, 1800–1867* (1993); *Transcontinental
America, 1850–1915* (1999); *Global America, 1915–2000* (2004).
See Reginald C. Stuart, "A Boltonian Revival? D.W. Meinig and
Upper North American History," *American Review of Canadian
Studies*, 36, no. 2 (summer 2006): 329–41, for a retrospective and
historiographical commentary.

10 Randy William Widdis, *With Scarcely a Ripple: Anglo-Canadian
Migration into the United States and Western Canada, 1880–1920*
(Montreal and Kingston: McGill-Queen's University Press 1998). Orono
pamphlets are Lawren McKinsey and Victor Konrad, *Borderland
Reflections: The United States and Canada* (no. 1, 1989); Roger Gibbins,
Canada as a Borderlands Society (no. 2, 1989); Seymour Martin Lipset,
*North American Cultures: Values and Institutions in the United States and
Canada* (no. 3, 1990); Clark Blaise, *The Border as Fiction*, and Russell
Brown, *Borderlands and Borderlines in English Canada: The Written
Border* (no. 4, 1990); Patrick McGreevy, *The Wall of Mirrors: Nationalism
and Perceptions of the Border at Niagara Falls*, and Chris Merritt,
Crossing the Border: The Canada United States Boundary (no. 5, 1991).

See also Robert Leckie, ed., *Borderlands: Essays in Canadian-American Relations* (Toronto: ECW Press 1991).

11 Edward Grabb and James Curtis, *Regions Apart: The Four Societies of Canada and the United States* (Toronto: Oxford University Press 2004); Bruno Ramierez, *Crossing the 49th Parallel: Migration from Canada to the United States, 1900–1930* (Ithaca: Cornell University Press 2001); Nick Mount, *When Canadian Literature Moved to New York* (Toronto: University of Toronto Press 2005); Eric R. Crouse, *Revival in the City: The Impact of American Evangelists in Canada, 1884–1914* (Montreal and Kingston: McGill-Queen's University Press 2005; Jeffrey D. Brison, *Rockefeller, Carnegie, and Canada: American Philanthropy and the Arts and Letters in Canada* (Montreal and Kingston: McGill-Queen's University Press 2005); Marianne P. Fedunkiw, *Rockefeller Foundation Funding and Medical Education in Toronto, Montreal, and Halifax* (Montreal and Kingston: McGill-Queen's University Press 2005).

12 Edward P. Kohn, *This Kindred People: Canadian-American Relations and the Anglo-Saxon Idea, 1895–1903* (Montreal and Kingston: McGill-Queen's University Press 2005).

13 See Elizabeth Mancke, *The Fault Lines of Empire: Political Differentiation in Massachusetts and Nova Scotia, ca 1760–1830* (New York and London: Routledge 2005); Stephen J. Hornsby, *British Atlantic, American Frontier: Spaces of Power in Early Modern British America* (Hanover and London: University Press of New England 2005); Hornsby and John G. Reid, eds., *New England and the Maritime Provinces: Connections and Comparisons* (Montreal and Kingston: McGill-Queen's University Press 2005).

14 Bukowicz et al., *Permeable Border*, and Dimitry Anastakis, *Auto Pact: Creating a Borderless North American Auto Industry, 1960–1971* (Toronto: University of Toronto Press 2005).

15 McManus, *The Line Which Separates*; Warren M. Elofson, *Frontier Cattle Ranching in the Land and Times of Charlie Russell* (Montreal and Kingston: McGill-Queen's University Press 2004); and David G. McCrady, *Living with Strangers: The Nineteenth-Century Sioux and the Canadian-American Borderlands* (Lincoln: University of Nebraska Press 2006).

16 Three recent works confirm this argument and the similarities of native experience regardless of which side of the border they found themselves on. See Tony Rees, *Arc of the Medicine Line: Mapping the World's Longest Undefended Border across the Western Plains* (Lincoln and Vancouver: University of Nebraska Press and Douglas & McIntyre 2007); Andrew R. Grayhill, *Policing the Great Plains: Rangers, Mounties, and*

the North American Frontier, 1875–1910 (Lincoln: University of Nebraska Press 2007); Garrett Wilson, *Frontier Farewell: The 1870s and the End of the Old West* (Regina: University of Regina Press/Canadian Plains Research Centre 2007).

PART ONE

First Nations

2

Do Borders Matter
in Native American History?

An American Perspective

ROGER L. NICHOLS

After a brief glance at North American history since 1800, it might seem easy to conclude that borders made little impact on Native history. At the broadest level of generalization Native peoples' experiences appear depressingly similar. In both the United States and Canada they faced invasion, disease, loss of most of their lands and resources, attempted forced acculturation, and frequent marginalization. To this day some of their descendants live on reservations or reserves where most of the population consists of the undereducated, the unskilled, and the unhealthy. Or, to put it another way, they include the very old, the very young, the very sick, and the very poor. Focusing on those images, in 1969, Vine Deloria, Jr, a Standing Rock Sioux, wrote *Custer Died for Your Sins,* denouncing American actions toward tribal groups. That same year, Harold Cardinal, a Cree from the Sucker Creek Reserve in Alberta, leveled similar charges at the Canadian government in *The Unjust Society.*[1]

Their attacks expose similar attitudes and actions in each country. Yet they tell only a part of the story. A careful analysis of tribal and band experiences in the two societies makes it clear that borders did make a difference for some native people, some of the time, and under some circumstances.[2] This was particularly true in the era between American independence in the 1780s and the establishment of the Confederation of Canada about eighty years later. After that, except for treaty making, the two governments' dealings with native groups came to resemble each other more closely. Contrasts remain, however, down to the present. Throughout the two histories one

can see variations and subtle distinctions in policies and in their local or regional implementation. Some of the variations resulted from
the dissimilar chronologies of national development. Others had to
do with the contrast in physical geographies and the number of
Native and invading peoples in each country.

Often by the end of the eighteenth century Canadians and Americans held divergent ideas about Indians. In the United States many
citizens considered tribal groups as a military and physical threat.
Certainly American pioneers feared Native people as potentially
dangerous, and at times the tribes became just that. At least as important, Indians stood between the land and its resources and the
invading settlers. Such ideas helped shape US citizens' thinking, actions, and demands on their federal government, and they influenced
its policies directly for most of the nineteenth century. In British
North America, the colonial authorities, if not the European settlers
themselves, had another perspective. For them Indians had been important economic partners in the valuable fur trade and had served
as military allies as well. Officials met band leaders in council frequently. At such meetings they offered encouragement to tribes near
the border with the United States and traded presents rather than
threats. When questioned about expenses, they defended their gift-
giving to native leaders as a reasonable cost of maintaining tribal
allies in the face of potential American aggression. Down into
the 1840s they saw First Nations people mostly in positive terms.
What Canadian pioneers thought about their tribal neighbours
was another matter.

Military relations between Euro-Americans and Native Americans
provide one clear example of the border's significance. From George
Washington's first administration in the late 1780s until the 1890
action at Wounded Knee, Indians fought repeatedly against the
United States and its citizens. In the early decades after independence
the federal government considered the tribes almost entirely in military and diplomatic terms. What eventually became the Bureau of
Indian Affairs began its life as an office within the War Department.
It remained there until 1849, when the Interior Department came
into being and the bureaucracy shifted from military to civilian oversight. Nevertheless, the most serious fighting in the West took place
after this development. A similar shift from military to civilian responsibility occurred in Canada at nearly the same time, but without
the repeated military campaigns against the Indians. Even a cursory

glance at any history of the frontier and Western America finds
repeated incidents of violence and warfare between Whites and
Indians. In Canadian history, in contrast, one finds relatively few
examples of such conflict. Miners and road-builders in British
Columbia provoked some violence, and in the Western Interior the
battles with the Plains Cree, which coincided with the 1885 Métis
rebellion, offer another example. When all is said and done, however, settling the Canadian West lacked the repeated military cam-
paigning and Indian wars occurring in the United States.[3]

Because of this sharp distinction, American and Canadian officials
expressed nearly opposite views of their relationships with Native
people. In the United States federal programs came and went, often
working in direct opposition to one another and rarely showing
much success. As a result social reformers called repeatedly for
policy changes and levelled angry charges of incompetence and cor-
ruption at the government. Meanwhile Congress struggled ineffec-
tually to solve the "Indian Problem." At the same time Canadian
leaders liked to contrast these failures south of the border with their
own enlightened actions. As Prime Minister Alexander Mackenzie
reported in 1877, Canadian policy was both inexpensive and "above
all, a humane, just and Christian" way to deal with the native
groups.[4] Like many other Canadians, he took pride in pointing out
that Canadian policy was more effective than that being carried out
in the United States at the time.

Native views about US and Canadian societies provide another
sharp contrast. From the era of American independence on, many
tribal people looked north to Canada for help and shelter. In
the 1780s, when Mohawk leader Joseph Brant complained that
the British had abandoned their tribal allies to the tender mercies
of the Americans, officials in Canada invited him to migrate north
across the border. He led eighteen hundred Iroquoians north and
settled near the present Brantford, Ontario.[5] This began a process of
sporadic Native American migration from the United States north
into Canada that lasted for much of the nineteenth century. In the
years after the War of 1812, Winnebago (Ho Chunk), Sauk, and
Mesquakie people from Illinois and Wisconsin travelled across
Michigan to visit Canadian officials at Malden across from Detroit.
They did this in such large numbers and so often that the route became known as the Great Sauk Trail. During the Removal Era of the
1830s many Potawatomi left their homes in Illinois, Indiana, and

Michigan and fled north into Ontario. Within a decade so many
Native people from the United States had entered Canada that
Canadian authorities launched an investigation. The officials responsible for dealing with tribal people defended their efforts and
reminded the critics that during the War of 1812 British policy had
been to promise sanctuary to Indian allies fleeing from the United
States. They also pointed to an 1841 order that they encourage such
migration.[6] Other examples of northward flight include bands of
Minnesota Sioux in 1862, Lakota leader Sitting Bull's trek in 1877,
and Nez Perce Chief Joseph's abortive flight that same year. Along
the southern border before 1820 groups of Creeks and Seminoles
fled into Spanish Florida. Farther west Kickapoo, Comanche, and
Apache all migrated from the United States into Mexico at one time
or another in the last half of the nineteenth century.[7]

By contrast there were only a few examples of tribal people fleeing
south as refugees from Canada into the United States. During the
Northwest Rebellion of the 1880s some Cree, Blackfoot, and Métis
moved into Montana, where a modest number of these groups remain at the Rocky Boy Reservation. Farther east in North Dakota,
Métis people drifted south across the border to join their Ojibwa
relatives. Their descendants now reside on the Turtle Mountain
Reservation there.[8] Despite these two exceptions, it seems clear that
for much of the nineteenth century US military activity and harmful
policies drove many Indians across the border to Canada, where
they sought better treatment.

Although both countries worked toward the acculturation of
native people, American officials decided to segregate them on a
massive scale as a method to reach that goal. Faced with more than
one million settlers living between the Appalachian Mountains and
the Mississippi Valley by the 1820s, Presidents James Monroe
and Andrew Jackson called for the removal of the Eastern Indians to
the West. In 1830, after a bitter fight in Congress, this policy became
law. During the next fifteen years the government forced dozens of
tribes and tens of thousands of people to leave their ancestral homes
and move beyond the Mississippi. The migration west led to the
disastrous Cherokee Trail of Tears and the dislocation and demoral-
ization of many other native groups. Its results included political
turmoil for years, and the significant 1831 *Cherokee v. Georgia* decision. It also helped bring about the 1832 Black Hawk War in Illinois
and the 1835–42 Seminole War in Florida.[9]

North of the border, Sir Francis Bond Head, the lieutenant-governor of Upper Canada, opted to copy the American Removal scheme. He chose this action because he believed that "whenever and wherever the Two Races come into contact with each other it is sure to prove fatal to the Red Man."[10] To him segregation made sense. He hoped that if the Ojibwa people could be moved north to Manitoulin Island, near the north shore of Lake Huron, they might learn to become farmers. One chief objected that his people already raised their own crops. If the government forced them to those islands, he said, "we could not live, soon we should be extinct as a people."[11] Despite this complaint and the bitter opposition of the Wesleyan Missionary Conference in Upper Canada, Bond Head moved ahead with the program. The missionaries appealed to social reformers such as the Aborigines Protection Society in Britain for help in halting the removal, but without success. By 1836 hundreds of Indians had been pushed onto the island, where they soon established two new settlements. Internal dissension and infertile soil made life there difficult, so the effort failed. While some remained on the island, others left, and whatever acculturation programs the missionaries had begun ended. There is no way to know how the experiment might have worked, because the Canadian rebellions of the late 1830s turned public attention elsewhere. While raising issues similar to those in the United States at the time, Bond Head's efforts moved only a few hundred First Nations people from their homes. South of the border by the 1840s, the Removal Policy had forced tens of thousands of Indians west. Thus it was far easier for Native people to retain their traditional homelands if they lived in Canada than south of the border.

At least in theory, the legal and constitutional positions of Native people in the United States and in Canada stood poles apart. Court rulings in the two countries established opposite relationships between the tribes and the rest of each society. In the United States, the oft-quoted 1831 *Cherokee v. Georgia* decision declared that the tribes were "domestic dependent nations."[12] This defined them as distinct groups, subservient to the federal government and quite apart from the rest of American society. Following this decision, federal actions moved toward isolating and segregating the tribes. Just eight years later, in 1839, Justice James Macaulay of the Court of King's Bench in Upper Canada ruled that Indians there had no claim to any separate identity or nationality. Rather, he stated that First

Nations people were Canadians. They had no other identity as part
of some separate group.[13] Therefore, in theory at least, they had
access to both civil and criminal courts, could sign contracts,
and could appeal for legal help in defending their property. If
implemented, Macaulay's idea would have had far-reaching consequences, but it appears to have had little influence on either legislation or its application.

Issues related to identity came to differentiate people on each side
of the border gradually. At first, in 1846 the *United States v. Rogers*
ruling defined Indians as people with some native blood, living
among a tribe, and recognized as members by others in the group.[14]
Four years later, in 1850 legislators in Canada East (Quebec) used
these same criteria and added being married to a tribal member or
having been adopted by the group to the definition.[15] Up to that
time the native people played a dominant role in the determination
of group membership and identity. However, in 1868 the government of the newly confederated Canada defined native families as
being headed by an Indian male.[16] As a result native women married
to Euro-Canadians lost their Indian status and band membership, at
least as far as the government was concerned. That divided Native
people into several distinct categories. Status or registered individuals had full legal standing for government and band benefits. The
rest – non-status or unregistered people – might have been as fully
native by blood and culture, but they became ineligible for benefits.
Although this gender discrimination in the Indian Act was eventually removed in 1985 thanks to the Charter of Right and Freedoms
and the threat of United Nations sanctions, at the beginning of the
twentieth century it created a dramatic contrast between the two
countries. One study showed that in British Columbia over 90 percent of the mixed race individuals there lived as part of the general
population. By contrast, in Washington State, directly to the south,
virtually all such people were considered to be Indians.[17]

The Métis, or mixed-race descendants of fur trade men and native
women, had a clearly different status in each country. In the late
nineteenth century the Canadian government formally recognized
Aboriginal land rights for Métis people in the Manitoba Act, 1870,
which allocated 1.4 million acres for them. Unfortunately, most of
the land scrip was diverted in various ways to European settlers.[18]
Occasionally in the United States the federal government set aside
small land grants for selected "half-breed" families. In the 1830s it

even made several brief attempts to create "half-breed reservations," but they quickly disappeared.[19] Today in Canada, Métis are recognized in the Canadian Charter of Rights and Freedoms as Aboriginal people, but they have no tribal or band affiliation and therefore no land base. In the United States, unless they choose otherwise, nearly all mixed-race people are tribal members and receive whatever benefits come to the group.

During the last third of the nineteenth century both nations turned to acculturation as a means to solve the "Indian problem." But even while working toward similar goals, occasionally they used almost opposite approaches. In the United States reservations were supposed to be temporary enclaves meant to bring about successful acculturation. Clearly, this policy failed, or took far too long. So both reformers and bureaucrats supported the Dawes Severalty Act, a program meant to break up tribal land holdings. Each family was to receive an allotment – usually 160 acres – on which it could begin a family farm. Of course the land often lacked water, lay in infertile regions, and remained far from potential markets. In addition, this effort to create thousands of new family farms came at a time when tens of thousands of American homesteaders, most with greater capital and experience, had failed in their attempts to build successful farms. Between 1887 and the early 1890s the US government forced most people on the Western reservations to accept allotment regardless of their circumstances or desires. White farmers and ranchers swept onto the former reservations to occupy the now "surplus" land not needed for allotments.[20]

In Canada the government toyed with such a program even earlier. But even with similar objectives, the implementation and results differed. Both the 1869 Enfranchisement Act and the 1876 Indian Act that followed set up machinery for encouraging acculturation and for a gradual breaking down of tribal reserves. Rather than the government stepping in and forcing everyone on a reserve to take land, however, this program usually remained gradual and focused primarily on the more nearly acculturated Eastern bands. To become enfranchised – that is to be admitted to full Canadian citizenship – tribal members had to demonstrate that they could read and write either English or French. They had to show that they were debt-free, and they were asked for written proof of their good moral character. At that point the individual got a location ticket for land on the home reserve and had to undergo a three-year probationary period to prove economic competence. For several decades only a few dozen people bothered going through this system.[21] Thus, at least for a time, the system operated on a voluntary basis, quite unlike the individual allotments forced on Native Americans in the United States. During the twentieth century the border came to make less difference in the policies or their implementation in either country. However, several actions occurred on one side of the border and not the other. The Acknowledgement Program, the first of these, began in 1978 in the United States. It grew out of the earlier workings of the Indian Claims Commission that ended that same year. As a part of the claims process, Native people presented evidence of past federal mistreatment. If they proved their case they received some level of payment and benefits. At that point numerous groups of people claiming to be Indians appeared and tried to present claims to the commission. They got nowhere. When the hearings ended, however, the government put machinery in place to investigate their status. Since 1978 some one hundred or so groups have lined up to present their story of why they should be considered Native people. So far the bureaucrats have worked their way through about thirty of these cases. Half the petitions have failed.[22]

There are many reasons for these failures. Existing tribes oppose adding new groups, because they fear having to share existing federal dollars with them. The government has turned down larger groups, such as the Lumbee in North Carolina and the Houma in Louisiana, at least in part because it hoped to avoid the added costs. To some extent the negative decisions came about because the claimants did not fit national stereotypes of how Indians should look and act. They lacked both horses and tepees and looked like rural poor rather than stereotypical Native people. The Acknowledgement Program continues to operate, but at such a glacial pace that nearly all the concerned parties hope that the process can be streamlined. No such program operates in Canada.

Another contemporary example of an action being taken on only one side of the border is the 1999 establishment of Nunavut as a huge, separate, Inuit-based territory in northeastern Canada. Whatever combination of motivations led to this action, no such thing has happened or is going to happen within the United States. In 1970, when the Nixon administration returned a few dozen acres of land and tiny Blue Lake to the Taos Pueblo in New Mexico as a religious site, it trumpeted its generosity toward native people. But this action did not set in motion any other efforts to return or turn over administrative control of other lands to Native groups. For example, the demands of the Lakota Sioux for the return of the Black Hills in South Dakota got nowhere. The Claims Commission awarded them $15 million for the land and told them to take it or leave it. It was clear that they got the cash, but no land. The tribe continues to insist on the return of their land, so their cash award remains unclaimed.

The border also made a difference in how literature, the popular press, and the entertainment industry depicted Indians during the last 150 years. Canada's less violent and therefore less colorful frontier experiences provided few incidents or individuals for writers to exploit. As a result, practically all of the images produced by dime novelists, Buffalo Bill's Wild West shows, popular literature, motion pictures, and television come from the American, not the Canadian, side of the border. For example, famous nineteenth-century novelists such as Mayne Reid, George Fronval, and Karl May, while depicting Indians as either noble or savage all, placed their characters south of the forty-ninth parallel. In more recent times, even European-made Western films and television programs have located their plots within the United States. From these examples it seems clear that the substantial differences in the two national histories helped to produce the present worldwide stereotypes about Native people in North America.

So, in the last analysis, did the border make a difference? On occasion it had only a modest impact, because broad policy goals and their implementation remained similar in both nations. Yet at the same time the variations in the application or enforcement of policy decisions had numerous and daily impacts on Native people. For that reason, if not others, one must conclude that for some people, at some times, and in some circumstances the border did, indeed, make a difference for people living on opposite sides of the Medicine Line.

NOTES

1 Vine Deloria, Jr, *Custer Died for Your Sins: An Indian Manifesto* (New York: Macmillan 1969); Harold Cardinal, *The Unjust Society: The Tragedy of Canada's Indians* (Edmonton: Hurtig 1969).

2 Unless specifically noted, the basic information for the next several paragraphs of this discussion comes from three sources. For Canada see J. R. Miller, *Skyscrapers Hide the Heavens: A History of Indian White Relations in Canada* (Toronto: University of Toronto Press 1989). For the United States see Francis Paul Prucha, *The Great Father: The United States Government and the Indians*, 2 vols. (Lincoln: University of Nebraska Press 1984). For comparisons between the two nations see Roger L. Nichols, *Indians in the United States and Canada: A Comparative History* (Lincoln: University of Nebraska Press 1998).

3 See Desmond Morton, "Cavalry or Police: Keeping the Peace of Two Adjacent Frontiers, 1870–1900, *Journal of Canadian Studies,* 12:2 (1977), 27, for a comparative calculation of conflicts between the US Army and Native Americans in the United States and between the RCMP and First Nations in Canada.

4 Alexander Mackenzie, 8 Feb 1877, Canada, *Debates of the House of Commons*, 3.

5 George F.G. Stanley, "The First Indian 'Reserves' in Canada," *Revue d'historie de Amerique française* 4 (September 1950):148–210; and Charles M. Johnson, "Joseph Brant, the Grand River Lands and the Northwest Crisis," *Ontario History* 55 (December 1963):267–82.

6 James A. Clifton, *A Place of Refuge for All Time: The Migration of American Potawatomi into Upper Canada, 1835–1845,* Mercury Series (Ottawa: National Museum of Man), 1975, 34–90.

7 For a concise account of the Sioux migration into Canada see Beth Ladow, "Sanctuary: Native Border Crossings and the North American West," *American Review of Canadian Studies* 31 (spring/summer 2001): 25–42. The Kickapoo experience is told in Arrell M. Gibson, *The Kickapoos: Lords of the Middle Border* (Norman: University of Oklahoma Press 1963), 180–253.

8 For some of this movement see David P. Delorme, "History of the Turtle Mountain Band of Chippewa Indians," *North Dakota History* 22 (October 1995):121–34; and Stanley N. Murray, "The Turtle Mountain Chippewa, 1882–1905," *North Dakota History* 51 (January 1984): 14–37.

9 The most thorough treatment of Removal in the United States is Ronald N. Satz, *American Indian Policy in the Jacksonian Era* (Lincoln: University of Nebraska Press 1975). See also Roger L. Nichols, *Black Hawk and the Warrior's Path* (Arlington Heights, IL: Harlan Davidson 1992).

10 Quoted in Duncan C. Scott, "Indian Affairs, 1840–1867," in Adam Shortt and Arthur G. Doughty, eds., *Canada and Its Provinces*, 23 vols. (Toronto: Publishers Association of Canada 1913–17), 5:338.

11 Quoted in Donald B. Smith, *Sacred Feathers: The Reverend Peter Jones (Kahkewaquonaby) and the Mississauga Indians* (Lincoln: University of Oklahoma Press 1987), 162–3.

12 Supreme Court of the United States, 1831, 30 US 1 (5 Peters) 15–20, Lawyers Edition.

13 Scott, "Indian Affairs, 1840–1867," 332, 335, 350.

14 Felix S. Cohen, *Handbook of Federal Indian Law*, new ed. (Albuquerque: University of New Mexico Press 1971), 3.

15 According to D.C. Scott, the two Canadas did not share a common Indian policy until 1857. Scott, "Indian Affairs, 1840–1867," 352.

16 Canada, *Statutes of Canada, 1869,* 31 Vic, c.6, 11–12.

17 Jean Barman, "What a Difference a Border Makes: Aboriginal Racial Intermixture in the Pacific Northwest," *Journal of the West* (July 1999): 14–20.

18 The classic discussion of this issue is Marcel Giraud, *The Métis in the Canadian West,* 2 vols., translated by George Woodcock (Lincoln: University of Nebraska Press 1986), 2:380–5. A more recent treatment of this issue is J.R. Miller, *Skyscrapers Hide the Heavens,* 159–61.

19 Gregory J. Johansen, "To Make Some Provision for Their 'Half Breeds': The Nemaha Half-Breed Reserve, 1830–1866," *Nebraska History,* 67 (spring 1986):8–29, and R. David Edmunds, "'Unacquainted with the Laws of the Civilized World': American Attitudes toward the Métis Communities in the Old Northwest," in Jacqueline Peterson and Jennifer S. H. Brown, eds., *The New Peoples: Being and Becoming Métis in North America* (Lincoln: University of Nebraska Press 1985), 185–93

20 For an excellent recent study of this process, see Bonnie Lynn-Sherow, *Red Earth: Race and Agriculture in Oklahoma Territory* (Lawrence: University Press of Kansas 2004).

21 John S. Milloy, "The Early Indian Acts: Development Strategy and Constitutional Change," in A. L. Getty and Antoine S. Lussier, eds., *As Long as the Sun Shines and Water Flows: A Reader in Canadian Native Studies,* 56–64 (Vancouver: University of British Columbia Press 1983), and John L. Tobias, "Protection, Civilization, Assimilation: An Outline History of Canada's Indian Policy," *Western Canadian Journal of Anthropology* (special issue, 1976): 13–30. Sarah Carter, *Lost Harvests: Prairie Indian Reserve Farmers and Government Policy* (Montreal: McGill-Queen's University Press 1990) is the most thorough analysis of these issues.

22 Roger L. Nichols, "Indians in the Post-Termination Era," *Storia Nordamericana* 5 (1988): 71–87.

3

The Border and First Nations History

A Canadian View

ROBIN FISHER

From the Canadian side, the border with the United States is usually seen as delineating distinctions in the treatment of First Nations people. This has, generally speaking, been both the historians' interpretation of the past and the current view among Canadians. In particular, the settlement of the two Wests is viewed differently both in Canadian historical writing and in the popular mind. Canadian historians see a peaceful and orderly process in Canada leading to a less destructive impact on First Nations cultures. While the Western has faded from the movie screen, many Canadians grew up with the view, nurtured by Hollywood, that the American West was very violent and that the Indians always lost – even if heroically. On this issue, as on others, Canadians think themselves different.[1] Recent, more detailed discussions of the comparative history of dealings with First Nations people have focused on the border area and on Aboriginal groups that straddle the international boundary. Much of this work suggests that that the distinctions between Canada and the United States have been overdrawn. And if we were to look more broadly at the two countries as a whole we might find that the differences are less clear and that the border does not matter so much.

The international boundary line is, of course, an artifact of the colonial polities, and it is important to remember that it bears no relationship to the boundary lines between the traditional Native cultures of North America. Defined linguistically, the divisions between Native groups ran as much north/south as they did east/west, particularly in the Far West, where cultural lines followed the north/

south configurations of geography. Right across the continent Native people freely crossed the line that would later become the border in search of resources or in pursuit of enemies.

During the fur-trading phase of Native and newcomer relations, North America was all of a piece and more in tune with Indigenous cultures. Because colder climates produced better furs, the trade tended to focus farther north, but French fur traders and, later on, the Northwest and Hudson's Bay Companies, traded all across the continent. Inland water routes and relations with the various groups of Native people, rather than the evolving boundary line between what would become Canada and the United States, determined lines of trade. In the Pacific Northwest, for example, the Western headquarters of the Hudson's Bay Company was at Fort Vancouver on the Columbia River and considerably south of the forty-ninth parallel. As it was established, piece-by-piece from sea to sea, the border was a product of the settlement frontier and diplomatic discussion, and it reflected the decline of the fur trade. With the establishment of agriculture to the south, the fur trade retreated north, where it continued, at least for a time, and this development added to the sense that the border mattered because it marked a distinction.

From the Canadian perspective, the border has been important as a divider both in history and in historiography. The two are connected of course, and that connection begins with the fur trade. The fur-trading period was longer in Canadian than in American history, and it is one subject where Canadian historiography has been more sophisticated than that of the United States. There have been vigorous debates in Canada about the fur-trading relationship, the role played by Native people, and the impact of the newcomers on their cultures. Those debates have fallen out largely, though not unanimously, on the Native agency side of the argument. This view sees the trade as a reciprocal relationship in which Native people were to a large extent the agents of their own destiny, and although there was cultural change, it is not seen as necessarily destructive. Canadian historians also tend to believe that the effect of the reciprocity of the fur trade was to perpetuate more cordial relations during the settlement. This view goes back at least to Francis Parkman.[2]

The traditional historiographical picture of the settlement phase is of a relatively peaceful, orderly, government-controlled settlement process in Canada, compared to a violent, chaotic, and uncontrolled frontier in the United States.[3] More recently, Canadian historians have also argued for a continuation of Native agency after the fur trade, although some have observed that this argument can be carried too far. It has been suggested that Native people were not entirely passive during the process of subjugation and that in Western Canada some groups played a significant role in the post-settlement economies.[4] Historians of Western Canada, from George Stanley on, have generally taken the view that, while the processes of settlement and dispossession were not good for Native people, they were not as bad as in the United States. The border thus became important, because it marked a dividing line across the continent, if not between good and evil, at least between better and worse.

To show how this interpretation is developed in more detail, we may take the case of the Pacific Northwest.[5] With the extension of the forty-ninth parallel to the Pacific Ocean by the Oregon Treaty in 1846, so the argument goes, the border separated two rather different colonial cultures that established control over the area by different processes. The region, from Alaska to California and from the Pacific to the Rockies, was home to a great diversity of First Nations cultures and, whatever generalizations historians may make, different individuals and different cultures reacted differently to the coming of settlers. I have maintained, and would still argue, that it is the different colonial cultures, rather than the distinctions between Native cultures, that mostly accounts for the way Native/newcomer relations developed south and north of the border.[6]

Settlers started arriving to the south before the international boundary was established in 1846, and the transition from fur trade to settlement was sharper in the south than it was to the north. Seeing what was coming, the Hudson's Bay Company moved its Western headquarters from Fort Vancouver on the Columbia north to the new Fort Victoria on Vancouver Island in 1843. The company understood that there would be a new order of things in the south with the coming of settlers, and HBC chief factor James Douglas referred to the Oregon agreement as "this monstrous Treaty" when it became clear that the Hudson's Bay Company would lose access to the territory it claimed between the Columbia River and the forty-ninth parallel.[7] Indeed, the representatives of the new settlement frontier could not wait to get the old fur traders out of the area. Many Native people also understood that the new international line reflected an immediate transition from fur trade to settlement in the south. When a group of Cayuse killed Marcus Whitman and members of his party at Waiilatpu in 1847, the attack was partly motivated by the fact that the missionaries had identified closely with the incoming settlers. So people at the time clearly understood that the border would define differences for both Natives and newcomers.

To the north the fur trade continued for a time; to the south the incoming settlers ran ahead of the governments' will and ability to control them. The territorial governments of first Oregon and then Washington Territory were in the hands of the military and had to deal with the clash over land after settlers had occupied choice areas. Officials did not take a consistent approach. First they tried removal of Native people on a grand scale with unsuccessful, but very unsettling, attempts to move coastal peoples into the interior. These removals upset both the groups that were to leave their traditional territory and those that were to have foreign people relocated on their land. Then the governments started negotiating treaties with large and mixed groups of Native people that purported to cover extensive areas of land. These treaty negotiations were usually done in great haste, with little concern for Native interests, and they were accompanied by clear threats about the consequences of not signing. The governor of Washington Territory told Native people who resisted taking treaty that "they [would] walk in blood knee deep" if they did not agree to what was offered to them.[8] However, once Native leaders were convinced to sign treaties, the documents were sent to Washington, DC, where they were not ratified. This lack of good faith left Native people angry, and they turned to violence to try to stem the tide of settlers moving onto their lands. The result was constant warfare on the American side of the border through the 1850s. Hostilities continued into the 1870s as Native groups such as the Nez Perce, who had initially tried to live with the settlers and the treaties on their land in the Wallowa Valley, were eventually driven to violence and then defeat. The US military and the volunteer groups who fought against the Native people were particularly brutal. Even Philip Sheridan, later in his career infamous for his remark about "the only good Indian...," was shocked at the excessive violence in the Pacific Northwest.[9] Probably inevitably, these wars led to the defeat of the Native groups and their final confinement on small, miserable reservations.

North of the border, in the colonies of Vancouver Island and British Columbia, the techniques of dispossession were somewhat

different. There the transition from fur trade to settlement was less
abrupt and former Hudson's Bay Company men managed the early
settlement phase. James Douglas, as governor first of Vancouver
Island and then of British Columbia, was the governing factor. He
clearly and consciously drew on his fur-trading experience when dealing with Native people as the representative of the new order. With
escalating violence south of the border during the 1850s, he also referred to American policy as a negative example. Douglas once observed in a letter to the senior naval officer in British Columbia that
"Nothing would be more disastrous than if we were reduced in the
opinion of the Indians to the level of Americans."[10] His comment was
an early example of a significant difference between the two sides of
the border that persists to the present. Canadian Native policy has
often been defined in relation to what is happening in the United
States, but American Native policy was seldom made with reference
to Canadian examples. This pattern reflects how, more generally,
Canadians compare themselves to Americans, but the opposite does
not happen nearly so much. Certainly James Douglas felt that he must
learn from mistakes made south of the border.

In contrast to the wholesale, often after-the-fact approach in the
Oregon and Washington Territories, the Douglas approach north of
the border was more piecemeal and local and to some extent it ran
ahead of settlement. He began by signing treaties on Vancouver
Island that covered small areas that Europeans wanted to settle.
Because men connected with the Hudson's Bay Company negotiated
these treaties, the First Nations people may have seen them as more
like trade deals than as permanent surrenders of land. After he became governor of the new mainland colony of British Columbia in
1858, which was created by the British government in response to
the Fraser River gold rush, Douglas could no longer use Hudson's
Bay Company resources to pay for treaties. Reserves were therefore
laid out, and, so the government believed, title extinguished without
formal agreements. Douglas did, however, continue the policy of lay-
ing out small reserves for local First Nations groups based on a deliberate effort to divide and rule. Douglas also applied British law
reasonably even-handedly, and within the limits of his power and
resources, he used force to control both Natives and the newcomers
(virtually all of them gold miners) who resorted to violence. He also
tried to contain conflict by taking limited and effective action against
individuals, rather than by mounting wholesale attacks on large

groups. These measures could not eliminate violence altogether during the gold rush and the settlement phase that followed, but at least they kept it under control. There were individual assaults and murders from time to time, and the Chilcotin attack on a road party in Bute Inlet threatened to escalate into something larger in 1864, just after Douglas left office, but there was not constant, warfare as existed south of the border.

In this early phase, the British Columbia frontier was one of top-down control, with ultimate responsibility residing in the Colonial Office in London.[11] This kind of colonial administration usually results in better treatment of Native people than the local autonomy and grassroots law that prevailed south of the border. In British colonies the transition to responsible government and then self-government put more power in the hands of settlers, and in virtually all cases it had an adverse effect on First Nations people. In British Columbia, governors attentive to white settlers' demands retreated from Douglas's policies after 1864. When his successor as governor of British Columbia faced a minor conflict with a Native group, he wrote to the Colonial Office that he might have to follow the American example and have Native people shot on sight. He was essentially told not to be silly.[12] But the comment was a sign that growing local autonomy would not necessarily be a good thing for the First Nations. After Douglas, Joseph Trutch, as chief commissioner of lands and works reduced the size of reserves that had been allocated to Native groups and alloted new reserves that were much smaller. This change in policy, which was the result of an unwillingness to consider First Nations' interests, was imposed through greater levels of coercion. The colonial policy of removal without treaty meant that British Columbia did not deal with Native title to the land and was left with a problem that is largely unresolved to the present day.

By the end of the initial settlement phase, First Nations people, both north and south of the border, had been dispossessed and marginalized. But if the result was generally similar, the process was different, and many Native people understood that at the time. Some Native people from the south crossed the border thinking they would be treated better in Canada. During the conflict of the 1850s, the Yakima leader, Kamaikin, escaped across the border to avoid retribution in Washington Territory. American vigilantes also crossed the border in pursuit of Native people who they believed had broken laws in the United States.[13] Later there were better-known examples of Native leaders and their people who thought that things would be preferable in Canada. Chief Joseph and the Nez Perces just failed to make it across the border in 1877. Sitting Bull crossed the border but did not find a permanent refuge in Canada. Some of the Sioux people, such as the community of Standing Buffalo in the Qu'Appelle Valley, have remained to the present day. There is little evidence of traffic in the other direction, of First Nations (as opposed to Métis) people from Canada seeking sanctuary and establishing communities in the United States.

By the time the westernmost extension of the international boundary was established from the Rockies to the Pacific, there was already a history of different treatment of Native people in the United States and Canada, and the differences also played out in the Pacific Northwest during the settlement phase. As in other parts of the continent, once settlers were established and the Native people pushed aside, there continued to be some distinctions of attitude, policy, and treatment. It is these distinctions that have been emphasized in the literature on Native history on both sides of the border.[14] If a historian may speak to the future, it may also be said that the differences between the two countries will grow greater with the coming demographic trends. There are some provinces of Canada and the Northern Territories where the indigenous populations already form a larger proportion of the whole than anywhere in the United States. In Saskatchewan, for example, there are now predictions that the First Nations population will comprise something like 20 to 25 percent of the whole in the 2020s. There is a similar trend in Manitoba. These relatively large First Nations population levels will have enormous implications for these regions and for Canada, and they may make its future even more different from the United States than is its past.

Yet the emphasis on differences on either side of the border should not lead us to ignore the similarities. Certainly the process of colonization after the establishment of the last stretch of border on the West Coast showed that neither nation-state had learned much from earlier experience with relations with Native people. Just as happened earlier to the east, Native interests were largely ignored in the rush to settle the land and exploit its resources. After the initial process of removal it may well be that the treatment of First Nations people became more similar north and south of the border through the late nineteenth and early twentieth centuries.

And though Canadians like to think that the history of the establishment of their settlement frontier was different, we are left with the
intractable question of why, if the process was so different, the outcomes were in so many ways similar. In very general terms at least
the result of settlement was that First Nations people were removed
from their land, marginalized in the new society, and denied political
power in both Canada and the United States.

With that thought in mind, perhaps we should reconsider the
argument about historical difference. In Native history, as in other
areas of history, there is actually less comparative work on the two
national experiences than one might expect. Comparative history
requires some knowledge of more than one national history and a
willingness to make broad generalizations, neither of which is necessarily encouraged, particularly among graduate students. One
exception is Jill St Germain's book on treaty making and the period that followed on the Canadian prairies and the US plains.
St Germain suggests that there are fewer differences in the treaty-
making process between the two countries than we might think and
that there is little reason for Canada to be self-righteous about its
treatment of Native people. More recently, her preliminary examination of post-treaty policy suggests that there were even fewer differences on either side of the border.[15] Of course if one looks at the
areas immediately adjacent to the border, one might expect to find
more similarities. In particular geographic regions along the forty-
ninth parallel, where there are cultural affinities north and south,
there is a greater likelihood of comparable histories and outcomes.
But in Canada there is also the sense that the border, or at least the
consciousness of it, extends to the whole country. The American fact
is ever-present. But the international dividing line should not lead us
to ignore the differences within Canada in the history of relations
with First Nations people. They are significant, based on both east/
west and north/south regional boundary lines. Indeed, the internal
distinctions within Canada may be as historically significant as those
between it and the United States, making the border a good deal less
important than it is thought to be.

The vertical boundaries between regions within Canada are important, first, because they often bear more relationship to cultural
divisions between First Nations groups. Just as the international
border was imposed by Europeans, distinctions between different
parts within Canada were also created by colonial cultures. In

Western Canada there is, for example, a major distinction between the three Prairie Provinces, where treaties were negotiated with the First Nations people, and British Columbia, where, with a few exceptions, they were not. This distinction was important at the time of settlement and is still important today. The numbered treaties on the Prairies represented a moment when the First Nations People were recognized as the owners of the land, even if only to then extinguish their title, and treaties have provided a legal baseline for current litigation over Aboriginal rights. In British Columbia, Native title was not extinguished in any formal way, and therefore ownership of the land remains unfinished business to the present day.[16] Many First Nations in the westernmost province are engaged in negotiations with the federal and provincial governments to try to settle that outstanding issue at the treaty table, but it is proving a long and difficult process. Such regional differences within Canada from east to west are perhaps obvious. Less obvious, however, or at least less apparent from the literature, are the distinctions from south to north.

Discussion of the importance of the international border inevitably focuses on the forty-ninth parallel, but are the two countries more similar or more different farther away from the border – farther north in the case of Canada or farther south in the case of the United States? In the case of the far north there is, first of all, another border to consider – that between Alaska and the Yukon. There has been even less comparative history written with that border in mind, but because of the general similarities of the Native cultures, because they share a similar geography and environment, and because both are remote from the national centres of power, there were fewer differences between the Yukon and Alaska at the 141st line of longitude than between Canada and the United States at the 49th line of latitude. Though in Canada there is, once again, the argument that the Yukon gold mining frontier was more peaceful and orderly than the rush for gold in Alaska, the impact of both on Native people was little different. More recently, in both that US state and the adjacent Canadian territory, native people have had more leverage over governments than groups in the south, because they form a larger proportion of the population in a sparsely settled area.

In Canada, historians of the North tell us that the Northern experience is very different from that of the South, and this is arguably particularly so in the area of Native and newcomer relations. The

non-Native population of Canada tends to be concentrated in the
South around the border, whereas the Native population is both
greater and a much greater percentage of the whole in the North.
There the fur trade also lasted for a longer period and is not a distant memory. Even after the fur trade the tenor of relations between
Native and newcomer was different, as cultural lines were less
rigidly drawn and there was more intermarriage and more shared
economic activity. Native people retained more of their traditional
culture and lifestyle farther north and, perhaps as a result, have
often been at the forefront of asserting Native politics and asserting
Native rights.

The Nisga'a, who live along the Nass River in northwestern British
Columbia, have maintained much of their culture because of the
strength of their traditions, but also because they are somewhat
removed from major centres of European population. From dele-
gations to the provincial government in the late nineteenth century
through to the landmark *Calder* case that went to the Supreme
Court of Canada in the early 1970s, they have always been at the
forefront of efforts to redress matters of Native rights. Now, after
twenty years of negotiating, they have recently become the first
group to negotiate a modern treaty in British Columbia. The Nisga'a
Treaty was initialed just before, and signed just after, the turn of the
twenty-first century. In the context of British Columbia's history of
dealing with First Nations people over land rights, this treaty is an
unprecedented achievement, which does nothing less than turn the
history of the province on its head. And it is no accident that it
has happened in the North. Other accommodations between First
Nations people and Canada, such as the James Bay Treaty and the
recent creation of Nunavut out of the eastern section of the North
West Territory, have also occurred in the North. In British Columbia
treaties will be easier to negotiate in more remote northern areas,
where there is not such a large population and there is still land and
resources to share, than they will be around the urban centers to the
south. To the extent that the North leads the way on First Nations
issues, there could be two effects on comparisons between Canada
and the United States. If these developments are largely confined to
the North and given that Canada has more remote regions than the
United States, they could increase disparities within Canada and
diminish the importance of the international border as a dividing
line. On the other hand, if the experience in the North provides an

example that is followed in the South, then Canada as a whole may become more different from the United States.

Though there are few detailed comparisons between Canada and the United States in the literature on Native history, Canadians, both in the past and in the present, tend to be fixated on the border. They have, moreover, both then and now, tended to assume that the border delineates distinctions: that Canada has been and remains different in the way it treats its Native people. The historical literature has, until recently, certainly provided a good deal of support for this general impression. But perhaps that fixation is also a distraction. Now and in the future there may be reasons to believe that the international border is less significant than we have thought. Some historical research points us to the conclusion that, if we look at areas around the border, we will see as many similarities as differences. At the same time, distinctions within Canada may be becoming as significant as, or more significant than, those between Canada and the United States. We should also bear in mind that First Nations political and legal issues have more and more become international questions and that growing connections across the fourth world will diminish national distinctions. The border has been and continues to be important, but not as important as we think.

NOTES

1 Michael Adams, *Fire and Ice: The United States, Canada and the Myth of Converging Values* (Toronto: Penguin Canada 2003).

2 Parkman to Whiting, 6 March 1845, in Wilbur R. Jacobs, ed., *Letters of Francis Parkman* (Norman: Oklahoma University Press 1960); Francis Parkman, *The Conspiracy of Pontiac* (Boston: Little, Brown and Company 1870).

3 This view has a long historiographical tradition on both sides of the border. See, for example, George F.G. Stanley, "Western Canada and the Frontier Thesis," *Canadian Historical Association Report* (1940), 111; Paul F. Sharp, "Three Frontiers: Some Comparative Studies of Canadian, American and Australian Settlement," *Pacific Historical Review* 24 (1955): 373.

4 Robin Brownlie and Mary-Ellen Kelm, "Desperately Seeking Absolution: Native Agency as Colonialist Alibi?" *Canadian Historical Review* 75, 4 (December 1994): 543–56; John Tobias, "Canada's Subjugation of the Plains Cree," *Canadian Historical Review* 64 , 4 (December 1983): 519–48; Ralph Knight, *Indians at Work: An Informal History of Native*

Indian Labour in British Columbia 1858–1930 (Vancouver: New Star Books 1978).

5 The following section is based on Robin Fisher, "The Northwest from the Beginning of Trade with European to the 1880s," in Bruce G. Trigger and Wilcomb E. Washburn, eds., *The Cambridge History of the Native Peoples of North America*, vol. 1, *North America*, part 2 (Cambridge: Cambridge University Press 1996), 148–62.

6 Robin Fisher, "Indian Warfare and Two Frontiers: A Comparison of British Columbia and Washington Territory during the Early Years of Settlement," *Pacific Historical Review*, 50 (February 1981), 31–51.

7 James Douglas and John Work to Governor and Committee, 7 December 1846, Inward Correspondence from HBC Posts, Victoria, 1845–69, A-11/72, Hudson's Bay Company Archives, Winnipeg.

8 Quoted in Robert H. Ruby and John H. Brown, *The Cayuse Indians: Imperial Tribesmen of Old Oregon* (Norman: University of Oklahoma Press 1972), 203

9 P.H. Sheridan, *Personal Memoirs of P.H. Sheridan, General United States Army* (New York 1888), vol.1, 88.

10 Douglas to Robert L. Baynes, 17 December 1859, CO. 305/6, microfilm, University of British Columbia Library.

11 Barry Gough, "The Character of the British Columbia Frontier," *BC Studies* 32 (winter 1976–77): 28–40.

12 Seymour to Edward Cardwell, 4 October 1864, Cardwell to Seymour, 1 December 1864, CO. 60/19, microfilm, University of British Columbia Library.

13 Keith Thor Carlson, "The Lynching of Louie Sam," *BC Studies* 109 (spring 1996): 63–78.

14 See, for example, Roger L. Nichols, *Indians in the United States and Canada: A Comparative History* (Lincoln and London: University of Nebraska Press 1998); Jill St Germain, *Indian Treaty-Making Policy in the United States and Canada, 1867–1877* (Toronto: University of Toronto Press 2001), xvii–xxii.

15 St Germain, *Indian Treaty Making*, an unpublished paper given at Comparative Native History Conference, University of Saskatchewan, May 2003.

16 For a more detailed discussion of the implications of this difference see Robin Fisher, "With or without Treaty: Indian Land Claims in Western Canada," in William Renwick, ed., *Sovereignty and Indigenous Rights: The Treaty of Waitangi in International Contexts* (Wellington: Victoria University Press 1991), 49–66.

PART TWO

Identities and Culture

4

Borders and Brows

Mass Culture and National Identity in North America since 1900

REGINALD C. STUART

Will converging North American culture cause national identities to converge? Americans dismiss this question, but in Canada borders, as barriers to guarantee divergence or as conduits to channel convergence, remain powerful images. These dichotomies, however, confuse more than clarify. Fears of "Americanization" have been a staple of cultural policy-making in Canada since the 1920s. But such rhetoric has as often masked self-interest as it has explained an ostensibly cultural issue. The concept of "Americanization" rests upon delusions about what culture is and how it differs (or does not) between Canada and the United States. Walter Lippman, the US progressive journalist, argued that culture was "what people are interested in, their thoughts, their models, the books they read and the speeches they hear, their table talk, gossip, controversies, historical sense and scientific training, the values they appreciate, the quality of life they admire. All communities have a culture. It is the climate of their civilization."[1] American cultural commentators in the 1930s and 1940s playfully classified people into "brows": high, middle, and low. Highbrows read Voltaire and attended opera, middlebrows read Raymond Chandler and took in Broadway musicals, and lowbrows read comic books and leered at burlesque shows. The "brow" school identified taste as the principal criterion of a person's cultural orientation. Although Canadians seem to have sorted out into very similar categories, these divisions have rarely been applied in Canada.

This is but one example of how Canadians and Americans shout past each other whenever discussions occur about culture. The archetypal case is the Canadian decision in the 1920s to subsidize magazines and to protect them from their US competitors.[2] Americans were mystified as to why their neighbours would think this necessary. The *New York Times* assured Canadians editorially that "they are not in danger of cultural extinction."[3] Myriad Canadian domestic debates over culture followed, most with ramifications for bilateral relations with the United States, such as whether the state or free-market forces should govern radio broadcasting, movie making, or television production. Canadian policymakers came to believe that any cultural expression or product was essential to national identity and therefore non-negotiable. Americans replied that cultural expressions were commodities, as negotiable as any other. Canadian promotional and protectionist cultural policies won fervent support from aspiring or actual high-culture practitioners. Most Canadians, however, were far removed from such highbrow considerations.

The real distinction lay not between "Canadian" and "American" culture but between elite and mass tastes. Like Americans, Canadians have sought entertainment and information that diverted them from workaday lives and found it within a complex North American mass entertainment system. This process had little impact on the development of national identities in either country, because the mass of people in both separated their sense of self and their allegiance from their entertainment. Highbrows, the elites, remained highbrows on both sides of the border. Localized diversions were continentalized and transformed into middlebrow and lowbrow mass entertainment.

The foundations for North American mass entertainment lie in a shared English and European heritage, mostly similar ethnic groups, a mostly common working language, a polyglot musical and literary heritage, and shared ideas about what was funny, heroic, or villainous. Since the nineteenth century, a North American infrastructure of waterways, railways, roadways, airways, and airwaves connected concentrated urban-industrial populations with sufficient incomes to indulge leisure activities. Circuses were the opening acts in this largely a-national North American mass-entertainment system. In 1846, New York's Mammoth Circus entrained animals, equestrians, clowns, acrobats and a Negro band for Toronto. After huge crowds watched Phineas T. Barnum's circus in Brooklyn in 1873, Barnum loaded his show on a special train to tour New England and eastern Canada. A hundred such troupes toured North America by 1903.[4] During this period, bureaucratic revolutions reshaped government and show business in both countries.[5] In 1894 the Vaudeville Managers of America, organized in Albany, New York, booked acrobatic, animal, magic, comedy, and song and dance acts into theaters, opera houses, and music halls in cities large and small in the northeastern Canadian-American borderlands.

Copycat agencies soon followed. New York City became the eastern center, and Chicago served the mid-west and western Ontario as North America's first mass-entertainment system evolved into what became known as Vaudeville.[6] Broad cross-sections of early-twentieth-century urban society – working and middle class, boys and girls, men and women – sought laughter and enjoyment in Vaudeville, not in highbrow enlightenment such as the Chautauqua circuits or "legitimate" theatre offered. Elites in both the United States and Canada sneered at vaudevillians, but missed the significance of what had taken place: the birth of North American mass entertainment. Audiences saw essentially the same act no matter where they were. Vaudeville performers knit together geographically dispersed audiences in a shared experience. Movies later did the same thing, and radio and television went one step further to reach mass audiences simultaneously. From its inception, this was a cross-border entertainment system. American Vaudevillians referred to Canada as the "Death Trail" because of the cold, but they found responsive audiences. Canadian favorites included Fred Allen, Jimmy Durante, and Groucho Marx. Bob Hope played Winnipeg, as well as Toronto, in a career that illustrated the continuity of the mass entertainment genres through the twentieth century.[7]

After the wind-up phonograph appeared in about 1910, records allowed middle-class families to enjoy and share entertainment in their parlors. In the 1920s radio and "talkie" movies brought Broadway bands, singers, instrumentalists, and orchestras to mass North American audiences.[8] But to interpret this as the "Americanization" of Canada is to follow a false trail. Mass audiences made judgments based on taste, instead of national identity, and although mass entertainment originated in the United States, the result was less Americanization than North Americanization.[9] Canadian performers took full part from the beginning. Eva Tanguey, from

Marbleton, Quebec, wowed New York audiences with a risqué stage act and made a fortune. Norma Shearer of Montreal won the third Best Actress Oscar in 1930, and Marie Dressler of Cobourg, Ontario, won the award the following year.[10] Toronto's Gladys Smith, renamed Mary Pickford, was dubbed "America's Sweetheart" by a studio publicist. Mack Sennett (who invented the Keystone Cops), Jack Warner, and Louis B. Mayer joined Pickford and a host of lesser-known actors, directors, technicians, and production people among Hollywood's founding generation. Canadians Norma Shearer, Raymond Massey, Walter Huston, and Deanna Durbin even reached stardom and acquired North American followings. In another example, when news of Rudolph Valentino's death spread, women in Vancouver as well as Los Angeles wept. And undershirt sales in both countries slumped when Clark Gable bared his chest in *It Happened One Night*.[11]

Hollywood treated Canada and the United States as single market and used the Motion Picture Distributors and Exhibitors of Canada to ensure that its films ran on over 90 percent of all movie screens in Canada by 1930. While Canadians flocked to the movies, newspaper editors bemoaned how Canada's youth, "rather than drinking in Canadian and British ideals, is imbibing American ideals." Canadian groups such as the Imperial Order of the Daughters of the Empire urged a quota policy to ensure that British films were shown, but legislation to this end failed in the Ontario (1931), British Columbia (1932), and Alberta (1933) legislatures. The MPDE lobbied local politicians and noted that Canadians had already voted on this issue at box offices by seeing movies from Hollywood.[12] No quota laws appeared, and the National Film Act of 1933 suggested that Ottawa policy-makers understood Canada had become an integral part of this North American mass-entertainment market. That was in large measure why the National Film Board trained filmmakers to create documentaries and leave the feature films to Hollywood.[13]

Ottawa's approach to the film issue reflected the pattern established in radio broadcasting. In 1924 the US Department of Commerce had identified 101 frequencies and set aside 6 of them for Canada. A year later, over 90 Canadian and hundreds of US stations reached the widest mass audience in history with information and entertainment. Canadian stations remained low-powered, so at night, when atmospheric conditions for transmission improved, Canadians drew 80 percent of what they heard from US broadcasters.

In 1927 Ottawa cobbled together a temporary network of private
stations to air sixtieth anniversary celebrations of Confederation
from coast to coast. At the same time, many of those stations were
already part of the Columbia Broadcasting System and imported the
American programs their local listeners demanded.[14]

This US "invasion" of the airwaves had seemed to Canada's nationalist highbrow policy-makers an electronic version of Manifest
Destiny. As a defense, they promoted a version of the British
Broadcasting Corporation under government control that the John
Aird Royal Commission of 1929 had recommended. The commission declared US programs to be empty of the high moral tone and
public purpose essential to build a Canadian nation. It was the state
or the United States. The Canadian Radio Broadcasting Corporation, set up in 1933, was intended as a cultural bulwark. But the
nationalists were helpless because improved receivers allowed most
Canadians to continue to tune in US programs. So when the
US Federal Communications Act of 1934 set up the Federal Communications Commission to regulate the free market radio system,
its policies and activities applied de facto to a North American
mass market.[15]

Canadian performers fit into North American radio as they had
vaudeville and the movies. Orchestra leader Guy Lombardo and his
sidemen emigrated from London, Ontario, to Cleveland, then to
Chicago and New York City as Lombardo's popularity grew.
Lombardo and his Royal Canadians provided North America's New
Year's Eve music for decades from the Waldorf Astoria Hotel. *Amos
'n Andy* was the most popular show in both countries in the 1930s.[16]
While the CBC captured the ears and hearts of Canada's professional
and intellectual classes, the mass of ordinary people demanded a
wide range of programming and entertainment. North American listeners tuned in to Cecil B. DeMille's *Radio Theater*, or *Inner
Sanctum*, which opened with Canadian actor Raymond Massey's
eerie laugh. Mass North American audiences followed the trials of
soap opera characters like *Ma Perkins* and *Big Sister*. Because the
movies and radio had drawn old vaudeville audiences, vaudevillians
made the transition to sound stages in Hollywood and broadcast
studios for radio. Bob Hope's *Pepsodent Show* is the longest-running
example. Live musical performances were recorded for sales and
broadcast and reworked into movies. All musical genres – classical,
jazz, crooning, bands, orchestral, later folk, rock and roll, and

innovative forms – reached succeeding generations of mass North American audiences through recordings and the mass media.[17]

After 1945, Canadian and American children grew up with the same radio programs, movies, and then television programs as their window on the world beyond their homes. Many favorites, such as the Lone Ranger and his sidekick Tonto or Sergeant Preston of the Yukon, appeared simultaneously in comic books, novels, radio, and television. Domestic comedies such as Ozzie and Harriet and Fibber McGee and his cascading closet ran for years. Youngsters in Vancouver or Seattle, Winnipeg or Minneapolis, Boston or Halifax joined a dispersed, invisible cross-border mass audience. They gave no thought to Canadian or American content, nor did their parents when they spent Saturday at matinees where Republic serials presented Flash Gordon and Federal Bureau of Investigation agents (Mounties made rare appearances), along with Warner Brothers or Walt Disney cartoons. The CBC's valiant attempts at entertainment programming failed miserably to reach a wide audience. Canadian performers, however, used the CBC as a platform to move beyond local and even national venues. Paul Anka, Giselle Mackenzie, and Robert Goulet (an expatriate American) contributed to the cliché that Canadians saw their own as successes only once they had made a name south of the border. Many of these Canadians played on the vaudeville-style variety programs of US television such as Ed Sullivan's Toast of the Town and Sid Caesar's Show of Shows.[18]

By 1948, 100 US television stations broadcast national news, public affairs, and entertainment to over 120 million North American viewers. Canadian television broadcasting under the aegis of the CBC began in 1952 in Montreal, and Canadians had purchased seven million sets by 1953. By mid-decade the CBC broadcast TV signals from Halifax to Vancouver, but only for few hours each day. So Canadians picked up nearby US stations, as they had with radio. Ottawa regulators allowed private stations to carry US programs, provided they took ten and a half hours of content weekly from the CBC. By 1960, 94 percent of Canadians owned a television. Canadian television thus evolved within a North American system focused on mass entertainment, because even nationalist politicians knew that any effort to bar US signals would be both futile and politically dangerous.[19]

CBC TV supplied news and public affairs, but other than Hockey Night in Canada, most mass-audience entertainment came from the

United States, just as it had with radio. Popular US programs had long runs: *Gunsmoke* for two decades, *Ed Sullivan* for twenty-three years, *Bonanza* (with Canadian Lorne Greene in a lead role) for fourteen years. Family programs such as *Father Knows Best*, *The Donna Reed Show*, and *Ozzie and Harriet* reflected the suburbanization of both countries and created a North American stereotype of the family that both Canadians and Americans accepted as a representation of their own lives. Walt Disney created a multi-mass-entertainment operation through TV programs, related commercial products, and tourism, with Disneyland in Anaheim, California, and Disney World in Orlando, Florida.[20]

Radio regained its place as a mass-entertainment medium when Alan Freed became the first of thousands of North American disc jockeys who promoted rock 'n roll to teenagers. Small transistor radios allowed teenagers to hear the latest hits anywhere and at any time as rock 'n rollers commuted among the various media. Elvis Presley performed on tour, on television, on radio, on records, and in movie roles created specifically for him.[21] However much highbrow critics in both countries bemoaned the entire process, North American mass entertainment for teenagers followed the pattern that vaudeville had established, albeit more quickly and on a vastly grander (and more profitable) scale.

Young people from both countries purchased the same records, saw the same movies, and identified with or yearned for the characters that James Dean played in *Rebel Without a Cause* and *East of Eden*. Wannabe Deans on both sides of the border took their dates to see *The Blob*, *Blackboard Jungle*, *Crime in the Streets*, or Sandra Dee's "Gidget" films.[22] Canada's cultural policies of the 1950s and 1960s made little or no difference to what people listened to or watched. Canadian actors and moviemakers honed their skills in local production companies but sought advancement, steady work, or stardom in New York and Hollywood. Aspiring country music performers in Ontario and Nova Scotia chose Nashville, not Toronto. Feature filmmakers such as Norman Jewison, David Cronenberg, and Ivan Reitman migrated to Hollywood, as many had before them.[23]

The border made very little difference for entertainment genres such as comedy. As was the case with the vaudeville acts, Americans and Canadians consistently found the same things funny. Vaudeville comedians such as the Marx Brothers expanded and extended their audiences through radio and movies. Jackie Gleason, George Burns,

and Gracie Allen worked in all media. Canadians Johnny Wayne and
Frank Shuster simultaneously became Canadian icons on CBC television and amused a mass North American audience through their
sixty-seven appearances on the Ed Sullivan show.[24] Canadian comedians slid into an American setting, because as children and ado-
lescents they had seen enough US TV to grasp instinctively what
made North Americans laugh. Canadian Rich Little's impression of
Richard M. Nixon resonated in both countries, but he reserved his
satire of Prime Minister John Diefenbaker for Canadian audiences.
The CBC provided most Canadian comedians with a start, but over
90 percent of TV comedy was filmed in the United States. Dan
Ackroyd, John Candy, Jim Carrey, Rick Moranis, Martin Short, and
Tom Green thus built careers in North American mass entertainment, while their home fans cheered them on from in front of television screens.[25] If Canadians worked south of the border, American
comedians such as Bob Newhart came north on tour, on radio, in
film, and on TV.[26] Popular taste, not nationality, created, shaped,
united, and separated audiences, and the border and national identity were largely irrelevant to the process.

North America's mass-entertainment system has offered stardom
to Canadians and Americans alike. On its own, Canada had limited
opportunities and lower incomes, just as many parts of the United
States did. In Southern California or New York relative unknowns
might, with hard work and luck, find mass audiences. Through mass-
market TV shows, movies, and recordings successful Canadian expatriates "returned" to Canadian viewers. Lorne Greene and William
Shatner started in Ontario's Stratford Shakespeare Festival, but they
achieved fame and wealth in the United States and still played before
Canadian audiences on screens and on stage tours. The two starred in
long-running genre series: Greene in *Bonanza* and Shatner in *Star
Trek*. Pa Cartwright and Captain Kirk endured for decades in North
America's re-running mass-entertainment system.[27]

Quiz and game shows became mass entertainment as well. The
CBC rejected Canadian Monte Hall's proposed game show when
highbrow critics and officials disliked the pilot. Hall headed for New
York, sold *Let's Make a Deal* and hosted 4,700 episodes. Alex Trebek
and *Jeopardy* followed a similar path. Some ambitious Canadian TV
journalists found the CBC similarly stifling and Canada too confined
to hold their interest. Greater opportunities and higher salaries

beckoned Morley Safer, Robert MacNeil, Peter Kent, and others to mass audiences on US channels.[28]

The TV *Guide* listings announced the integrated cross-border nature of television programming, as cable, and eventually satellite, transmission put increasing numbers of channels and niche shows on screens in both Canada and the United States. TNT, ABC, CBS, NBC, and all-news channels such as CNN appeared in both countries, albeit with different commercials. Canadian voices and stories largely vanished outside Canada because they served only their domestic viewers. Interested Americans received Canadian channels via satellite, and US cable companies in towns and cities near the border often carried CBC and CTV channels. When a Seattle cable company cancelled a Vancouver CBC channel, protests and petitions forced the company to reverse its decision. More importantly, Canadian companies made films to tap North America's mass-entertainment market on television. By 1997 Canadian film exports of cartoons, science fiction, police, and law firm dramas and romances earned over Can$1 billion annually. A Toronto company teamed with Disney to make *Road to Avonlea* from Lucy Maud Montgomery's "Anne of Green Gables" stories. These lasted seven original seasons and more on reruns, as *Avonlea* won awards in both countries, found millions of viewers and earned millions of (US) dollars.[29]

Highbrow? Lowbrow? No brow! The programs on these media conveyed that, language aside, the historical patterns show national origin and that the border mattered little or not at all for the content and character of North American mass entertainment. At the same time, highbrows, arts groups and intellectuals, Canadian Radio and Telecommunications Commission members, and Heritage Ministry officials wanted the border to matter. They scorned the mass entertainment revolution that engulfed them, but failed to grasp how various North American entertainment genres had collected continental audiences through various media over many decades. Vincent Massey, steeped in cosmopolitan European and English upper-class tastes, headed a Royal Commission on the Arts (1949–51) that concluded that Canada needed highbrow cultural policies to sustain its national identity. On its recommendation, Louis St Laurent's Liberal government funded the Canada Council and other programs. These in turn nurtured high- (and middle-) brow culture in many genres and supported and developed Canadian academics, writers, intellectuals, artists, and publishers. The mass of the Canadian population, however, displayed little interest in such productions. Outside French-speaking Canada, which developed homegrown popular entertainment, Canadians chose North American mass entertainment more often than the CBC.[30]

As they had in the 1920s, Canadian and American officials talked past one another in rancorous, circular discussions that made little difference to what ordinary Canadians consumed from the North American mass-entertainment system. But the cleavage that mattered was taste, and tastes in mass entertainment in the 1950s had cross-border constituencies, highbrow as well as lowbrow. Just as Canadian highbrow cultural nationalists did, American critic Dwight Macdonald denounced Hollywood for making culture a branch of mass production, marketing, and consumption. If the Soviet Union saw its masses through a communist ideological prism, Macdonald argued, America saw its masses through a free-market prism and forced taste down to its lowest formulaic common denominator. Dwight Macdonald and Vincent Massey were thus cross-border allies futilely defending high culture from the mass entertainment that captivated the masses. If US highbrow logic had some intellectual coherence, however, its Canadian counterpart seemed strained at times. If national origin mattered above all else, why did the CBC's live broadcasts from the Metropolitan Opera House in New York City never raise nationalist eyebrows? But the cleavage that mattered was that between highbrow and middle or low, and the cleavage in taste ignored the border.[31]

The Canadian Radio and Telecommunications Commission, regulator of Canadian private and public broadcasting, nevertheless cast itself as the defender of Canadian culture. Its "Canadian content" regulations for broadcasting licenses restricted certain US TV channels, and siphoned funds from Canadian cable TV providers to subsidize aspiring film producers, songwriters, and singers in the 1960s. This support helped launch some Canadian performers, and let others limp along. But many successful performers, like singer Gordon Lightfoot, argued that "the CRTC did absolutely nothing for me ... Canadian content is fine if you're not doing well. But I'm in the music business and I have a huge American audience. I'm going to do Carnegie Hall for the second time. I like to record down there, but I like to live up here."[32] Lightfoot's national identity was Canadian.

He saw his art as North American. The border mattered for the first, but not the second.

Beginning in the 1970s, the border began to matter less than it ever had for the production and consumption of popular culture, movies in particular. Colleges such as Capilano in Vancouver and Sheridan in Toronto developed training programs in all phases of media production, and their graduates found work not just in local but in North American mass-entertainment industries. When computers came to dominate film animation, Canadian colleges revised their courses, and graduates went to work for the Disney Company when it opened branch studios in Vancouver and Toronto. Graduates also fanned out to find careers in mass-entertainment productions by California's Industrial Light and Magic, Lucasfilms, and Disney on blockbusters such as the *Star Wars* films, *Terminator 2, Jurassic Park, The Mask,* and various TV series.[33] Canadian animators had begun working on national themes for the NFB; by the end of the twentieth century they were in all corners of North America's mass-entertainment industry as Canadian film companies forged cross-border alliances. By the 1990s cross-border integration in feature filmmaking was a reality.[34] The fundamentals of the US-Canada relationship – proximity, a mostly common language, shared intellectual and social values, mingled peoples with common tastes – created an asymmetrical interdependence that ignored the border insofar as mass entertainment was concerned. By the 1980s Los Angeles counted as the fourth- or fifth-largest "Canadian" city by population, because so many expatriates worked and lived there. Canada's consuls general in Los Angeles even characterized themselves as Canada's ambassadors to Hollywood.[35]

Many provincial and municipal governments in Canada established film offices to attract production companies north from Hollywood. Between 1978 and 2000, US film and television production spending in Canada rose from US$12 million to US$1.18 billion.[36] With the Canadian dollar at a 30 to 40 percent discount, US dollars bought more on a Canadian location. The border also mattered when Hollywood unions began to complain that "runaway" production in Canada took jobs from US-based members. In August 1999, a crowd of five thousand protested such "runaways" on Hollywood Boulevard, and California politicians and Washington lobbyists charged that provincial incentives to attract production companies amounted to subsidies and were therefore an unfair trade practice. Rhetoric swirled, but little happened, and the rhetoric cooled.[37] Politics was one thing, the realities of office another, the high stakes in North America's mass-entertainment industry yet another.[38] Policy-makers in all jurisdictions responded to domestic concerns, but the complex and interwoven interests of North American mass entertainment kept the system operating.[39]

The border also mattered to Canadians with interests in the entertainment business, who felt threatened by American competition and wanted what they called the status quo – free Canadian access to the US market but controlled US access to their own market. The CRTC and cable companies also wanted to control Canadian markets and supported each other to exclude American competition in the name of protecting Canadian culture. So they opposed having the popular (and often highbrow) Home Box Office channel in Canada under any circumstances.[40] Gordon Ritchie, a Canadian free trade negotiator, suggested that satellite broadcasters, which Canadian interests dubbed "Death Stars," would expose what he termed the incestuous and mendacious relationship of communications and entertainment industry leaders.[41] On both sides of the perforated border the debate was about the money that mass entertainment produced, not national culture, because tastes, not political jurisdictions, defined North America's markets.

Technological change runs as a leitmotif through this story. Entertainment media had converged by the 1990s, and the Internet reinforced how much things had changed since vaudeville days. The immediate connection between performers and audiences had largely disappeared from mass entertainment, because technology had created the paradox of an atomized mass audience. Television broadcast movies, shows about movies. Magazines advertised and explained the latest productions and their stars. Radio and TV broadcast music and entertainment talk shows. Movies had websites in early production stages to build audiences. Individual Canadians remained embedded in all aspects of this North American system. How many Americans knew that Jim Carrey, Shania Twain, or Alanis Morrisette were Canadian-born? The citizenship of performers, producers, or other entertainment workers mattered less than how audiences received them. And North American mass entertainment was relentlessly commercial. Even the CBC sold advertising space and imported US programs to build audiences and improve its revenue. There was one audience in two countries for all but news, localized public affairs shows, and sportscasts of the Canadian Football League and curling.[42]

Did North American mass entertainment subvert, erode, or in some way dilute a Canadian identity? Despite almost a century of doomsday rhetoric from Canadian industry lobbyists and cultural elites in Canada, the few empirical studies contradict such assertions.[43] And successive polls since the 1980s demonstrate that ordinary Canadians have asserted a strengthening sense of their identity within North America that deepened by 2004.[44]

Studies do find traces of nationally defined differences in preferences in mass culture. Canadians watch about 30 percent less TV over a given period than Americans do. Canadians also, until recently, disdained such US staples as morning news magazines and late-night talk shows. And their tastes varied from US viewers in other ways. In the fall 1999 season, for example, low audience ratings led US networks to cancel *Action*, a comedy about a reptilian Hollywood producer in which no character had redeeming moral virtues. But Canadians liked its sardonic humor and kept the only seven episodes in reruns for a few weeks, despite an utter lack of Canadian content. That was also the case with *The X-Files,* which at first discouraged American viewers, as did *The Simpsons* cartoon comedy. Canadian interest kept these shows alive until ratings picked up in the United States. Canadians also watched *The West Wing* and *L.A. Doctors* in larger relative audience numbers than Americans. It seemed a leap of faith for nationalists and intellectuals to claim that Canadians had higher-toned taste than Americans or that a combination of the sophisticated and the silly were in some indefinable way national traits.[45] In most respects, however, Canada became a regional market within the North American mass-entertainment context.

The border did seem over time to shape a distinct variation on one feature of modern mass entertainment: celebrity. Celebrity began in the late nineteenth century, when editors put faces above names in newspapers in order to compete on newsstands. Baseball players and prizefighters joined industrialists and political figures as national and, before long, international celebrities. The emergence of the star system in mass entertainment during World War I further diluted the qualifications for celebrity. By the 1920s entertainment figures spoke on radio, acted in movies, and made appearances on tour or at staged "events." People tuned in or attended events not

just to hear or see a baseball game, a boxing match, or a movie but
to cheer their favorites. Celebrity became a commodity in North
America's mass entertainment system, and citizenship mattered far
less than audience appeal. Stars from either country could get their
start in the other, yet both could become North American. Canadians
Mary Pickford in the 1920s and Shania Twain in the 1990s both
gained fame first with American audiences. Quebec's French language isolated local celebrities unless they learned English, where-
upon they could enter the North American mass-entertainment
system, as Celine Dion has demonstrated.[46]

Celebrity status ignored the border. In 1990 *Maclean's* magazine
asked Canadian and American women and men which of six prominent personalities they would choose as sex symbols. Tom Cruise
and Michelle Pfeiffer topped the choices in both countries. When US
"shock" radio host celebrity Howard Stern came onto Montreal airwaves in 1997, Canadian commentators howled with indignation
(as many had in New York) at his vulgarity. But Stern's reputation
preceded him, and he drew Canadian listeners in droves.[47]

Partly in response to sentiment that Canada should honor its own
celebrities, Toronto arts and entertainment leaders created a Walk of
Fame in 1998 and annually awarded maple leaf plaques set in a the-
ater district sidewalk (*à la* the avenue of stars on Hollywood
Boulevard). True, Canadian "stardom" had an inclusive character.
Olympic skater Barbara Ann Scott, Grand Prix race driver Jacques
Villeneuve, writer Pierre Berton, pianist Glenn Gould, and ballerina
Karen Kain had plaques alongside actors Jim Carrey and Christopher
Plummer, director Norman Jewison, and singers Anne Murray, Dion,
and Twain. On the whole, Canadians also seemed abashed about
celebrity status, whereas Americans readily accepted being famous
as sufficient unto itself.[48]

In sum, the history of North American mass entertainment suggests that to interpret the border as a dividing line between discrete
Canadian and American national cultures confuses rather than
clarifies the complex and messy nature of relations between Canadians and Americans and between the United States and Canada in
the realm of mass entertainment. When nationalist elites in Canada
have insisted on highbrow policies and programming to deflect or
repel American assaults on an alleged national culture, they have
both ignored and underestimated the interests and tastes of the mass
of Canadians. Whatever bitter battles rage between Ottawa and

Washington, North Americans happily consume mass entertainment, whatever its national origin and regardless of who produced, directed, or performed it. Ottawa's policies and regulations had no impact on what the mass of Canadians defined as entertainment. Nor did what they read, heard, or saw dilute their national civic identity.[49]

Canadian cultural practitioners of every brow in almost every medium have achieved international reputations over the past decades. The distinction and the cleavage that matters in cross-border cultural issues lies between mass entertainment and elite tastes, not national identity. The pretence that the sky will fall on Canadian culture or that Canadians' civic identity has been undermined because American entertainment is everywhere on the airwaves, screens, compact discs, or the Internet has been proven flat wrong.[50] To understand this paradox, it is essential to sort out how and where the border between Canada and the United States matters and where it does not, in order that policy-makers can focus on practical and achievable goals. A glance at the history of North American mass entertainment will give them a good starting point.

NOTES

Acknowledgment: The author thanks the Canada-US Fulbright Program and the Woodrow Wilson International Center for Scholars in Washington, DC, and most particularly David Biette, director of the Canada Institute, and Mount Saint Vincent University for their collective support on the larger project from which this paper has come.

1 Michael Kammen, *American Culture American Tastes: Social Change and the Twentieth Century* (New York: Alfred Knopf 1999), xvii, 26; Gilbert Gagne, "North American Integration and Canadian Culture," in George Hoberg, ed., *Capacity for Choice: Canada in a New North America* (Toronto: University of Toronto Press 2002), 159–83.

2 Mary Vipond, "Canadian Nationalism and the Plight of Canadian Magazines in the 1920s," *Canadian Historical Review*, 58 (March 1977): 43–63.

3 "Canadian Culture," *New York Times*, 7 March 1923, 14.

4 "The Newly-Arrived Elephants," *New York Times*, 22 July 1871, 8; "Barnum's Success in Brooklyn," *New York Times*, 20 April 1873, 2; "Empress, the Old and Gentle Elephant, Retires to a Home," *Washington Post*, 8 July 1906, SM 7; "The Art of the Circus," *Guide*

to the Performing Arts, www.theartofperforming.com.circus; *Maclean's*,
6 October 2003, 38–42.

5 Robert Wiebe, *The Search for Order, 1877–1920* (New York: Hill &
Wang 1966)

6 Bruce Lenton, "The Development and Nature of Vaudeville in Toronto:
From 1899 to 1915," PHD diss., University of Toronto, 1983; Hilary
Russell, "All That Glitters": A Memorial to Ottawa's Capitol Theatre and
Its Predecessors, Canadian Historical Sites 13, Occasional Papers in
Archaeology and History, Ottawa: Indian and Northern Affairs, 1975.

7 "Vaudeville Managers Combine," *Washington Post*, 24 November 1894,
12; Tina Loo and Carolyn Strange, "The Traveling Show Menace:
Contested Regulation in Turn-of-the-Century Ontario," *Law Society
Review* 29 (1995): 639–67; "French Canadian Stage," *New York Times*,
2 August 1903, 5; Anthony Slide, *The Vaudevillians: A Dictionary of
Vaudeville Performers* (Westport: Arlington House 1981), xi–xiv; John E.
Dimeglio, *Vaudeville U.S.A* (Bowling Green: Bowling Green University
Press 1973), 166–7, 192–202; *Bob Hope and American Variety*
(Washington: Library of Congress 2002), a brochure for an exhibition in
the Bob Hope Gallery of American Entertainment; James Cowan, "The
Greatest of All Time," *National Post*, 29 July 2003, B4.

8 Daniel J. Boorstin, *The Americans: The Democratic Experience* (New
York: Random House 1973); Samuel E. Moffett, *The Americanization of
Canada* (Toronto: University of Toronto Press 1972), 56–67.

9 Russell, "All That Glitters"; Seth Feldman, "And Always Will Be: The
Canadian Film Industry," in Helen Holmes and David Taras, eds., *Seeing
Ourselves: Media Power and Policy in Canada* (Toronto: Harcourt Brace
& Company), 99–115; Robert Sklar, *Movie Made America: A Cultural
History of American Movies* (New York: Random House 1994 [first pub-
lished 1975]).

10 Robert Everett Green, "Play It Again ... and Again ... and Again," *Globe
and Mail*, 14 June 1997, C7; Kate Taylor, "Stratford Festival Antes Up
for Gamble on Broadway," *Globe and Mail*, 7 November 1998, C7;
Frank Moher, "Why New York Tells Canadian Theatre 'Don't call
us...,'" *National Post*, 27 March 2000, D6.

11 Charles Foster, *Once upon a Time in Paradise: Canadians in the Golden
Age of Hollywood* (Toronto: Dundurn 2003); Feldman, "And Always Will
Be"; Ted Magder, *Canada's Hollywood: The Canadian State and Feature
Films* (Toronto: University of Toronto Press 1993).

12 Kerry Seagrave, *American Films Abroad: Hollywood's Domination of the
World's Movie Screens* (North Carolina and London: McFarland &

Company 1997), 2, 12, 19–27; (quote 19); 57–8; 103. Peter Morris, *Embattled Shadows: A History of the Canadian Cinema 1895–1936* (Kingston: McGill-Queen's University Press 1978); See also Magder, *Canada's Hollywood*, chaps. 1, 2.

13 Seagrave, *American Films Abroad*, 149–51; Henry Garrity, "Book Review Essay: Searching for Identity in Canadian Film ... Again," *American Review of Canadian Studies* 33 (autumn 2003): 415–18; Pierre Berton, *Hollywood's Canada: The Americanization of Our National Image* (Toronto: McClelland & Stewart 1975).

14 Susan Smelyan, *Selling Radio: The Commercialization of American Broadcasting, 1920–1934* (Washington and London: Smithsonian Institution Press 1994); Bill McNeill and Morris Wolfe, eds., *Signing On: The Birth of Radio in Canada* (Garden City: Doubleday 1982); Frederick Lewis Allen, *Only Yesterday* (New York: Harper Brothers 1931), 116.

15 Margaret Prang, "The Origins of Public Broadcasting in Canada," *Canadian Historical Review* 46 (1965): 1–25; Frank Peers, *The Politics of Canadian Broadcasting, 1920–1951* (Toronto: University of Toronto Press 1969), 4–12, 19–40, 228–9, 276–84; Anthony Smith, ed., *Television: An International History* (New York: Oxford University Press 1995), 89–91.

16 Michele Hilmes, *Hollywood and Broadcasting: From Radio to Cable* (Urbana and Chicago: University of Illinois Press 1990).

17 Doug Owram, *Born at the Right Time: A History of the Baby Boom Generation* (Toronto: University of Toronto Press 1996), 152–6; Martin Laba, "No Borders, No Problems: Mixed Media, Cultures of Youth, and Music in the Marketplace," in Holmes and Taras, *Seeing Ourselves*, 73–83; Peter Fornatale and Joshua E. Mills, "The Emerging Teen Culture in Radio in the Television Age," in Peter Fornatale and Joshua Mills, eds. *Radio in the Television Age* (Woodstock: The Overlook Press 1980), chap. 3; Deirdre Kelly, "Back in the Swing," *Globe and Mail*, 27 June 1998, C1, 3; Geoff Pevere and Greig Dymond, *Mondo Canuck: A Canadian Pop Culture* (Scarborough: Prentice Hall 1996) 8–11, 142–4.

18 Owram, *Born at the Right Time*; John Clare, "The Scramble for the Teenage Dollar" (*Maclean's*, 14 September 1957), in *Canada in the Fifties: Canada's Golden Decade* (Toronto: Penguin Books 1999), 184–91; Laba, "No Borders, No Problems."

19 Theodore Caplow, Louis Hicks, and Ben J. Wattenberg, eds., *The Measured Century: An Illustrated Guide to Trends in American, 1900–2000* (Washington, DC: AEI Press 2001), 100–1; Paul Rutherford, *When Television Was Young: Primetime Canada, 1952–1967* (Toronto: University of Toronto Press 1990), 41.

20 Richard Collins, *Culture, Communications and National Identity: The Case of Canadian Television* (Toronto: University of Toronto Press 1990).

21 Owram, *Born at the Right Time*, 88–93, 155.

22 Ibid., 143–52.

23 Feldman, "And Always Will Be," 105–8; Magder, *Canada's Hollywood*, chaps. 6–10; Seagrave, *American Films Abroad*, 187–9, 226–7, for Quebec see 262–3; Marci McDonald, "The Paramount Connection," *Maclean's*, 25 April 1994, 17–18; Peter Birnie, "Bordering on Hollywood," *Vancouver Sun*, 2 October 1996, F4; Robin Mathews, "Canadian Culture and the Liberal Ideology," in Robert Laxer, ed., *Canada Ltd.: The Political Economy of Dependency* (Toronto: McClelland & Stewart 1973), 213–31; Martin Knelman, "Telefilm's Hollywood Deal Full of Promise," *Toronto Star*, 11 April 2004, www.thestar.com; Peter Howell, "Arcand's Oscar boost," *Toronto Star*, 2 March 2004.

24 Christie Davies, *The Mirth of Nations* (New Brunswick, NJ: Transaction Publishers 2002) and *Jokes and Their Relation to Society* (Berlin and New York: Mouton de Gruyer 1998); Beverley Rasporich, "Canadian Humor in the Media: Exporting John Candy and Importing Homer Simpson," in Holmes and Taras, *Seeing Ourselves*, 84–98; Liam Lacey, "The Yucks of the Canucks" *Globe and Mail*, 8 August 1995, C1, 2; Siobhan Roberts, "Science of Mirth," *National Post*, 13 August 2001, A6; Rick Moranis, "It Is to Laugh," *Weekend Post*, 20 November 1999, 1–3.

25 Rutherford, *When Television Was Young*; Rasporich, "Canadian Humor," 333–4; "Culture and Communications," http://tv.cbc.ca/national/pgminfo/border/culture/html; Pevere and Dymond, "TV Nation: SCTV," "Mr Michaels Takes Manhattan: Saturday Night Live," "No Joke: The Canadian Sitcom Paradox," *Mondo Canuck*, 188–93, 194–9, 204–8; Morton Ritts, "Boobs on the Tube," *Maclean's*, 23 December 23 1996, 77, 79.

26 Michael Posner, "There's Something Funny Going On Here," *Globe and Mail*, 31 October 1998, C1, 2; Andrew Clark, "The Land of Laughs," *Maclean's*, 1 February 1999, 66, 68; Jeffrey Simpson, *Star Spangled Canadians: Canadians Living the American Dream* (Toronto: Harper Collins 2000), 309–17; Canadian Press, "Conan O'Brien"'s Toronto Show a Ratings Winner," 11 February 2004, www.ctv.ca/servlet/ArticleNews/story.

27 Simpson, *Star Spangled Canadians*, 317–21; William Shatner (with Chris Kreski), *Star Trek Memories* (New York: Harper Collins 1993); *Star Trek: Movie Memories* (New York: Harper Collins 1994); J. Kelly Nestruck, "Kicking Kirk," *National Post*, 2 September 2003, B9.

28 Mary Jane Miller, *Rewind and Search: Conversations with the Makers and Decision-Makers of* CBC *Television Drama* (Montreal and Kingston: McGill-Queen's University Press 1996); Matthew Fraser, "Is CBC relevant? Not to Young Canadians," *Financial Post*, 25 May 1999, C7; Simpson, *Star Spangled Canadians*, 217–30.

29 Martin Knelman, "Made for TV Movies," *Report on Business Magazine*, May 1994: 63–8; Barbara Wickens, "Romancing the Small Screen," *Maclean's*, 22 August 1994: 54–5; Knelman, "Mickey on the Road to Avonlea," *Financial Post Magazine*, March 1996: 22–8; Doug Saunders, "Exporting Canada's Culture," *Globe and Mail*, 25 January 1997, C1, 3; Anthony Keller, "Have Can-con, Will Travel," *Globe and Mail*, 13 September 1997, C3; Chris Cobb, "Pop Icons Bring Wealth into Canada," *National Post*, 21 June 2001, A8; Canadian Press, "South Park to Poke Fun at Canada Once Again," 24 January 2004, www.ctv.ca/servlet/ArticleNews; Dan Brown, "The Trailer Park Boys Return," CBC *News*, 6 April 2004, www.cbc.ca/arts/features/trailerpark.

30 Paul Litt, *The Muses, the Masses, and the Massey Commission* (Toronto: University of Toronto Press 1992); Robert Fulford, "How Massey Smothered the Arts," *National Post*, 22 December 2001, A16; Ramsay Cook, "Cultural Nationalism in Canada: An Historical Perspective," and Roger Frank Swanson, "Canadian Cultural Nationalism and the Public Interest," in Janice L. Murray, ed., *Canadian Cultural Nationalism: The Fourth Lester B. Pearson Conference on the Canada – United States Relationship* (New York: New York University Press 1977), 15–44, 55–82.

31 Dwight Macdonald, "A Theory of Mass Culture," in Bernard Rosenberg and David White, eds., *Mass Culture: The Popular Arts in America* (New York: Free Press 1957), 59–73.

32 Robert A. Wright, "'Team, Comfort, Memory, Despair': Canadian Popular Musicians and the Dilemma of Nationalism, 1968–1972," *Journal of Canadian Studies* 22 (winter 1987–88): 27–43 (Lightfoot cited 30); Pevere and Diamond, "Paul Anka: Highway to My Way"; "Rock of Ages: The Endurables"; "Another Fine Messer: The Down-Home Tradition That Will Not Die"; "A Great Broad: Anne Murray," *Mondo Canuck*, 8–11, 46–9; 136–41; 146–7.

33 Chris Wood, "Canadian Made," *Maclean's*, 24 June 1996, 38–43; Joe Chidey, "Dawn of *Spawn*," *Maclean's*, 11 August 1997, 52–3; Karen Mazurkewich, *Cartoon Capers: The History of Canadian Animators* (Toronto: McArthur & Company 2000); *National Post*, 3 September 2001, A11; Jonathan Gatehouse, "Cartoon Time for Canuckleheads," *National Post*, 19 February 19 2000, B3.

34 Brenda Bouw, "Of Mice and (Bronf)man," *National Post Business* (September 1999): 74–8; Daryl-Lynn Carlson, "Turning the Silver Screen into Gold," *The Wealthy Boomer*, 2, 1 (2000): 68–70; Mike King, "Montreal Becoming a 'Famous Player' as Hollywood of the North," *National Post*, 2 October 1999, A11; Michael Posner, "A Really Big Show," *Maclean's*, 11 August 11 1997, 38–9; Cori Howard, "Canadian Film Production Has Banner Year" and "Canadians of the Academy," *National Post*, 11 February 2000, C3, 23 March 2000, B3; Brian Steinberg, "Lions Gate Finds Own Territory in Hollywood Jungle," *National Post*, 30 July 2002, 3; Mark Anderson, "Selling Toronto," *Financial Post Magazine*, March 1996, 31–3, 36, 61; Kathryn Leger, "Montreal Film and TV Production Booming," *National Post*, 7 July 1999, A8; Stephen Handelman, "Will Canada Be Reeling?" *Time,* 30 September 2002, 33.

35 Ron Graham, "Born Again in Babylon," Thomas S. Axworthy, ed., *Our American Cousins: The United States through Canadian Eyes* (Toronto: James Lorimer 1987, 190–205). First published, *Saturday Night* 98 (June 1983): 23–39.

36 Ian Bailey, "Film Agencies Worry about New Tax Bite," *Montreal Star*, 13 January 1999, B2; Ian Jack, "Ottawa, Hollywood Move toward Tax Compromise," *National Post*, 23 January 1999, D1, 2; Robert Remington, "Canada Warned Tax Hikes on Actors Jeopardize Industry," *National Post*, 27 December 2000, A5; Sinclair Stewart, "Martin Moves to Kill Tax Shelter,"*National Post*, 24 September 2001, D1, 2; Mike Gasher, *Hollywood North: The Feature Film Industry in British Columbia* (Vancouver: University of British Columbia Press 2002).

37 Cori Howard, "This Love Affair Had to End Sometime," *National Post*, 20 August 1999, B2; Ian Bailey, "US Unions Target 'Runaway' Film and Television Production," *Montreal Star*, 5 July 5 1999, C10; 23 January 2000, B5; Tichard Blackwell, "Canadian Film Industry Worried," *Montreal Star,* 9 October 2003; Eric Reguly, "Runaway Film Work Running Away," *Globe and Mail*, 9 March 2004.

38 "Film Shoot in Toronto Slammed by US Congress," *CBC Arts News*, 8 April 2004, www.cbc.ca/arts/stories/runaway; Frank Ahrens, "Hollywood in Canada Splits Unions," *Washington Post*, 16 April 16 2004, E1.

39 Rory Leishman, "Hollywood Strikes Back over Canada's Subsidies," *Globe and Mail*, 21 August 1999, D5; Robert Russo, "Canada Stealing US Film Jobs, Gore Report Says," *National Post*, 19 February 2001, A5; Peter Morton, "US Film Groups Call for Taxes against Studios," *Financial*

Post, 5 December 2001, 6; Jeffrey Simpson, "Hollywood's Case against Canada," *Globe and Mail,* 4 December 4 2001, A23.

40 Gordon Ritchie, *Wrestling with the Elephant: The Inside Story of the Canada-US Trade Wars* (Toronto: Macfarlane Walter & Ross 1997), 217–22.

41 Mark Stokes, "Canada and the Direct Broadcast Satellite: Issues in the Global Communications Flow," *Journal of Canadian Studies* 27 (summer 1992): 82–96; John Meisel, "Escaping Extinction: Cultural Defence of an Undefended Border," in David Flaherty and William McKercher, eds., *Southern Exposure: Canadian Perspectives on the United States* (Toronto: McGraw-Hill Ryerson 1986), 152–68; Ritchie, *Wrestling with the Elephant,* 230–4.

42 Nicholas Jennings, "Cross-border Shopping," TV *Times,* 26 August to 2 September 1994, 1; Chris Dafoe, "TV Hopefuls Go Due South," *Globe and Mail,* 7 March 1998, C1, 2.

43 Jason Bristow, "Symbolic Tokenism in Canada-US Cultural Sector Trade Relations," *Canadian-American Public Policy* 55 (November 2003) (Orono: The Canadian-American Center).

44 Annual *Maclean's* polls since 1984; Michael Adams, *Fire and Ice: The United States, Canada and the Myth of Converging Values* (Toronto: Penguin Canada 2003).

45 Tony Atherton, "Our Taste in TV from Ridiculous to Sublime,"*National Post,* 10 January 2000, D6; John McKay, "CRTC Eyes Homegrown TV Output," CH, 22 February 2001, C7; Jeffrey Simpson, "Watching the Bigger Picture through US Eyes," *Globe and Mail,* 26 February 2002, A7; Kate McNamara, "Off the Dial," *Financial Post,* 25 June 2002, FP9.

46 Brenda Bouw, "Star Light, Star Bright, " *Financial Post,* 14 August 1999, D5; "Princess Diana and the Cult of Fame," *Globe and Mail,* 13 September 1997, D9; Daniel Boorstin, *The Image: A Guide to Pseudo Events in America* (New York: Vintage Books 1961); Tyler Cowen, "The Gift of Fame," *National Post,* 27 May 2000, B1, 2.

47 Kate Taylor, "Shooting Stars," *Globe and Mail,* 22 May 1993, C1, 2; Gina Mallet, "Starved for Stars," *Globe and Mail* 17 January 1998, D1, 3; Rae Corelli, "A Desert Isle Desires," *Maclean's* 25 June 1990, 72–3; "True North Strong and Geeky," *National Post,* 28 December 2000, B6–7.

48 Christopher Harris, "But Can We Walk the Walk?" *Globe and Mail,* 20 June 1998, C1, 12; Shiovan Govani, "The End of Shame, but Not of Fame," *National Post,* 23 September 2000, E1, 4; Rebecca Eckler, "Inside Canada's Star Chamber, " *National Post,* 17 January 2001, B5;

Maclean's, 1 July 2003, 29–49; John Porter, *The Vertical Mosaic: An Analysis of Social Class and Power in Canada* (Toronto: University of Toronto Press 1965).

49 Chris Cobb, "Pop Icons Bring Wealth into Canada," *National Post,* 21 June 2001, A8; Michelle MacAfee, "Canadians Feel Culture Threatened by Americans: Poll," *Chronicle Herald,* 1 July 2002, B4; Charles Gordon, "The New Challenge Threatening Culture," *Maclean's,* 1 February 1999, 13; Terrance Wills, "What's Canadian? What's Culture?" *National Post,* 6 April 1999, B5.

50 Stephen Godfrey, "Is Culture Truly Excluded from Free Trade? " *Globe and Mail,* 12 January 1990, C1, 3; Charles Gordon, "The New Challenge Threatening Culture," *Maclean's,* 1 February 1999, 13; Heather Scoffield, "Arts Community Feels Culture Battle Is Lost," *Globe and Mail,* 19 June 1999, A2; Dallas Smythe, *Dependency Road: Communications, Capitalism, Consciousness, and Canada* (Norwood, NJ: Ablex Publishing 1981); an NDP MP passed on the Windsor election anecdote; Wills, "What's Canadian? What's Culture?" *National Post,* 6 April 1999, B5; Tyler Cowen, "Cashing In on Cultural Free Trade"; Purvis, "Marquee"; Micheline Charest and Ronald A. Weinberg, "Youthful Vision," *Time,* 9 August 1999, 64–6.

5

Dancing with Our Neighbours

English Canadians and the Discourse of "Anti-Americanism"

JENNIFER MACLENNAN

According to Canadian historian W.L. Morton, "the intimacy of the relations and the disparity of power between [Canada and the United States] make it inevitable that American indifference and power will provoke Canadian resentment from time to time."[1] This resentment – if that's the correct term for this pattern of resistance – routinely shows up in popular discourses on the Canadian identity, from such classics as Farley Mowat's *My Discovery of America* and Al Purdy's *The New Romans*[2] to more recent offerings like Rick Mercer's *Talking to Americans* and Molson Breweries' "I Am Canadian" advertising campaign.[3] English-speaking Canadians' insistence on cultural difference, and in particular their cultural protectionism, are frequently portrayed, and in some quarters accepted, as nothing more than "anti-Americanism." Indeed, some have claimed that a Canadian identity exists *only* as a kind of anti-Americanism.[4] It is true, as Margaret Atwood points out, that Canadians can be "like itchy underwear"[5] on the topic of Canadian difference. It is also true that they are frequently guilty of portraying their American neighbours in ways that may be, in the words of Canadian historian and media personality Pierre Berton, "manifestly unfair."[6] Such "American-bashing," however, is actually a much more complex phenomenon than it at first appears.

There can be little doubt, as J.L. Granatstein argues, that "Canadian anti-Americanism has for two centuries been a central buttress of the national identity," but despite the "central place that anti-Americanism has played [sic] in all our history,"[7] the

Canadian reaction to the pervasive American presence has not been purely or exclusively negative. Indeed, as much as Canadians routinely repudiate American values and American cultural influences through a cultural "anti-language" of resistance and difference,[8] they continue at the same time to freely and enthusiastically embrace those very influences, as Frank Manning acknowledges when he characterizes Canadians as "insatiable consumers of American culture."[9] Like Manning, Northrop Frye maintains that Canadians, firmly fixed "in the American orbit," could not resist the pull of American mass culture "even if they wanted to," and, he emphasizes, "not many of them do want to."[10] Thus, even as we cheer for "Joe Canadian" or laugh at Rick Mercer's "Talking to Americans," we continue to embrace American mass culture, and there seems little inclination to change those habits. In fact, *Maclean's* columnist Mary Janigan recently characterized Canadians as "US-obsessed."[11]

To understand how it is that strongly resistant discourses such as David Orchard's *The Fight for Canada: Four Centuries of Resistance to American Expansionism,*[12] Maude Barlow and Bruce Campbell's *Take Back the Nation,*[13] Mel Hurtig's *The Vanishing Country,*[14] or even the satirical television program *This Hour Has 22 Minutes* can co-exist alongside often quite vocal admiration for things American[15] requires a careful look at the scene in which such paradoxical acts of embrace and resistance take place. The remainder of this chapter offers a new paradigm for understanding the dynamics of identity as they are re-enacted in Canadian public discourse through the construct of the "cultural Island," whose relationship to its cultural "mainland" is inevitably one of conflict and paradox.

Canada, for all its huge landmass, is nevertheless an island, with a cultural sensibility that has been thoroughly "Islandized." Newfoundland novelist Wayne Johnston's Joey Smallwood might have been describing the Canadian predicament in his assertion that "for an islander, there had to be natural limits, gaps, demarcations ... Between us and them and here and there, there had to be a gulf."[16] Its geographic singularity makes the Island a natural pocket of resistance against the influences of the surrounding dominant culture, providing an effective, perhaps an inevitable, metaphorical and mythopoeic identification for any culture threatened by overwhelming outside influences.

And there can be little doubt that this is Canada's predicament. From the products Canadians purchase, to the stores in which they shop, from the movies and television programs they watch to the magazines they read, Canadians are, in the words of satirist and social commentator Mary Walsh, "endlessly bombarded by American culture and American images and American dreams and American everything."[17] Even in schools and universities, Canadian students read primarily from American textbooks that feature the naturalized values of American culture rather than those of their own. As a result, they are as familiar with American history, culture, and politics as with Canadian – and often more so. As media analyst John Meisel explains, "popular culture, sports, politics, even tourist attractions south of the border are part of the mental map of most Canadians and are frequently as important to us, if not more so, than corresponding indigenous counterparts."[18]

While few countries in the world have remained unmarked by the influences of American globalization, Canada's situation makes it more vulnerable than most, combining as it does a geographic proximity to the cultural powerhouse of the United States, a small population scattered in a few metropolitan centres across a huge land mass, a lesser economic clout, and close personal, political, and economic relationships with its southern neighbour. John Meisel expresses the concern that, as a consequence of American cultural inundation, "our perceptions, values, ideas, and priorities will become so dominated by those of our neighbours that the distinctiveness of Canada will, to all intents and purposes, vanish."[19] He is not alone in this fear, which was articulated forcefully in the reports of two Royal Commissions: the 1929 Aird Commission, which warned that heavy reliance on American media might "mould the minds of the young ... to ideals and opinions that are not Canadian,"[20] and the 1951 Massey Commission, which suggested that because "we face, for the most part without any physical barriers, a vast and wealthy country to which we are linked not only by language but by many common traditions,"[21] this overwhelming American cultural influence could very likely "refashion ... us in its own image."[22]

Identification with the concept of an Island is one way for a threatened culture with no natural boundaries to impose a division between "here" and "there," and to maintain a strong and necessary sense of "us" amid the prevailing influence of "them." In her study of Cape Breton Island, for example, Carol Corbin explains how the tangible boundaries of the Island function not only geographically but also conceptually to impose a sense of definition and to enable its culture to "retain its identity while being bombarded by media messages – primarily American media messages – produced by different cultures in distant places."[23] Although the Island therefore manifests qualities that can legitimately be seen as "anti-mainland," at heart its expressions are not really about the mainland at all but about the articulation and authentication of unique identity by a culture marginalised on the rim of a larger, more aggressive neighbour. In the case of Canada, it is this very bombardment that *makes* us a culturally expressive Island.

Understanding Canada's ethos as "Islandized" allows us to encompass, and to account for, other celebrated conceptions of Canadian identity. One feature of the Island mythos is, of course, the inevitable motif of survival, famously identified by Margaret Atwood as the central unifying symbol of Canadian culture.[24] For the Islander, the ever-present threat to identity emanates from "the mainland." For a Canadian, the threat is the result of "ubiquitous and inescapable"[25] American influence. The Canadian concern with identity and cultural survival that has "obsessed the media and the politicians and a great many ordinary, thinking Canadian people"[26] is therefore not the product of some "identity crisis,"[27] as some have argued, nor is the Island as metaphor something that must be outgrown. It is instead a mature cultural mythos that captures Canada's permanent predicament – geographic, economic, and cultural. Far from casting off its Island sensibility, Canadian popular culture continually reaffirms it through such phenomena as the overt nationalism of Stompin' Tom Connors,[28] the exuberant celebration of Canadian Olympic gold in hockey at the 2001 Olympics,[29] Molson's "I am Canadian" series, and such books as Frank E. Manning's *The Beaver Bites Back* or Michael Adams' *Fire and Ice*.[30] These expressions and many more like them illustrate the power that an assertion of cultural difference still has to evoke strong emotion from the majority of Canadians – even when the source is a beer advertisement.[31]

A main feature of the "Island view of the world" that marks Canadian identity discourse is, of course, its resistance to "outside" values that threaten to subsume it. This pattern of resistance is something more complex than, and perhaps altogether different from, mere anti-Americanism. Instead, it is an attempt to redefine the figure-ground relationship, to make Canadian distinctiveness visible as figure and to cast the overwhelming influence of American cultural imports as ground. As Margaret Atwood points out, the process is one of learning to "pay some attention to what ... occurs *only* here," rather than simply "studying what also occurs here, like Ford motor cars."[32]

Given "the pervasive presence of American popular culture in Canada"[33] and the resultant Canadian preoccupation with American cultural influence, it should not be surprising that so much of our energy is spent on affirming our unique and separate identity nor that much of that effort is specifically devoted to distinguishing ourselves from the United States. Our agonistic stance is an inevitable response to the very real concern that, as Pierre Berton explained to his mythical American correspondent Sam, "we are in danger of being swamped by you."[34] Or perhaps crushed, as implied by Pierre Trudeau's famous remark to the Washington Press Club in 1969: "Living next to you is in some ways like sleeping with an elephant. No matter how friendly and even-tempered is the beast, if I can call it that, one is affected by every twitch and grunt."[35]

Much as resistance is the keynote of the Island mythos, however, its dominant appeal for Canadians lies in its ambiguity. For any Islander, the pattern of resistance to the dominant culture, while pervasive, is not seamless. Even as Islanders take pride in celebrating their distinctiveness, they remain – however marginally and whether they like it or not – members of the broader culture, just as Canadians are members of a broader "North American" culture. It is this ambivalent membership in the broader culture that leads John Meisel to assert that "inside every Canadian, whether she or he knows it or not, there is, in fact, an American. The magnitude and effect of this American presence in us all varies considerably from person to person, but it is ubiquitous and inescapable."[36] Thus, even in the midst of their resistance, Canadians, like all Islanders, may still instinctively look to the dominant culture for recognition and validation of their experience. This "recognition anxiety" makes the process of identity formation a complex and ironic one for Islanders – and for Canadians. On one level, the inevitable rejection of Island values by "mainstream" culture, whether it comes in the form of ignorance or outright repudiation, serves as an ironic confirmation of Island difference. As long as this rejection continues, Islanders can be sure that they have successfully resisted assimilation and that Island identity is affirmed by mainland ignorance. At the same time, however, Islanders desire, even seem to crave, acknowledgment from the mainland culture of which they are inevitably a part, and they feel

resentment at being overlooked. Unfortunately, too often the price
of acceptance is assimilation, a condition that Islanders themselves
in turn reject. Thus, either response from the mainland – acceptance
or rejection – serves to confirm the Islander's sense of difference and
to prompt further acts of resistance that in turn reaffirm a sense of
the Island's separate identity. Even as they resent the indifference of
the "mainland," Islanders read its repudiation of their culture as a
form of validation.

The pattern of seduction and repudiation evident in Island ambivalence results in a celebration of mainland displays of ignorance
about Island ways – a prototype of the Canadian fascination with
tales of American ignorance of Canada.[37] For example, as Rick
Mercer points out, "Canadians know almost everything there is to
know about America. We're inundated with every sordid little detail
about their culture." By contrast, explains Mercer, "Americans know
nothing about Canada."[38] As a result, despite the closeness of the
relationship, Canadians are rarely heard by the very culture whose
influence threatens to swamp their own indigenous expressions.
"Canadians are used to being ignored by their neighbours," says J.L.
Granatstein,[39] but the ignorance still rankles, and one of the features
that marks Canadian popular culture as "Islandized" is the commonplace that has been described as "one of our longest-running jokes –
Americans' lack of knowledge of their next-door neighbours."[40] This
phenomenon is frequently evident, for instance, in Canadian editorial
cartoons and helps to explain the incredible popularity of Mercer's
"Talking to Americans."[41] It also helps to explain the negative reaction to the same program among some Canadians.[42]

The commonplace of American ignorance provides a focus for
much of the rhetoric of Canadian identity. Margaret Atwood explains why: "Americans don't usually have to think about Canadian-
American relations, or as they would put it, American-Canadian
relations. Why think about something which you believe affects you
so little? We, on the other hand, have to think about you whether we
like it or not."[43] One result of this lack of understanding, according
to the patterns of Canadian identity discourse, is that our interests are
misunderstood, ignored, or worse, trampled by a ubiquitous figure
that represents the second commonplace of Canadian cultural discourse: the American bully.[44] As Pierre Berton observes, "when the
Globe and Mail in a lead editorial refers to 'the American bully' ...
it tells you something about the depth of Canadian feeling" on such

issues,[45] as does comedian Mary Walsh's interview, in character as "Dakey Dunn," with Canada's foreign affairs minister. In it, the belligerent Dunn crudely characterized Canada's ongoing role in North America as "playing 'bum boy' to the Americans."[46]

Mainstream media also exploit this commonplace. It appears routinely in editorial cartoons,[47] and the weekly newsmagazine *Maclean's* freely features on its cover such headlines as "Darn Yankees"[48] or a provocative illustration of the Canadian one-dollar coin bearing the image of George Washington, over the slogan "Say It Ain't So – Canadian Sovereignty: Is the Loonie Next to Go?"[49] The accuracy of the stereotype implied by such headlines and images is beside the point; what matters insofar as the language of resistance is concerned is whether the pattern of American dominance and Canadian exploitation functions as a recognizable and naturalized commonplace of Canadian cultural resistance. Clearly, it does.

One more feature of the Island's complex identity process is worthy of note, because it is so directly echoed in the Canadian mythos. Despite the ironic validation provided by the mainstream rejection that Islanders both resent and welcome, the phenomenon of Islandized identity is more complex yet, as the confident assertion of Island difference is routinely undermined by an accompanying fear among members of the marginalised culture that their culture may actually *be* inferior. That is, Islanders – Canadians – may covertly doubt the legitimacy of their own cultural experience because it appears to be invalidated by more "genuine" experiences reported from outside. Mary Walsh, for example, speaks of growing up with the "feeling that the real world was taking place somewhere else, that the real things, the important things, were happening somewhere else, and that I was so far away from it that I might never partake of a real life."[50] This Canadian sense of cultural disenfranchisement is confirmed by, among others, Margaret Atwood, Pierre Berton, and Northrop Frye. Atwood observes that growing up Canadian meant believing that "'there' is always more important than 'here' or that 'here' is just another, inferior version of 'there,'"[51] while Berton notes the distinctively Canadian habit "of seizing on the American model and believing it to be the only one,"[52] and in response judging our own culture inferior. Like them, Northrop Frye observes that "one of the essential Canadian moods" is a feeling of "insecurity and inferiority," and declares that "it seems to me very characteristic of Canada that its highest Order [the Order of Canada] should have for its motto: 'looking for a better country.'"[53] Thus, despite the well-defined sense of difference that marks the Island's sense of self, there remains a deep ambivalence in its relationship to the mainstream culture of which it is also a part. It is easy to extrapolate to Canadian culture in general, and especially to the "everlasting, frustrating, humiliating question"[54] of Canada's celebrated inferiority complex.

But need we be humiliated? It's easy to misread the Canadian pattern of cultural dissociation as a manifestation of inferiority, to see in the Canadian anti-language something "obsessive, even fetishistic" and therefore "unhealthy."[55] Needless to say, such a characterization is mistaken, reflecting not only a misunderstanding of Canadian identity formation but of the dissociative nature of identity formation in general. As the great rhetorical theorist Kenneth Burke explains, the process of cultural identification itself is inevitably "antithetical,"[56] involving "some kind of congregation that also implies some related norms of differentiation."[57] In other words, cultural identifications – like other social identities – are built up dissociatively as well as associatively. Such "identification by antithesis" Burke regards as an inescapable product of human experience, and he argues that we cannot fully understand identity formation if we fail to recognize the extent to which every "'unification' implies [a corresponding] *diversity*."[58] Like Burke, cultural theorist John Fiske emphasizes the importance of a "sense of oppositionality" to any culture's self-definition, explaining that "all social allegiances have not only a sense of *with whom* but also of *against whom*."[59]

One of the features of Canadian identity rhetoric that invites charges of anti-Americanism is this sheer persistence and repetition of its repudiative themes. However, as Kenneth Burke explains, such repetition is a normal and necessary part of maintaining any kind of identity.[60] Human identities – from the personal to the cultural – are reiterative by nature and are sustained through such ritual reenactments, which remind us of who we are by creating recognizable patterns that emerge across discourses in the same tradition. These patterns then become conventionalized forms that both preserve and fulfill our understanding of ourselves. At the cultural level, we affirm our membership by enacting the familiar pattern, and by so doing we renew ourselves as part of the community. In a sense, then, all our expressions of identity can be seen as a "restatement of ... the same thing in different ways, the sustaining of an attitude."[61] Canadian cultural identity is no exception, but because of the constant threat of its potential disappearance, it is marked by greater intensity. Philosopher and conservative Canadian nationalist George Grant explains: "national articulation is a process through which human beings form and re-form themselves into a society to act historically. This process coheres around the intention realized in the action ... But a nation does not remain a nation only because it has roots in the past. Memory is never enough to guarantee that a nation can articulate itself in the present. There must be a thrust of intention into the future. When the nation is the intimate neighbour of a dynamic empire, this necessity is even more obvious."[62]

Most commentators on the subject have, perhaps mistakenly, supposed that the repudiative rhetoric of Canadian identity is an instrumental genre aimed at challenging American attitudes and on this basis have condemned it as nothing more than "glib, mindless prejudice."[63] But this assumption seems fundamentally mistaken. Whenever we attempt to understand the workings of a rhetorical genre – and the features of the rhetoric of Canadian identity are distinctive and consistent enough to make it a genre – we do well to ask what exactly is being said, by whom, and for what audience?

To answer this question, let us assume that what we are looking at is not an instrumental rhetoric designed to bring about practical ends but an epideictic genre whose role is to celebrate and affirm. The audience for such a rhetoric would then clearly not be Americans but a homegrown Canadian audience, for whom the repudiation of American culture is about something other than bashing Americans into recognizing Canadian difference. Once we make this assumption, we can begin to understand that Canadian statements of dissociation are not, and have in fact never been, statements about Americans, no matter how prominent their references to the United States might be. Although the United States, in particular American mass culture, plays a feature role in these discourses, the part it plays is purely symbolic. Understanding the rhetoric of Canadian identity means understanding that American culture forms a foil, a perceptual "ground" or "scene" within which the drama of Canadian difference is played out time and time again.

Canadian statements of dissociation are not really about Americans, or even really about America. Instead, the "United States" they talk about is an abstraction, a symbol of mass culture as invading force. This important distinction has been emphasized over and over in these very discourses of resistance. For example, Margaret Atwood assures us that Canadians "do know the difference between an individual and a foreign policy. Americans as individuals can be enthusiastic, generous, and optimistic in ways undreamt of by your average Canadian."[64] Mel Hurtig, too, emphasizes that, although "Canadians despair over the Americanization of Canada [and] ... the overwhelming majority of Canadians don't want to become Americans ... almost all Canadians recognize that there are many good things about the US and millions of wonderful Americans in all parts of the country. Without question, Canadians like Americans more than they like the USA."[65] An advertisement from the campaign against US split-run magazines, which appeared in many Canadian magazines in 1999, sums up the position exactly: "We Love Americans," it announced. "That doesn't mean we want to be them."[66]

The persistent concern of English-speaking Canadians about the extent and nature of American cultural influence in their own country should not be mistaken for a concern with Americans as an object of obsession. To assume so is entirely to miss the point of Canadian resistance rhetoric. If such Canadian preoccupation can be described as "obsession," it is obsession not with American but with their *Canadian* culture, and in particular with its chances of survival amid the overwhelming influence of American mass culture. It is therefore part of a sane culture's response to "the aggressive power of American popular culture and its infatuation with a missionary zeal that suits it well for certain types of international propaganda."[67]

In the end, this analysis leaves us with two questions. First, is the rhetoric of Canadian identity actually anti-American? If we limit our inquiry to repudiation and differentiation, it is undeniably so: "We know who we are *not* even if we aren't quite sure who we are," Pierre Berton tells his mythical correspondent, Sam; "we are not American."[68] But to simply answer "yes" and leave it at that is to leave the real dynamics of identity unexamined. Like all other identifications, cultural identities are, inescapably, as much a product of dissociative processes as they are of associative ones, and we necessarily begin to understand who we are only when we can recognize who, or what, we are not. As Mary Walsh advises, such a dissociative impulse provides "the real reason, apparently, that there is an us."[69] The gesture toward differentiation that is contained in our cultural expressions is better understood as agonistic than as antagonistic, the product of our "Islandized" culture, whose

relationship with the surrounding dominant culture is both ambivalent and ambiguous.

Indeed, far from being anti-American, Canadian resistance may
even be, as Northrop Frye suggests, "in the United States' best
interests,"[70] since the oppositional themes in our rhetoric of identity
are really directed not at genuine American culture at all, but toward
a pervasive "anonymous, mass-produced, mindless sub-culture ...
dominated by advertising and distributed through the mass media ...
[whose] effect on American culture is quite as lethal as its effect
everywhere else."[71] Although we are used to thinking of these mass
culture messages as "an Americanizing influence," Frye argues that
mass culture is a product of industrialization and therefore "is
American only to the extent that the United States is the world's
most highly industrialized society."[72] Frye's argument is echoed by
such cultural analysts as Neil Postman, who laments the "descent
into a vast triviality" brought about by mass culture,[73] and Daniel
Boorstin, whose classic treatment *The Image* rejects mass culture
as "a new category in human emptiness."[74] It appears that Mel
Hurtig is correct to suggest that as many "anti-American criticisms originat[e] from respected American sources, people who love
their country, but despair over what has been happening to it"[75] as
from Canadian sources, an assertion confirmed by, for example, the
work of Michael Moore[76] or Lewis Lapham.[77] In a similar vein,
Marshall McLuhan argues that Canada's position as a "borderline"
culture provides an advantage in perspective, since "sharing the
American way, without commitment to American goals or responsibilities, makes the Canadian intellectually detached and observant
as an interpreter of the American destiny."[78]

In other words, the Canadian anti-language that helps to establish
and maintain our sense of difference also allows us to function as a
kind of "cultural corrective" to the excesses of a mass culture that is
just as poisonous to genuine American culture as it is to us. Whether
or not we accept this assertion, we can still agree with Frye that "it
is of immense importance to the United States itself that there should
be other views of the human occupation of this continent, rooted in
different ideologies and different historical traditions."[79] It is for this
reason, perhaps, that to some at least, "English Canada at its best
represents to the rest of the world, if not to itself, America without
the power and the problems, America the way it used to be before it
lost its innocence."[80]

A second lingering question has to do with the complicated issue of whether Canada really is a "vanishing country," as Canadian nationalists have contended at least since George Grant wrote his influential *Lament for a Nation*.[81] Opinions on the subject remain divided; Mel Hurtig, for example, worries that "the Americanization of Canada" is being accelerated by the continentalist pressures and economic integration resulting from the North American Free Trade Agreement and has devoted yet another book to the subject.[82] Michael Adams, by contrast, insists in his recent offering that, far from becoming more Americanized, Canadian values are diverging even further from American ones, even as integrationist pressures increase.[83] Recent changes to public policy, and even law, regarding such issues as decriminalization of marijuana or gay marriage tend to support Adams' contention, as do some analyses of the outcome of the 2004 American election.[84]

What this analysis demonstrates is that a small country in the shadow of a larger, more extroverted and powerful nation cannot help but reach for discursive strategies that both define and preserve its sense of cultural distinctiveness. It cannot help, either, displaying ambivalence in its relationship to these pervasive foreign influences. No doubt the resistance and the ambivalence will remain dominant features of our public enactments of identity. Kenneth Burke describes symbolic acts as "the dancing of an attitude," and perhaps it is these very acts that have made us and that will continue to make us, in the words of Mary Walsh, "so inexorably ourselves that at this point I don't really think we can become anything else."[85] The neighbours aren't going anywhere, and neither are we; inevitably, we will continue to dance an identity that asserts difference even as it incorporates the ambiguity of an Island view of the world.

NOTES

1 W.L. Morton, The *Canadian Identity* (Toronto: University of Toronto Press 1961).
2 Farley Mowat, *My Discovery of America* (Toronto: McClelland and Stewart 1985); Al Purdy, ed., *The New Romans: Candid Canadian Opinions of the US* (Edmonton: Hurtig 1968).
3 "Talking to Americans." *Wikipedia,* online: <en.wikipedia.org/wiki/Talking_to_Americans> (accessed 13 April 2004). The "I Am

Canadian" ad can be heard online at <www.adcritic.com/content/
molson-canadian-i-am.html> (accessed 28 March 2001).

4 Robert Fulford, "Anti-American Cant a Self-inflicted Wound," *National
Post,* 22 September 2001, online: <www.robertfulford.com/Anti-
Americanism2.html>; Theodore Plantinga, "Anti-Americanism and
Canadian Identity," *Myodicy* 3 (April 1997), online: <www.redeemer.
on.ca/~tplanti/m/MAM.HTM>; Jamie Glazov, "The Sickness of Canadian
Anti-Americanism," *FrontPageMagazine.com,* 7 March 2003, online:
<www.frontpagemag.com/Articles/Printable.asp?ID=6535>. For a more
thoughtful treatment, see Jack Granatstein, *Yankee Go Home? Canadians
and Anti-Americanism* (Toronto: HarperCollins 1996).

5 Margaret Atwood, "Canadian Looks at American Looking at Us," *Advocate,*
4 May 1985, 1B.

6 Pierre Berton, Why *We Act Like Canadians,* 2d ed. (Toronto: McClelland
1987), 70.

7 Granatstein, *Yankee Go Home,* 4.

8 Anti-languages, as Norman Fairclough explains, are cultural codes that are
"set up and used as conscious alternatives to the dominant or established
discourse types." Norman Fairclough, *Language and Power* (New York:
Longman 1989), 91. An anti-language functions to subvert the power of a
dominant culture by insisting on difference as a means of repudiating its influence, and thereby also asserts an alternate set of values. While all cultures incorporate a sense of "the other," anti-languages are an especially
prominent feature of cultural identification for marginalised cultures.

9 Frank E. Manning, "Reversible Resistance," in *The Beaver Bites Back?
American Popular Culture in Canada,* ed. David H. Flaherty and Frank E.
Manning (Montreal and Kingston: McGill-Queen's University Press
1993), 3.

10 Northrop Frye, *"Sharing the Continent" Divisions on a Ground* (Toronto:
Anansi 1982), 64.

11 Mary Janigan, "We're US-Obsessed," *Maclean's,* 29 March 2004, 14.

12 David Orchard, *The Fight for Canada: Four Centuries of Resistance to
American Expansionism* (Toronto: Stoddart 1993).

13 Maude Barlow and Bruce Campbell, *Take Back the Nation* (Toronto: Key
Porter Books 1991).

14 Mel Hurtig, *The Vanishing Country: Is It Too Late to Save Canada?*
(Toronto: McClelland and Stewart 2002).

15 Dimitry Anastakis, "Anti-American? What about anti-Canadianism?"
Toronto Star, 27 March 2003), online: <www.isp.msu.edu/Canadian
Studies/dimitry.htm> (accessed 20 February 2004).

16 Wayne Johnson, *The Colony of Unrequited Dreams* (Toronto: Vintage Canada 1999), 132.

17 Mary Walsh, "A Hymn to Canada," 1993 Spry Lecture, 8 December 1993, transcript (Toronto: CBC Radioworks 1993), 6.

18 John Meisel, "Escaping Extinction: Cultural Defence of an Undefended Border," in David Taras, Beverly Rasporich, and Eli Mandel, eds., *A Passion for Identity*, 2d ed. (Scarborough, ON: Nelson Canada 1993), 304.

19 Ibid., 153.

20 Sir John Aird, *Report of the Royal Commission on Radio Broadcasting (Aird Commission)* (Ottawa, ON: 1929), quoted from *Communication History in Canada*, ed. Daniel J. Robinson (Toronto: Oxford University Press Canada 2004), 267.

21 Vincent Massey et al., *Report of the Royal Commission on National Development in the Arts, Letters and Sciences* (Ottawa: King's Printer 1951) 11, 18.

22 Ibid., 50.

23 Carol Corbin, "Conversation and Culture," in *The Centre of the World at the Edge of a Continent: Cultural Studies of Cape Breton Island*, ed. Carol Corbin and Judith A. Rolls (Sydney, NS: University College of Cape Breton Press 1996), 178.

24 Margaret Atwood, *Survival: A Thematic Guide to Canadian Literature* (Toronto: Anansi 1972), 32.

25 Meisel, "Escaping Extinction," 152.

26 George Woodcock, *The Canadians* (Toronto: Fitzhenry and Whiteside 1979), 292.

27 "Canadian Nationalism and Anti-Americanism," online: <www.united-northamerica.org/antination.htm> (accessed 17 February 2004).

28 "What Other Folks Had to Say," *The Official Stompin' Tom Web Site*, online: <www.stompintom.com/> (accessed 15 September 2000 [253] 2000–08–17; [285] 2000–09–29).

29 *Maclean's*, for example, devoted its entire 11 March 2002 issue to the two hockey golds that Canada won in Salt Lake City. Articles included James Deacon, "How Sweet It Is," *Maclean's*, 11 March 2002, 16–23; Robert Sheppard, "Party Time," *Maclean's*, 11 March 2002, 24–7; Bob Levin, "Who're You Rooting For?" *Maclean's*, 11 March 2002, 60.

30 Michael Adams, *Fire and Ice: The United States, Canada, and the Myth of Converging Values* (Toronto: Penguin 2003).

31 Andrew Flynn, "Wave of Beer-Ad Patriotism Holds Strong into Canada Day Weekend," Canadian Press, 29 June 2000; Heather Sokoloff, "Finding a Job for Joe: His Name is Joe and He is Canadian; Can We

Lose Him to the US? Actor Made Famous by Beer Ads Opts to Stay in Hollywood," *National Post,* 15 February 2001, online: <www.national-post.com/>.

32 Margaret Atwood, "Alphabet," *Second Words* (Toronto: Anansi 1982), 94.

33 Manning, "Reversible Resistance," 4.

34 Berton, *Why We Act,* 71.

35 Pierre Trudeau, "Address to the National Press Club, Washington, DC" (March 1969), quoted in David Zarefsky and Jennifer MacLennan, *Public Speaking: Strategies for Success,* Canadian ed. (Scarborough: Prentice Hall Allyn & Bacon Canada 1997) 305.

36 Meisel, "Escaping Extinction," 152.

37 For some recent examples, see Wayne Johnston, "From Sir, With Love: Teaching Americans," *The Walrus* 1 (December 2004–January 2005):15–17; Anthony Wilson Smith, "The Irony of Our Identity Crisis" *Maclean's,* 20 May 2002, 2; Allan Fotheringham, "Boy, Are We Ever Naïve," *Maclean's,* 20 May 2002, 18; "Identity in Crisis" (Letters), *Maclean's,* 20 May 2002, 6; and Graeme Smith, "Many Americans Think Canada Is US State, Poll Finds" *Globe and Mail,* 7 May 2002, A10. Also of interest: Bob Garfield, "If Molson Tops Global Rivals for Top Lion, Blame Canada," *Advertising Age* 71 (19 June 2000): 20–1.

38 Rick Mercer, "Talking about 'Talking to Americans': Rick Mercer Puts On America," *Elm Street* 5 (February-March 2001): 27.

39 Granatstein, "Yankee Go Home," 3.

40 Derek Toth, "Mercer Elevates Art of Skewering Yanks" (Canadian Press), *Saskatoon Star Phoenix,* 31 March 2001, E8.

41 "Talking to Americans," *Wikipedia.*

42 Masked Movie Critic, "Why Should Americans Care? (or Can Rick Mercer Get Anymore [*sic*] Desperate?)" The Great Canadian Guide to the Movies & TV, online: <www.pulpanddagger.com/movies/essay_three.html> (accessed 13 April 2004).

43 Margaret Atwood, "Canadian-American Relations: Surviving the Eighties," *Second Words* (Toronto: Anansi 1982) 372–3.

44 For an examination of the phenomenon, see Jennifer MacLennan, "Brian Meets Rambo: The American Bully in Canadian Editorial Cartoons on Free Trade," *Proceedings of the Canadian Society for the Study of Rhetoric* 5 (1993–94): 111–22.

45 Berton, *Why We Act,* 6.

46 Mary Walsh, "Dakey Dunn Interviews John Manley, Minister of Foreign Affairs" (comedy segment), *This Hour Has 22 Minutes,* CBC broadcast, 19 March 2001.

47 See Guy Badeaux et al., *Portfoolio: The Year in Canadian Caricature* (Toronto: Macmillan of Canada [Annual]).

48 "Darn Yankees!" (cover headline) *Maclean's*, 14 August 1997, 12–19.

49 "Say It Ain't So – Canadian Sovereignty: Is the Loonie Next to Go?" (cover headline) *Maclean's*, 15 July 1999, 14–18.

50 Walsh, "Hymn," 2.

51 Atwood, *Survival*, 18.

52 Berton, *Why We Act*, 89.

53 Northrop Frye, "Conclusion to *Literary History of Canada*," *Divisions on a Ground* (Toronto: Anansi 1982), 78. The motto actually reads, "They Desire a Better Country," though the Latin translation on the medal has been disputed by Canadian language guru Bill Casselman. See "Nincompoop Heralds Bungle Motto on the Order of Canada Medal," online: <www.billcasselman.com/wording_room/latin_canada_motto.htm> (accessed 12 November 2004).

54 Hugh MacLennan, quoted in Robert M. Hamilton and Dorothy Shields, *The Dictionary of Canadian Quotations and Phrases* (Toronto: McClelland and Stewart 1979), 453.

55 Masked Movie Critic, "Why Should Americans Care?"

56 Kenneth Burke, "The Rhetorical Situation," in *Communication: Ethical and Moral Issues*, ed. Lee Thayer (London: Gordon and Breach Science Publishers 1973), 271.

57 Ibid., 268.

58 Ibid., 266.

59 John Fiske, *Understanding Popular Culture* (London: Methuen 1989), 24.

60 Kenneth Burke, "Container and Thing Contained," *A Grammar of Motives*, reprint ed. (Berkeley: University of California Press 1969), 19.

61 Kenneth Burke, *Counter Statement*, reprint ed. (Berkeley: University of California Press 1968), 125.

62 George Grant, *Lament for a Nation: The Defeat of Canadian Nationalism*, reprint ed. (Toronto: Macmillan 1965), 31.

63 Granatstein, *Yankee Go Home*, 287.

64 Atwood, "Can-Am Relations," 372.

65 Hurtig, *Vanishing Country*, 185.

66 Communications Committee, Bill C-55 Working Group, "We Love Americans: That Doesn't Mean We Want to Be Them" (advertisement); Jennifer MacLennan and John Moffatt, eds., *Inside Language* (Scarborough, ON: Prentice Hall Canada 2000), 127.

67 Manning, "Reversible Resistance," 4.

68 Berton, *Why We Act*, 72.

69 Walsh, "Hymn," 4.

70 Frye, "Conclusion," 75.

71 Frye, "Sharing," 64.

72 Ibid.

73 Neil Postman, *Amusing Ourselves to Death: Public Discourse in the Age of Show Business* (New York: Penguin 1985), 6.

74 Daniel Boorstin, *The Image: A Guide to Pseudo-Events in America*, re-issue ed. (New York: Vintage Books 1992), 49.

75 Hurtig, *Vanishing Country*, 185.

76 For example, Michael Moore, *Dude, Where's My Country?* (New York: Time Warner Publishing 2003) or *The Awful Truth*, videotape (New York: New Video Group 2002).

77 Lewis Lapham, *Waiting for the Barbarians* (New York: Verso Press 1997).

78 Marshall McLuhan, "Canada: The Borderline Case," in *The Canadian Imagination*, ed. David Staines (Cambridge, MA: Harvard University Press 1977) 226–48.

79 Northrop Frye, "Sharing," 70.

80 Martin Knelman, *Home Movies: Tales from the Canadian Film World* (Toronto: Key Porter Books 1987) 149–50.

81 George Grant, *Lament for a Nation: The Defeat of Canadian Nationalism*, reprint ed. (Toronto: Macmillan 1965).

82 Hurtig, *Vanishing Country*.

83 Adams, *Fire and Ice*.

84 For instance, Jeffrey Simpson, "The South Rises Again, Making Bush a Winner," *Globe and Mail*, 4 November 2004, A25; John MacArthur, "In God They Trust," *Globe and Mail*, 4 November 2004, A25; and Laurence Martin, "Triumph of Bible Belt Imperialism," *Globe and Mail*, 4 November 2004, A25.

85 Walsh, "Hymn," 6.

6

Allied Christian Soldiers

Convergence and Divergence in the Canadian and American Missionary Movements at the Home Base and in Korea, 1870–1960

RUTH COMPTON BROUWER

From the late nineteenth to the mid-twentieth centuries American, British, and Canadian Protestants were partners in a nearly global missionary enterprise. In the intricate web of relationships that developed in this North Atlantic missionary triangle, Canada was linked much more closely to the United States than it was to Britain, the imperial tie notwithstanding. Cross-border connections first emerged as the mainline Canadian denominations began organizing for foreign missions at the home base and selecting overseas fields. Appointment practices strengthened the links, as did the more intimate ties of marriage and family. Canadian-American cooperation and teamwork was evident at highly publicized international conferences and in ecumenical bureaucracies; cooperation and teamwork were vital to the staffing of costly "union" institutions for higher education and medical work, particularly in Asia. Indeed, so closely integrated was the North American missionary enterprise of the mainline Protestant churches that "'American' statistics customarily included Canadians."[1]

In Korea, as elsewhere, the dominant theme was teamwork. Still, as in other mission sites, there were instances of divergence and tension between Canadian and American mission policies and practices, especially in the interwar years, when fundamentalist-modernist controversies in the United States played themselves out in the field.

These theological controversies were most acute within American Presbyterianism, which established the strongest missionary presence in Korea. Inevitably, American Presbyterians' troubles spilled over into their relationships with their Canadian counterparts in the northern Korea mission of the Presbyterian Church in Canada (after 1925 a mission of the United Church of Canada). Expressed politely and in the form of distinctive responses to local challenges rather than in terms of national disagreements, these mission differences nonetheless foreshadowed patterns of national difference that would emerge between Canada and the United States in the post–World War II era in the sphere of secular international relations. While no systematic study of missionary influence on Canadian foreign policy exists, a few scholars, such as J.L. Granatstein, have spoken in passing of observable links and legacies.[2] In the case of Korea, there was significant continuity between liberal Protestants' conduct in foreign mission activity in the interwar years and Canadian foreign-policy makers' approach to international relations in the so-called golden age of the post-World War II era. An ongoing pattern of small differences between the Canadian and American actors in both spheres arose within an overarching and largely predictable pattern of convergence.

ALLIED CHRISTIAN SOLDIERS AT HOME AND ABROAD

By the end of the nineteenth century, all of Canada's major Protestant denominations had established significant overseas mission work.[3] So important were foreign missions to the denominations' self-image and so great a hold did they exercise on the imaginations of churchgoers that for decades some Protestant denominations paid greater attention to their self-imposed foreign obligations than to First Nations' work and missions to immigrants. Certainly this was the case with Presbyterians. The largest Protestant denomination at the time of the 1911 census, the Presbyterian Church in Canada, had eight overseas missions, the biggest in India and East Asia.[4]

From the outset, Canadian Presbyterians looked to their denominational counterparts in the United States for precedents and guidance. Thus, when two female school teachers came forward seeking appointments as missionaries to India in the early 1870s, the Toronto-based Foreign Missions Committee (FMC) sent them to serve temporarily with American Presbyterians and accepted that mission's guidance in deciding in 1876 to open work of its own in an as yet "unclaimed" field in the princely states of Central India. The FMC also emulated its US Presbyterian counterpart by calling into existence a women's missionary society to publicize and finance the work of women missionaries.

Canadian Methodists and Anglicans also turned to their US counterparts for precedents as they sought to capitalize on women's enthusiasm for missions. Denominational women's missionary societies quickly established local branches and regional structures, convened annual conferences, and launched mission periodicals. To a greater degree than was the case in Britain at the same period, missions-minded women in the United States and Canada joined women's missionary societies at the home base or volunteered for overseas service. Once on the ground they were pioneers in establishing Western-style schools and medical services and other agencies of "modernization." Although North American women volunteered in large numbers and established many firsts, they were not alone in seeing missions as congenial "women's work." By the late 1800s women also outnumbered men in many overseas missions established by Protestant agencies in Britain and Europe.[5]

Canadian men were less likely than Canadian women to volunteer for overseas missionary work, but when they did they were more inclined than their female counterparts to seek placements and opportunities that their own denomination's mission board either could not, or would not, accommodate. As a result, they served in significant numbers under US mission boards, and some later became celebrated "American" missionary heroes. The dramatized biography of India medical missionary William Wanless, written by his second wife, an American, was a striking example. Ontario-born but trained and appointed in the United States, Wanless won fame as a surgeon and was eventually knighted by the British government.[6]

Wanless's marriage to an American was by no means unusual among Canadian missionaries. Men and women who went to the United States for professional training as a step towards a missionary appointment frequently became engaged to a fellow student with similar ambitions. Furthermore, Canadians married or, like Wanless, remarried in the mission field to American partners whom they had met in shared mission spaces such as union institutions for higher medical and educational work or at missionary conferences or hill stations. Although Canadians also married British missionaries in the course of preparing for or conducting their work, such unions were considerably less frequent. There were more opportunities for close associations to form among Canadians and Americans, and they had similar cultural backgrounds. In many ways, the international border was of little consequence for Canadians and Americans with a shared commitment to the world of overseas missions.

This was true not only in terms of individual appointments and personal relationships but also in regard to recruitment and promotional strategies. From the outset the Student Volunteer Movement for Foreign Missions (SVM), which began in the United States in the 1880s with John R. Mott, a young Methodist layman, as its first organizer, sent recruiters to college and university campuses in both countries. Even small institutions such as Prince of Wales College in Charlottetown, Prince Edward Island, felt SVM outreach.[7] Since recruitment and promotional organizations like the SVM, the Young People's Missionary Movement, and the Laymen's Missionary Movement (organized in the United States in 1906) were ecumenical, easily crossing denominational lines, it was hardly surprising that they should have been international as well.[8] The YMCA and YWCA were also important sources of cross-border mission stimulus, particularly for the liberally inclined. Many of the books and pamphlets such organizations published were intended for a North American market. Some of the books sponsored by these ecumenical organizations – Van Buskirk's 1931 *Korea: Land of the Dawn*, for instance – seem to have reached an audience well beyond the missions constituency, in part because they were among the few readily available print sources about the lands and peoples they described.[9]

The growth of ecumenical and international recruitment and promotional strategies in the late nineteenth century gave rise to bureaucracies. The bureaucratization of missions accelerated after World War I with the growth of specialized agencies to promote ecumenical work in higher education, medicine, agriculture, and the production of didactic literature. The US-based Foreign Missions Conference of North America (FMCNA), an umbrella organization of mission boards, appeared in 1893, its rotating presidency sometimes filled by an executive member of a Canadian board. Geographic considerations made it far more practical for Canadian boards to be affiliated with the FMCNA than with its overseas counterpart, the Conference of British Missionary Societies (CBMS), even though many Canadian missionaries and mission bureaucrats were only a generation removed from the British Isles and still had family ties there. Both the FMCNA and the CBMS were, in turn, part of the International Missionary Council (IMC), established in 1921, with head offices in London and New York and affiliated work in Geneva. Organizations like these and their many specialized sub-committees facilitated the establishment, growth, and staffing of union institutions in major mission sites and promoted other tasks that benefited from a shared, if non-institutionalized, approach, such as literacy drives. These groups also had an important role to play in lobbying government officials and indigenous leaders for financial support and concessions and in arguing against policies with real or potential harm for mission work or for the local peoples, Christian and non-Christian, in whose interests they claimed to speak. Men like Joseph Oldham, the London-based first secretary of the IMC, and John R. Mott, its chairman, whose leadership roles also included the YMCA, the SVM, and the World Student Christian Federation, had ready access to national leaders, as well as to imperial and foreign-policy bureaucrats. Speaking of Mott, William R. Hutchison refers to "one red-letter day in 1923 ... [when] this particular lion of the religious establishment 'began with William Howard Taft at 9:30, lunched with President Coolidge, and visited with his old friend Woodrow Wilson at 3:30.'"[10] In the interwar period, men like these and occasionally women like Margaret Wrong, the Canadian secretary of the IMC's London-based International Committee on Christian Literature for Africa, also developed close ties to the Rockefeller Foundation and other foundations with an interest in the practical work of missions.[11]

Bureaucrats like Wrong generally worked behind the scenes. At the highly publicized ecumenical conferences that were a feature of the early twentieth century, however, mission statesmen like Mott shared public platforms with national leaders and prominent businessmen who supported the missionary cause. President William McKinley was among those who addressed the 1900 Ecumenical Missionary Conference in New York, at which representatives of over two hundred missionary agencies had gathered. Numerous agencies, many of them American, were also represented at the Fourth International Convention of the SVM, held in Toronto's

Massey Hall in 1902, with support from such prominent local lay-men as Timothy Eaton and Chester Massey.[12] Indeed, even when a Canadian conference was nominally just "national," as with the National Missionary Congress organized by the Canadian Council of the Laymen's Missionary Movement in 1909 to get men more actively involved in missions, no fewer than 1,774 "honorary com-missioners from the United States" were among the approximately 4,000 delegates in attendance at Massey Hall. Some of them, like Robert E. Speer, secretary of the largest Presbyterian mission board in the United States and an early itinerant for the SVM, spoke on more than one occasion. Speer's friend N.W. Rowell, a prominent lawyer and future political leader, was chairman of the Canadian Council of the LMM. In his introduction to the subsequently pub-lished volume of Congress addresses, Rowell expressed his hope that they would inspire readers "to firmer faith and larger effort in the work of world conquest."[13]

Rowell was present the following year at the landmark World Missionary Conference at Edinburgh in 1910, which opened with a "message of greeting and encouragement" from the new king, George V. Four years later World War I would begin, permanently shattering optimistic missionary assumptions and disrupting mis-sion unity. In retrospect, the Edinburgh conference would come to be seen as a watershed in the history of the modern missionary movement. Participation in the movement by mainline Protestant North American denominations increased for another decade, but there was less evidence of royal and presidential patronage and more circumspection about claims to Western Christian superiority at these international conferences.[14] Prominent liberal laymen like Rowell, while still involved, altered their discourse and outlook significantly. Rowell eschewed further talk of Christian "world conquest" and instead supported secular organizations such as the League of Nations, which worked parallel to the practical and cooperative efforts of missions, now often envisioned in terms of Christian internationalism. Much more famously and controversial-ly in the United States, John D. Rockefeller Jr became an advocate of cooperation among all world religions.[15]

In the full-time bureaucracies that sustained these major ecumen-ical and international organizations and in the conferences that pub-licized their goals, Canadians seldom occupied roles at the top. They were, however, more than junior partners and were well represented.

Indeed, Canadian men and women may have been over-represented
in these bureaucracies, for several possible reasons. In proportion to
the size of their country, Canadians were over-represented in the
overseas missionary movement as a whole. So it is not surprising to
find them turning up in leadership positions in mission bureaucracies at the British and North American home bases and abroad, particularly in agencies with specialized roles. Furthermore, as American
funds and personnel increasingly dominated a movement in which
British Protestants had long been the pioneers,[16] new forms of tact
and diplomacy were required to negotiate the shifting balance of
power. In this context, Canadian appointments seem to have been
viewed as acceptably neutral by senior decision makers in London
and New York. Thus, when in 1929 the IMC's London-based secretary Joe Oldham recommended that Margaret Wrong become the
first secretary of the new International Committee on Christian
Literature for Africa (ICCLA), he gave as one reason her likely ac-
ceptability to American mission officials.[17] The notion of Canada as
a lynchpin between the two Anglo-Saxon superpowers had attracted
Canadian intellectuals dating back to the nineteenth century, so it
may be that missions-minded Canadians were predisposed to these
leadership roles in the transatlantic mission bureaucracies. Finally,
professional opportunities in the world of missions may have attracted proportionately more able young Canadians, and for longer,
than was the case in the more advanced, urbanized societies of
Britain and the United States.

ALLIED CHRISTIAN SOLDIERS IN KOREA

The extensive personal and professional linkages between Canadians
and Americans in the world of Protestant mainline missions and the
opportunities for Canadians to take leadership roles in ecumenical
union institutions and mission bureaucracies are strikingly evident
in the case of Korea. There, Christianity went from being virtually
unknown in the nineteenth century to becoming South Korea's
second largest religion by the second half of the twentieth century.[18]
The phenomenal growth of Christianity in Korea has been attributed to a number of factors. Korea's status as a colony of Japan from
1910 until the end of World War II was unquestionably one such
factor. Colonialism drove many Korean nationalists to appropriate
Christianity as an ideological weapon against Japanese imperialism.

Christianity, writes one historian, was viewed as "modern" but not "imperialist." Another observes that it "enabled Korean believers to feel both patriotic and modern at the same time."[19]

Christianity's eventual success is all the more remarkable in that the first Protestant missionaries to reside in Korea came only in the mid-1880s. American Presbyterians and Methodists arrived in the immediate wake of a treaty between the United States and the so-called Hermit Kingdom. By the end of the century, along with representatives of northern and southern US Methodism and Presbyterianism, there were Canadian and Australian Presbyterians and a small number of British Anglicans with officially established missions.[20] As in India, Canadian Presbyterians had taken their cue about where and how to establish a mission from their American counterparts. The three official founders, all Nova Scotians, had begun work in 1898 north of the thirty-eighth parallel. By the time their mission came under the jurisdiction of the newly established United Church of Canada in 1925, it was a robust, if perpetually financially challenged, enterprise committed to evangelistic, educational, and medical work.[21]

Even before the official founding of the Canadian Presbyterian mission, another Nova Scotian, the Reverend William John McKenzie, had undertaken independent missionary work in Korea. He died by his own hand after making converts in a small village where he fell ill and became deranged. His tragic death and the interest in Christianity his brief work stimulated ensured McKenzie a place in American as well as Canadian mission lore. In his history of early US Presbyterian missions in Korea, Harry A. Rhodes told McKenzie's story before going on to observe, "It is interesting that so many of the earlier missionaries ... were Canadians." Rhodes referred specifically to the Methodist medical missionary William Hall, the independent Baptist evangelist Malcolm C. Fenwick, and Presbyterians James Scarth Gale, Robert Hardie, and Oliver Avison.[22]

Several of these men illustrate a pattern that is already clear. Canadian missionaries frequently intermarried with Americans and/or accepted appointments under US denominational mission boards and then went on to high-profile careers. Sometimes, as in the case of the Hall family, there were two generations of cross-border marriages and of husband-and-wife teams of medical missionaries.[23] Oliver R. Avison was, like William Hall, a Canadian medical pioneer in Korea, but he had a longer and much more

influential missionary career. Born in England in 1860 and raised in
a Methodist home in Almonte, Ontario, Avison studied and taught
pharmacy at the University of Toronto and then took a medical
degree before accepting an appointment as a missionary to Korea
under a US Presbyterian board. Eager to establish a fully modern
facility for training Koreans in Western medicine, he spoke passion-
ately about his goals and his ecumenical vision at the large missionary conference held in New York in 1900. Listening in the audience
was a wealthy Cleveland layman, L.H. Severance, who subsequently
provided funds for Avison to build what became the first school of
Western medicine in Korea. Graduating its first class of fully trained
Korean doctors in 1908, the Severance Union Medical College and
Hospital was described in its early days as a scaled-down version of
Avison's "ideal of medical education ... the University of Toronto."
For both Severance and Avison it was to prove a fruitful investment
of money and effort, as well as a source of honour. In the early 1950s
the medical college was said to have trained more than one-third of
South Korea's supply of doctors.[24]

Men like Avison cultivated connections in Korea as well as North
America and on that basis built high-profile careers. As pioneer
American medical missionary Horace Allen had done before him,
Avison served as personal physician to members of the royal family
and cultivated their support. Prince Ito was invited to address the
first Severance graduating class. Avison also attracted the attention
of Syngman Rhee. When as a young man Rhee decided to break
with tradition by having his topknot cut off, Dr Avison performed
the symbolic surgery. Years later, living in retirement in Florida,
Avison remained in touch with Rhee, by then the first president of
South Korea.[25]

Some time after the topknot incident, when he had reached the
stage of being ready to seek baptism as a Christian, Rhee turned to
another prominent Canadian serving under American Presbyterian
auspices, the Reverend James Scarth Gale. In keeping with mission
protocol, Gale recommended instead that he be baptized by the
Methodists, since it was they who had given him schooling. Gale
also recommended that Rhee go to the United States to study.[26] By
the time Rhee approached him, Gale was already well known as a
writer and translator and a sympathetic interpreter of Korean culture.[27] Born in Ontario of Scottish parents, he studied French in
Paris with a view to evangelizing French Canadians. At the University

of Toronto, he was influenced instead to go as a YMCA-sponsored missionary to Korea. Three years later, in 1891, he began serving under an American Presbyterian board and the following year married Harriet Heron, the wealthy and locally well-connected widow of a US Presbyterian medical missionary.[28]

Their links with US mission boards by no means cut men like Avison and Gale off from the missionaries who came to Korea under the official sponsorship of the Presbyterian Church in Canada. Rather, Gale assisted the three founding fathers as they prepared to begin work in the north.[29] But he himself lived a comfortable and much more prominent life in Seoul. Working with a Korean colleague he translated *Pilgrim's Progress*. He also prepared a series of schoolbooks that drew heavily on Ontario's public school readers, and he wrote a well-received *History of the Korean People*, among many other works. Though he retired to England, the home of his second wife, in 1928, Gale maintained ties with his Canadian family and friends and was honoured by the United Church of Canada on a return visit in 1927.[30]

Clearly, several Canadians became "American" missionary celebrities in Korea. Did the national differences matter? Did it matter to the demoralized and vulnerable Korean royal family or to the young Syngman Rhee or to the few Korean schoolchildren who used Gale's readers until they were banned by Japanese colonial authorities that some of the key Christian missionary figures in their country were Canadians rather than Americans? It seems unlikely that they either knew or cared, for given the degree of social and political upheaval in Koreans' lives in the late nineteenth and early twentieth centuries, they would have been hard-pressed to identify distinctive national differences among the missionary newcomers, especially when those newcomers spoke the same language, dressed alike, and seemed to have such interconnected personal and professional lives.

And yet, over time, some differences *did* emerge between American and Canadian missionaries in Korea, even when they shared the same denominational identity. Differences between US Presbyterian missionaries and their Canadian Presbyterian/United Church of Canada counterparts are evident in their respective responses to three distinct phenomena: the March First movement for independence from Japan in 1919, the desire of some converts to travel to and study in the West, and the Shinto shrine controversy of the 1930s.

Writing of the non-violent protests against Japanese rule that began in Seoul in March 1919 and that led to mass demonstrations in hundreds of places in Korea, Bruce Cumings commented that "American missionaries were divided in their judgment of the March First movement," appalled by the violence with which it was suppressed, but also concerned that radicals and agitators had provoked that violence. Hamish Ion has maintained that "of all Western missionaries, Canadian Presbyterians were the most outspoken and critical of Japanese actions" against the nationalists.[31] Certainly, no American or other Westerner played as prominent and active a role in the movement as Dr Frank Schofield, a British-born Ontario missionary who taught bacteriology at Severance Union Medical College. Schofield was reportedly the only missionary who had advance knowledge of plans for the March First uprising,[32] which Woodrow Wilson's declaration about the national self-determination of peoples had stimulated. In the wake of the failed movement, Schofield was zealous, indeed over-zealous from the perspective of more moderate sympathizers, and publicized the atrocities that occurred when Japanese gendarmes suppressed a movement in which Korean Christians were heavily over-represented. He had many photographs documenting abuse of Korean activists that he presented to senior Japanese authorities in Korea and Japan and to the British Foreign Office, in an effort to persuade them to condemn the heavy-handed response to the March First movement.

Dr Schofield remained the most aggressive and persistent Canadian missionary in his condemnation of the Japanese response to the March First uprising both before and after his recall "on furlough" at the end of 1919. He would return to Korea to live and work in 1958, and following his death in 1970, he was buried "amid great pomp and ceremony – in the National Cemetery outside Seoul," an honour that was "truly extraordinary" for a Westerner.[33] But he was not alone among Canadian Presbyterian missionaries and home-base officials in his response to the events of 1919. Missionaries like William Scott and Dr Stanley Martin and the FMC's A.E. Armstrong, who was on tour in East Asia at the time, did a good deal to publicize the maltreatment of Korean nationalists, not only in Seoul but also in Yong Jung [Lungchingtsun], Manchuria. After their country became a Japanese colony, many Koreans had gone to live in Yong Jung, where they encountered Canadian Presbyterians doing educational and medical work. Dr Martin, who died in 1941, was posthumously honoured years later by South Korea's government for giving medical care to injured Korean nationalists. Unlike Schofield, neither his missionary colleagues nor Armstrong was critical of colonialism as a general phenomenon, but they did want Japan to improve its conduct in Korea by introducing beneficial reforms such as, they believed, the British were undertaking in their empire.[34]

Japan did make reforms in Korea in the wake of international criticism following the March First movement and introduced cultural policies aimed at "tutoring Koreans for a distant day of independence." Yet various forms of Korean nationalism grew, some of them expressed in militant activity at home and abroad, including significant communist activity. Meanwhile, one group of Protestant "self-reconstruction nationalists" adopted a peaceful, gradualist approach. They were among the modernizing young men – only some of them Christians – who looked to mission institutions for opportunities for advanced education, including study or travel abroad.[35]

Theological and national differences figured in mission responses to Korean Christians who sought such opportunities. In his account of the Presbyterian/United Church of Canada mission in Korea, William Scott, a long-serving liberal missionary in Hamhung, the mission's largest station, maintained that from the second decade of the twentieth century Canadian missionaries encouraged and funded Korean theological students to study abroad, first in Japan and later in Canada. "This was a venture not encouraged by other Presbyterian missions," he added, "because of the fear that students going abroad might come under the influence of too advanced theological thinking."[36] Donald Clark has noted this as one aspect of a critique of early American Protestant missions in Korea offered by contemporary Korean Christians in the "dissident/activist wing of the church." The charge, Clark wrote, was that they "opposed sending Korean converts abroad for higher education. They seemed to prefer to keep their protégés in Korea under their own influence, safe from liberal theology and the corruptions of modern life."[37] Of course, many thousands of Korean Christians did eventually make their way to the United States with or without missionary encouragement, far more indeed than ever came to Canada. Helen Kim, the first Korean woman to obtain a doctorate, and Syngman Rhee, who was in the United States at the time of the March First uprising, are prime examples. But the willingness of Canadian missionaries, as a matter of policy, to encourage their protégés seems to have been unusual, and lasting in its significance. "'To God's Country': Canadian Missionaries in Korea and the Beginnings of Korean Migration to Canada," a doctoral thesis by a Korean scholar, sees "the missionary connection ... as the predisposing influence in shaping the decision to migrate and the direction of the migration."[38]

Probably one of the earliest and strangest examples is described in the memoir of a worldly young Korean, Younghill Kang, whose determination to "modernize" and go to "America" led him to seek the assistance of missionaries despite his cynicism about their intellectual abilities and their motives for being in Korea. Kang studied at a mission school and sought out missionaries who would help him. Though he had been told that "missionaries neither would nor could take Koreans over," his goal was eventually facilitated by a recently widowed Nova Scotia missionary whom he identified as "Mr Luther." This was undoubtedly Luther Young, principal of the boys' academy in Hamhung. Kang, who met Young when he was temporarily working in another mission school, admired him as liberal, educated, and sincere. It may have been Young who arranged for Kang to study at Dalhousie University in Halifax. Though his narrative ends with his voyage across the Atlantic, other sources indicated that Kang eventually went on from Nova Scotia to the United States, the real "America" of his dreams. There he did what many missionaries feared young men like him would do. He chose a hedonistic life in the West rather than return to a life of Christian service in his own country.[39]

Undoubtedly the most significant area of difference between the Canadian and the US Presbyterian missionaries in Korea was in regard to their responses to the so-called Shinto shrine issue. The issue became controversial in the early 1930s when Japanese authorities tried to create widespread support for State Shinto activities. Colonial officials sought public participation, including compulsory participation by schoolchildren and their teachers, in ceremonies at Shinto shrines in Korea and Taiwan, such as was also being required in metropolitan Japan as a way of promoting loyalty to the state and solidifying reverence for the Emperor. Enforced attendance at these ceremonies was perceived by many Korean Christians as endorsement of Japanese rule, as well as a violation of their own religious beliefs. Thus, a good many of them took so strong a stand against the shrine rites that they endured imprisonment and, during the

World War II years, even martyrdom, rather than comply. For their part, US Presbyterians declined to accept the directive to take mission school children to shrine ceremonies, opting instead to close mission schools. Donald Clark writes that while even the Vatican chose to interpret shrine ceremonies as "political and not religious" and advised Korean Roman Catholics to comply, "the Presbyterian establishment at Pyongyang ... from the outset called it idolatry, setting the stage for a major confrontation between church and state, and also among members of the church who dissented from the views of the leadership."[40]

In his study of the Christian response to the Shinto shrine controversy in Korea, Sung-Gun Kim reported that, like the majority of American Presbyterian missionaries, Australian Presbyterians were "from the outset ... generally against participation in the shrine obeisance on religious grounds." Among the United Church of Canada missionaries, on the other hand, the liberal majority was "preponderantly in favour of conformity."[41] A liberal minority of US Presbyterian missionaries dissented from the position of the majority. By the same token, one of the three founders of the Canadian mission, Duncan MacRae, took a theologically conservative stand on the issue and spoke out strongly against shrine observances, even in retirement in the mid- and late 1930s from his Cape Breton home. But MacRae was far from representative. Most United Church of Canada missionaries seemed to share the view expressed by William Scott that local Korean Christians' interests were best served by a policy of regarding the Shrine observances as civic rites rather than religious observances, for in that way they could keep their mission schools open and fully functioning. Under Scott's leadership the mission in earlier years had also "registered" its advanced schools with the colonial government, since such a policy, while formally restricting Christian teaching in the schools, otherwise facilitated improvement of their standards and physical facilities and thus future prospects for their students. MacRae had also opposed that policy, believing that it had the practical effect of lessening the mission's commitment to direct evangelization.[42]

The pragmatic position taken by Scott on the shrine issue and, earlier, on registration of the schools was also that taken by the Foreign Missions secretaries in Toronto, A.E. Armstrong, James Endicott, and Jesse Arnup. Even MacRae's old friend and colleague Robert Grierson, writing in retirement from his home in Ontario, accepted the Japanese authorities' claim that "the observances were national only, and not religious."[43] Furthermore, the United Church mission's de facto emphasis in this era on providing Christian social services rather than giving priority to direct evangelism (whatever men like Armstrong may sometimes have written to the contrary) meant that their other institutions in northern Korea such as hospitals were also conducted pragmatically rather than along lines of theological rigidity. No one who has read Scott's history of the mission or the accounts left by missionaries such as Florence Murray, superintendent of the hospital at Hamhung, could doubt that they took their roles as Christian missionaries seriously or assume that they simply "sold out" in the face of Japanese pressure. Rather, their commitment to practical social service work and the value they placed on what might be called the evangelism of personal example, especially in a context where "local [colonial] officials and gendarmes ... had broad discretion in interpreting and implementing government regulations,"[44] meant that they could usually function effectively and in good conscience.

In these circumstances it is not surprising that some United Church missionaries stayed on in Korea in relative safety and comfort well after relations between Japan and the United States and Britain worsened dramatically at the end of the 1930s. More than 90 percent of Protestant missionaries are said to have left Korea by Christmas 1940, as advised by both the US consul in Seoul and the British consul general.[45] In Hamhung, however, four United Church missionaries remained until June 1942, when they were repatriated to Canada as part of an exchange of wartime detainees. While the two ordained men, Scott and E.J.O. Fraser, were kept under house arrest following Japan's attack on Pearl Harbor (and Fraser briefly jailed), Florence Murray and nurse Beulah Bourns were able to continue their hospital work until the day they left Hamhung, reportedly "the only persons so allowed in all Korea." In their account of their experiences, written while en route home, the four missionaries claimed that with a few exceptions the treatment of most enemy aliens was "reasonably fair and considerate" and that "much depended upon the local officials and upon the measure of goodwill that had been built up in time of peace."[46]

The Canadians' ability to remain longer in their station reflected that goodwill and was a by-product of their generally more pragmatic, less doctrinaire approach to relations with the colonial power than that taken by US Presbyterians, especially when theological issues came to the fore. An even longer lingering by-product of the theological controversies of the 1930s would be evident in South Korean Protestantism after World War II, when theological splits occurred between various conservative and "liberal" factions, splits that could be traced back to how particular church leaders and other Christians had responded to colonial directives to participate in State Shinto activities. Four major Presbyterian denominations would eventually emerge from these divisions.[47]

The Canadians who returned to Korea after the war to take up new work in South Korea could not escape being affected to some degree by the controversies. Scott, who returned in 1946 to begin teaching in a comparatively liberal seminary, was the Canadian most directly involved. Several years after his return he came under investigation by a much more conservative new seminary established by the General Assembly of the branch of Presbyterianism with which the Canadian mission had long been affiliated. The new General Assembly seminary, headed by an American, insisted on adherence to such beliefs as the inerrancy of scripture. It also prohibited links with the World Council of Churches. In these uncongenial circumstances the United Church of Canada mission broke away from its old association and in 1955 officially affiliated with a new and smaller body known as the PROK, the Presbyterian Church in the Republic of Korea.[48]

Other Canadian missionaries who settled in South Korea after World War II typically worked in long-established ecumenical institutions for medicine or higher education in and around Seoul. Both then and during and after the Korean War they would also do a great deal of relief work. Dr Florence Murray, by now among the most senior of the returned missionaries, served in supervisory roles, first in the medical college at Ewha Womans University under its first Korean president, Helen Kim, and then at Severance Union Medical College and Hospital. Few of Murray's colleagues were Americans, for Koreans increasingly occupied the senior supervisory and professional positions, as well as the lower levels of institutional work, in facilities founded by missions. But now the authority and omnipresence of the US occupying forces played a crucial role in Murray's personal and professional life. Indeed, even her return to Korea in 1947 had depended on the willingness of those in charge of an American transport and troop ship to accept her and two other

Canadian women missionaries as passengers.[49] In this context, she gave private – and occasionally public – expression to some deeply paradoxical views about Americans in Korea. Given her independence of mind and outspoken approach, she probably chafed more than most of her Canadian colleagues when the dominant American presence in postcolonial South Korea seemed overbearing or insensitive. But it seems reasonable to suppose that even Canadian missionaries less prickly than she occasionally resented the attitudes and behaviour that such an imbalance of power sometimes produced.[50]

During her two decades of medical work in northern Korea, Murray had occasionally made acerbic comments about American missionary colleagues whom she encountered at conferences or vacation sites. But on a daily basis she had mainly worked with Koreans in her role as superintendent of the hospital at Hamhung, an institution she worked tirelessly to modernize. Though it had not been easy, she had gradually learned to work with, and around, local colonial officials. In post–World War II Seoul, and again in the Korean War context, the challenges of being dependent on and surrounded by the new American occupiers were at once more direct and more frustrating. In these circumstances, she was frequently critical of the US occupying forces. They were, she maintained, wasteful, even wantonly destructive of supplies, at a time when Koreans were desperately in need. And US soldiers had a morally harmful influence, particularly by fathering children with desperately poor Korean women and then accepting no responsibility for them.[51]

Yet Murray was as concerned about communist incursions in South Korea as the American military government. When she was asked by military government officials to investigate internal difficulties at the new Seoul National University Hospital and then to serve as advisor to its beleaguered superintendent, she accepted the request and attributed many of the divisions and difficulties she subsequently found to communist agitators. She was openly as well as privately critical when in 1949 US troops were largely withdrawn following the controversial 1948 election that established the Republic of South Korea under Syngman Rhee, correctly anticipating that the new government would be vulnerable to attack from the North.[52] Required like other missionaries to leave Korea at the outbreak of the war in June 1950, she was back in the country in the fall of 1951. Back in Seoul by March 1952 (more than a year before the July 1953 armistice), she attempted to restore Severance's severely damaged medical plant, which US forces were temporarily using as a treatment center for Korean civilians in the service corps. In Seoul she welcomed homesick young American, as well as Canadian, soldiers to her makeshift home. When reconstruction was underway as the Korean War ended, she engaged in the protracted and delicate negotiations required to hold the US Eighth Army to its commitment to build a memorial hospital on the new Severance campus outside central Seoul. Both before and after the war she made what was perhaps her single most valuable contribution to Severance by serving as a conduit for requests for money and specialized personnel to the New York-based ecumenical board that significantly financed its work. Finally, in 1958, on behalf of the United Church of Canada mission, Murray became "chairman" of the new Wonju Union Christian Hospital Board, cooperating with US Methodists and using start-up funds from the United Nations Korean Relief Agency (UNKRA) to build a new medical facility in a mountainous region southeast of Seoul that had suffered severely from the war. Murray, in sum, epitomized, albeit in exaggerated form, a common pattern among Canadian missionaries working with Americans in Korea from the late nineteenth century: a general convergence of values and goals, disrupted occasionally by distinctive responses to particular challenges and by differences arising from the scale, context, and confidence of their respective enterprises.

MISSION LEGACIES IN THE GOLDEN AGE OF CANADIAN DIPLOMACY?

In *The Missionary Mind and American East Asia Policy, 1911–1915*, James Reed wrote that "over the course of a generation, the [Protestant] missionary enterprise ... produced a certain collective mentality that may be called the Missionary Mind. This collective mentality, consisting of a generalized sense of moral obligation towards Asia and towards China in particular, colored the attitudes of the foreign-policy public and shaped the policies pursued by government officials." Long after the missionary movement was on the wane, Reed maintained, the Missionary Mind continued to influence US foreign policy, producing a harmful "lack of clear-sightedness" and leading to such mistakes as prolonged support for the Methodist Chiang Kai-shek and a refusal to recognize Communist China, a policy that, in turn, "led to strains in America's relations with Britain,

Canada, France, and other allies." After mainland China was lost to US influence, Reed argued, "the American public would not tolerate the 'loss' of another Asian country. The Korean war and the Vietnam War become understandable in this context."[53]

Was there a time when Canadian foreign policy was influenced by the equivalent of a Canadian "Missionary Mind"? J.L. Granatstein has suggested that for a time after World War II Canada's Protestant mission community exercised a significant and positive influence on the conduct of external affairs. Canada's early involvement in peace-keeping, he maintained, "should be viewed as analogous to the mis-sionary impulse that was so much a part of Canada before the 1939 war ... The missionary impulse to serve abroad was enormously strong and genuine, and nowhere did it live on in deeper form than among the officers of the Department of External Affairs. Sometimes it seemed as if every post had at least one or two sons of missionaries on staff. The Department sprang full blown from the church and its outposts."[54]

Lester B. Pearson, a central figure in External Affairs as a diplomat and minister before becoming prime minister, was not himself a "mish kid." But as the son of a Methodist minister and as an under-graduate at the University of Toronto's Victoria College he would have been exposed to the values of Christian internationalism that the missionary movement was thought to represent.[55] Furthermore, through his later personal and professional relationships with liberal mission families like the Normans and Endicotts and with mission bureaucrats like Hume Wrong's sister Margaret Wrong, he would have known many people in the movement who were deeply and sympathetically knowledgeable about the parts of the non-Western world in which they lived or worked. Andrew Cohen focuses on Pearson, Wrong, and Norman Robertson in *While Canada Slept*, seeing them as "renaissance men" in "the golden age of Canadian diplomacy." Like Granatstein, Cohen identifies interconnections through friendship and kinship between the diplomats and their policies and the social-service-oriented foreign missionaries of the early twentieth century. Like Granatstein, too, he sees the diplomats' policies as a mixture of idealism and realism. They were, Cohen writes, "a company of pragmatists" in their approach to seeking in-fluence and being useful internationally.[56]

But how mindful of Canada's overseas missionary connections were foreign policy officials when it came to specific matters? It is clear that historic mission ties *and* pragmatic considerations were front and center in their deliberations in the fall of 1947 as they weighed the pros and cons of yielding to US pressure to have a Canadian representative serve on the United Nations Temporary Commission on Korea (UNTCOK) to monitor the anticipated national election. A memorandum for the Canadian delegation at the UN pointed out that "Canada's prewar interest in Korea was focused almost entirely in missionary activities," that Canadian missionaries had "played a role second only to the Americans in inclining Koreans towards the democratic way of life," and that men like Gale, McKenzie, Avison, and D.W. Chisolm (a Maryknoll father from Antigonish) had made particularly noteworthy contributions to the country. These facts were weighed against the shortage of External Affairs personnel available to serve in Korea and "possible Soviet charges that we would be an American tool."[57] John Price's article on Canada and UNTCOK (to which a representative was eventually appointed) acknowledges that officials in this case took the missionary connection into account. But earlier and longer studies of Canadian involvement in Korean affairs in the postcolonial and Korean War eras do not identify the missionary link as a factor bearing on External Affairs decision making. The common thread in these works is the extent to which American policy-makers sought to promote and shape Canadian involvement in Korean matters.[58]

It seems highly unlikely that there was an ideology-driven "Missionary Mind" shaping Canada's Korean policies in the years after World War II. On the other hand, it is certainly possible to identify parallels and analogies in the ways that Canada's missionary and foreign-policy communities approached challenges in Korea, especially vis-à-vis their US counterparts. There is evidence of a mixture of idealism and pragmatism on the part of both Canadian sets of actors and an awareness that they had limited room to choose alternative options. Thus, in responding to Japanese colonial directives on the matter of State Shinto activities the missionaries saw staying on and complying as the best way of serving their Korean Christian constituency, whereas their more doctrinaire US Presbyterian counterparts declined to comply, closing schools and in a few cases leaving the country. In the case of Canadian diplomats dealing with US pressure in 1947–48 to have a Canadian representative on UNTCOK, there was, as noted, initial hesitation about making such an appointment. There was also, for a time, reluctance to have the

appointee remain on the commission when it yielded to US pressure
to proceed with an election only in South Korea, a process Canadian
officials regarded as likely to result in a permanent division of the
peninsula and to signal approval of a rightist regime in the South.[59]
Then in 1950, with the Korean War, there was an initial attempt to
limit the size and nature of Canada's involvement in what was only
nominally a UN-led operation and, later, efforts at a "diplomacy of
constraint" in the face of actions contemplated by the United States
that would have escalated the conflict.[60] Just as the Canadian missionaries had done earlier, Canada's External Affairs officials in
these situations tried to pursue a somewhat independent policy,
though ultimately with less success.

Yet at the end of the day, Canada was largely on side with US policies on Korea, just as Canada's Presbyterian/United Church missionaries had largely been on side with their US counterparts in Korea
– and elsewhere – from the late nineteenth century onward. Like
Florence Murray on the ground in post–World War II Seoul,
Canadian diplomats may have had concerns about the extent and
assertiveness of US might, but on balance they saw it as right, as well
as practical, to support their much stronger ally. Because the best-
known "mish kids" and missionaries in the golden age of Canadian
diplomacy had been, or remained, left-wing – notably Herbert
Norman and James G. Endicott – and because the best-known
Canadian missionary in Korea was the anti-colonial crusader Frank
Schofield, it might seem appropriate to conclude this chapter by emphasizing that a distinctive and leftish mission legacy existed in
Canada in the early Cold War period. Certainly such men stand in
contrast to the presence on the contemporary American scene of a
grandson of missionaries whose name is synonymous with rigid and
moralistic Cold War diplomacy: Eisenhower's Presbyterian secretary
of state, John Foster Dulles.[61] Nonetheless, a less dramatic, more
convergent pattern existed in both the missionary and the diplomatic realms. Two statements by way of conclusion remind us of the
road most travelled in both cases. Writing about the Americans,
Canadians, and Australians who dominated in Protestant missions
in Korea, Donald N. Clark observed that while there were differences among and within these missions, "the watchword was mainly
'cooperation.'" Speaking about Canada-US relations in 1947 as minister of external affairs, Louis St Laurent observed that North
Americans had "travelled so much of the road together in close

agreement that by comparison the occasions on which our paths may have diverged seem insignificant."[62]

NOTES

My thanks to the editors for helpful suggestions during the process of revising this article.

1 William R. Hutchison, *Errand to the World: American Protestant Thought and Foreign Missions* (Chicago: University of Chicago Press 1987), 126n1.

2 J.L. Granatstein, "Canada and Peacekeeping: Image and Reality," in J.L. Granatstein, ed., *Canadian Foreign Policy: Historical Readings* (Toronto: Copp Clark 1986), 232–40.

3 John Webster Grant, *The Church in the Canadian Era*, updated ed. (Burlington, ON: Welch Publishing 1988), 12–13, 55–8. Monographs on specific areas of overseas work include Alvyn J. Austin, *Saving China: Canadian Missionaries in the Middle Kingdom, 1888–1959* (Toronto: University of Toronto Press 1986); Ruth Compton Brouwer, *New Women for God: Canadian Presbyterian Women and India Missions, 1876–1914* (Toronto: University of Toronto Press 1990); Rosemary R. Gagan, *A Sensitive Independence: Canadian Methodist Women Missionaries in Canada and the Orient, 1881–1925* (Montreal: McGill-Queen's University Press 1992); and A. Hamish Ion's two works, *The Cross and the Rising Sun: The Canadian Protestant Missionary Movement in the Japanese Empire, 1872–1931* (Waterloo: Wilfrid Laurier University Press 1990), and *The Cross in the Dark Valley: The Canadian Protestant Missionary Movement in the Japanese Empire, 1931–1945* (Waterloo: Wilfrid Laurier University Press 1999).

4 John S. Moir, *Enduring Witness: A History of the Presbyterian Church in Canada*, 2d ed. (n.p.: Presbyterian Church in Canada 1987). The next few paragraphs draw on Moir and on Brouwer, *New Women*, where full references are provided.

5 Hutchison, *Errand to the World*, 101.

6 Lillian Emery Wanless, *Wanless of India: Lancet of the Lord* (Boston: W.A. Wilde 1944). See also Christopher H. Grundmann, "Wanless, William J.," in *Biographical Dictionary of Christian Missions*, ed. Gerald H. Anderson (New York: Simon and Schuster and Prentice Hall 1998), 717.

7 C. Howard Hopkins, *John R. Mott, 1865–1955: A Biography* (Grand Rapids: William B. Eerdmans 1980); Florence J. Murray, *At the Foot of Dragon Hill* (New York: Dutton 1975), preface.

8 Brouwer, *New Women*, 24–5, 84–5; Hutchison, *Errand*, 132.

9 James Dale Van Buskirk, *Korea: Land of the Dawn* (Toronto: Missionary Education Movement of the United States and Canada, United Church of Canada Edition, 1931).

10 Brian Stanley, "Church, State, and the Hierarchy of 'Civilization': The Making of the 'Missions and Governments' Report at the World Missionary Conference, Edinburgh 1910," in Andrew Porter, ed., *The Imperial Horizons of British Protestant Missions, 1880–1914* (Grand Rapids: Wm. B. Eerdmans 2003), 58–84; Keith Clements, *Faith on the Frontier: A Life of J.H. Oldham* (Edinburgh: T&T Clark 1999); Hopkins, *John R. Mott*; William R. Hutchison, "Protestantism as Establishment," in William R. Hutchison, ed., *Between the Times: The Travail of the Protestant Establishment in America, 1900–1960* (Cambridge: Cambridge University Press 1989), 7, for the Mott anecdote, quoting Hopkins.

11 Ruth Compton Brouwer, *Modern Women Modernizing Men: The Changing Missions of Three Professional Women in Asia and Africa, 1902–69* (Vancouver: University of British Columbia Press 2002), chap. 4.

12 Mark A. Noll, *A History of Christianity in the United States and Canada* (Grand Rapids: William B. Eerdmans 1992), 294; *Hand-Book/Fourth International Convention/Student Volunteer Movement for Foreign Missions*, Toronto, Ontario, 26 February to 2 March 1902; Gagan, *Sensitive Independence*, 53.

13 *Canada's Missionary Congress* (Toronto: Canadian Council, Laymen's Missionary Movement [1909]), vi, ix. Rowell's extensive involvement in church and mission work is shown in Margaret Prang, *N.W. Rowell: Ontario Nationalist* (Toronto: University of Toronto Press 1975).

14 Prang, *Rowell*, 83; Hutchison, *Errand*, 125; Clements, *Faith*, chap. 5 (90, for quoted reference to George V); Stanley, "Edinburgh, 1910."

15 Hutchison, *Errand*, 125, 148; N.W. Rowell, "The League of Nations and the Assembly at Geneva," *International Review of Missions* 24, 2 (1921): 402–15. Rockefeller's involvement in Christian activism at home and abroad left him vulnerable on the left to charges of hypocrisy and, on the fundamentalist right, to charges of apostasy.

16 Noll, *History*, 533. Noll maintains that by 1925 "half of the world's 29,000 missionaries were Americans or Canadians."

17 Brouwer, *Modern Women*, 100, 166n21. This book also deals with two Canadian professional women whose medical missionary careers eventually led them into full- or part-time work for mission bureaucracies.

18 Donald N. Clark, *Christianity in Modern Korea* (Lanham: University Press of America, 1986), xi.

19 Clark, *Christianity,* xiii (for "'modern' but not 'imperialist'"); Sung-Gun Kim, "Korean Christianity and the Shinto Shrine Issue in the War Period, 1931–1945," PHD diss., University of Hull, 1989, 323.

20 Van Buskirk, *Land of the Dawn,* chap. 2; Allen D. Clark, *A History of the Church in Korea* (Seoul: Christian Literature Society 1971), chaps. 3–4 and map showing "Major Denominations in Korea."

21 United Church of Canada Archives Toronto (UCAT), William Scott, "Canadians in Korea: A Brief Historical Sketch of Canadian Mission Work in Korea," typescript, 1975; Brouwer, *Modern Women,* chap. 3; Ion, *Cross and the Rising Sun* and *Cross in the Dark Valley.*

22 Harry A. Rhodes, *History of the Korea Mission Presbyterian Church, U.S.A., 1884–1934* (Seoul: Chosun Mission Presbyterian Church [1934]), 140.

23 Sherwood Hall, *With Stethoscope in Asia: Korea* (McLean, VA: MCL Associates 1978).

24 Allen De Gray Clark, *Avison of Korea: The Life of Oliver R. Avison, M.D.* (Seoul: Yonsei University Press, [1979]), 13; O.R. Avison, "Some High Spots in Medical Mission Work in Korea: Part 4 – A Medical School," *Korean Mission Field,* 35 (July 1939), copy in Public Archives of Nova Scotia (PANS), Maritime Missionaries to Korea Collection (MMKC), vol. 2287, file 7; Library and Archives Canada (LAC), RG 25, vol. 5778, file 204-A (S), Pt. I.1, "Memorandum for the Canadian Delegation to the Second Session of the General Assembly, 21 October 1947," 10 (for Avison's honorary degree); Brouwer, *Modern Women,* 90.

25 Robert T. Oliver, *Syngman Rhee: The Man behind the Myth* (New York: Dodd Mead and Company 1955), 22–3, 94–5.

26 Oliver, *Syngman Rhee,* 95–7; Richard Rutt, ed., *James Scarth Gale and His History of the Korean People* (Seoul: Royal Asiatic Society 1972), introduction, 33. Rhee was baptized as a Presbyterian at a church in Washington in 1905, just after beginning studies at George Washington University.

27 Korea historian Bruce Cumings views him as "the greatest scholar among the foreign missionaries in Korea." Bruce Cumings, *Korea's Place in the Sun: A Modern History* (New York: W.W. Norton 1997), 136. See also 158, 173–4.

28 Rutt, *Gale,* introduction, 17. For Harriet Heron see Martha Huntley, "Presbyterian Women's Work and Rights in the Korea Mission," *American Presbyterians,* 65, 1 (spring 1987): 40.

29 Rutt, *Gale,* introduction, 32; Scott, "Canadians in Korea," chap. 5; Helen Fraser MacRae, *A Tiger on Dragon Mountain: The Life of Rev. Duncan M. MacRae, D. D.* (Charlottetown: A. James Haslam 1993).

30 Rutt, *Gale*, introduction.

31 Cumings, *Korea's Place*, 157; Ion, *Cross and the Rising Sun*, 14 for quotation and 188ff. for details.

32 Martha Huntley, *Caring, Growing, Changing: A History of Protestant Missions in Korea* (New York: Friendship Press 1984), 169.

33 Doretha E. Mortimore, "Dr Frank Schofield and the Korean National Consciousness," *Korea Journal* 17, 3 (March 1977): 37–47, quotation at 37.

34 Ion, *Cross and the Rising Sun*, 188–96. Likening Japan's treatment of Korean nationalists to the "'German [war] Machine" and to Turkish atrocities against Armenians, Armstrong wrote about the events to John R. Mott and to N.W. Rowell, by now a federal cabinet minister (189). For Martin see also UCAT, biographical file for Dr Stanley H. Martin.

35 Cumings, *Korea's Place*, 156–62 (including "tutoring" quotation); Kenneth M. Wells, *New God New Nation: Protestants and Self-Reconstruction Nationalism in Korea, 1896–1937* (North Sydney, Australia: Allen and Unwin 1990), 16.

36 Scott, "Canadians in Korea," 95. A brief biographical sketch of Scott accompanying this manuscript describes his leadership on this and related matters such as early devolution of leadership roles to Korean Christians.

37 Clark, *Christianity in Modern Korea*, 48. See Hutchison, *Errand*, 140, regarding American Fundamentalists' similar concern in the interwar era that Chinese Christians who had gone to the West for higher education were returning "infected with critical views of the Bible."

38 Jung-Gun Kim, "'To God's Country': Canadian Missionaries in Korea and the Beginnings of Korean Migration to Canada," Ed.D., Ontario Institute for Studies in Education, University of Toronto, 1983, quotation at vi.

39 Younghill Kang, *The Grass Roof* (New York: Scribner's 1931), 359–60 for the quotation, 311 for "Luther" as an exceptional missionary, and chaps. 23 and 24 for his arrangements with Young and the trip across the Atlantic. A handwritten note inside a copy of *The Grass Roof* in the Dalhousie University Library indicates that Kang studied there. See Cumings, *Korea's Place*, 203–4, 453–4 for Kang's later life as "a Greenwich Village poet and intellectual." For Young see UCAT, biographical file on Luther Lisgar Young.

40 Clark, *Christianity in Modern Korea*, 13, also 48. Allen D. Clark's *History of the Church in Korea*, chap. 9, gives a longer account, sympathetic to those who resisted the shrine policy.

41 Sung-Gun Kim, "Korean Christianity and the Shinto Shrine Issue in the War Period, 1931–1945: A Sociological Study of Religion and Politics,"

PHD diss., University of Hull, 1989, 320. See also Ion, *Cross in the Dark Valley*, 92–100, 330.

42 Scott, "Canadians in Korea," chap. 14; PANS, MMKC, MG1, vol. 2281, assorted files on Shinto shrine controversy. See *Tiger on Dragon Mountain*, chap. 25, for a sympathetic account of MacRae's position by his daughter Helen Fraser MacRae.

43 PANS, MMKC, MG1. Vol. 2281, assorted files, including file 1936, letter of Armstrong to MacRae, 5 Feb 1936; file 1938, James W. Falconer of Pine Hill Divinity Hall, Halifax, to Armstrong, 29 April 1938, and Robert Grierson to MacRae, 5 April 1938.

44 Ion, *Cross in the Dark Valley*, 330.

45 Sung-gun Kim, "Shinto Shrine Issue," 320, 321.

46 PANS, MMKC, vol. 2276, file 37, "Report of the Interim Committee of the Korea Mission of the United Church of Canada," August 1942, 4, 6. Brouwer, *Modern Women*, 85–6.

47 Allen D. Clark, *History of the Church*, chap. 10; Donald N. Clark, *Christianity in Modern Korea*, 2,13; Scott, "Canadians in Korea," 211–19.

48 Allen D. Clark, *History of the Church*, 274–6; Scott, "Canadians in Korea," 211–19.

49 Florence J. Murray, *Return to Korea* (Belleville, ON: Essence Publishing 1999), chap. 1. Murray died in 1975 while revising the manuscript for this book.

50 This section on Murray's relationship to the American occupying forces draws on my *Modern Women*, chap. 3, especially 86–92, and relevant endnotes.

51 Murray, *Return*, 15. Shocked by the foul language, drinking, and sexual behaviour of the young soldiers and the army wives on board ship en route from San Francisco in 1947 she had already been sarcastic about the ways they would be "commending the great American way of life" to Koreans.

52 Murray, *Return*, chap. 5.

53 James Reed, *The Missionary Mind and American East Asia Policy, 1911–1915* (Cambridge: Council on East Asian Studies, Harvard University 1983), introduction (quotations on 1–3). Reed's book focuses on a period when liberals and moderates were in the ascendant in the missionary enterprise, creating optimism about an eventual Christian and democratic China among many Americans from President Wilson on down.

54 Granatstein, "Canada and Peacekeeping," 237, 238. On "mish kids" in Canada's foreign service beginning with Herbert Norman see also John Hilliker, *Canada's Department of External Affairs*, vol. 1, *The*

Early Years, 1909–1946 (Montreal: McGill-Queen's University Press 1990), 191–2, 258.

55 *Mike: The Memoirs of the Right Honourable Lester B. Pearson,* vol. 1, *1897–1948* (Toronto: University of Toronto Press 1972). Pearson was not religiously observant as an adult, but as John English observes, he and his colleagues in External Affairs were nonetheless marked by their upbringing, "the secular heirs of spiritual parents"; English, *The Worldly Years: The Life of Lester Pearson, 1949–1972* (Toronto: Vintage Books 1992), 182.

56 Andrew Cohen, *While Canada Slept: How We Lost Our Place in the World* (Toronto: McClelland & Stewart 2003), especially 7 (quotation), 9, 12, 20, 36 (quotation), 74, 80, 199.

57 LAC, RG 25, vol. 5778, file 204-A(s), pt. 1.1. "Memorandum for the Canadian Delegation," 9–11, and "Commentary on the United States Draft Resolution on Korea," part 2, 24 October 1947, 4.

58 John Price, "The 'Cat's Paw': Canada and the United Nations Temporary Commission on Korea," *Canadian Historical Review* 85, 2 (June 2004): 297–324; Denis Stairs, *The Diplomacy of Constraint: Canada, the Korean War, and the United States* (Toronto: University of Toronto Press 1974); Martin Kitchen, "From the Korean War to Suez: Anglo-American-Canadian Relations, 1950–1956," in B.J.C. McKercher and Lawrence Aronsen, eds., *The North Atlantic Triangle in a Changing World: Anglo-American-Canadian Relations, 1902–1956* (Toronto: University of Toronto Press 1996), 220–55; Meroslav Galan, "Canada-Korean Relations, 1947–1955: The Continentalization of Canadian Foreign Policy," PHD diss., McGill University, 1981.

59 In his closely argued revisionist article Price argues that the Canadian decision makers, and Pearson in particular, quickly "fell into line" with the US determination to have UNTCOK monitor an election just in South Korea: "The 'Cat's Paw,'" 321.

60 Stairs, *Diplomacy of Constraint*; Kitchen, "From the Korean War."

61 Roger W. Bowen, ed., *E.H. Norman: His Life and Scholarship* (Toronto: University of Toronto Press 1984), part 1; Stairs, *Diplomacy of Constraint*, 259–62; Frederick W. Marks, III, *Power and Peace: The Diplomacy of John Foster Dulles* (Westport: Praeger 1993), chap. 1.

62 Donald N. Clark, "Sources of Historical Information on the Foreign Community in Korea," *Korea Journal*, 25, 3 (March 1985): 20; St Laurent, as quoted in Norman Hillmer, "The Foreign Policy That Never Was, 1900–1950," in Serge Bernier and John MacFarlane, eds., *Canada, 1900–1950: Un pays prend sa place/A Country Comes of Age* (Ottawa: Organization for the History of Canada 2003), 141–53 (quotation at 152).

PART THREE

Conflict and Cooperation

7

Addressing Cross-border Pollution of the Great Lakes after World War II

The Canada-Ontario Agreement and the Great Lakes Water Quality Agreement

PHILIP V. SCARPINO

The environmental history of the Great Lakes is as complex and challenging as the lakes themselves – one minute deceptively calm and the
next requiring overwhelming efforts to make sense of the intertwined
histories of people and nature on those vast freshwater seas. Rarely
are environmental issues neatly circumscribed by political boundaries, and in the case of the Great Lakes, physical geography and
human and natural history argue strongly for an international, comparative approach. Although Lake Michigan is contained wholly
within the United States, the remaining four lakes – Superior, Huron,
Erie, and Ontario – are boundary waters that straddle the Canadian/
US border for about 1,900 kilometers (1,187 miles).[1] The Great
Lakes are bordered by two nations, eight states, one province, and
scores of cities and towns. As such, political boundaries have ren-
dered management of the lakes a complicated business.

Although water quality has been an important theme in the environmental history of the Great Lakes since the late nineteenth
century, its significance increased dramatically in the decades after
World War II. Following the war, the Canadian and US economies
experienced prolonged prosperity. Cities and industries expanded,
swelling the flow of untreated wastes into the Great Lakes. New
technologies, especially phosphate-based detergents, altered the
composition of the pollutants and by the late 1960s created a high-
profile crisis while science increased knowledge and understanding
of the causes and consequences of water pollution. Grassroots

environmental movements in both countries drew inspiration from
a popularized understanding of the science of ecology and created a
political constituency for protecting and enhancing water quality in
the Great Lakes.

In the post–World War II period, the signing of two landmark
agreements, the Canada/Ontario Act (1971) and the Great Lakes
Water Quality Act (1972), represented the first successful international attempt to ameliorate a growing water pollution crisis.[2]
Analysis of the process whereby Canadians and Americans crafted
these accords offers a useful example of international response to
environmental change and to negotiating the authority and responsibility for regulating the environment between two interrelated, but
different, federal systems.

The journey that culminated with the signing of these two agree-
ments actually began decades earlier. In 1909, the United States and
Britain, acting on behalf of Canada, signed the Boundary Waters
Treaty, which addressed all boundary waters shared by the two

nations. The treaty established the general framework and institutional mechanisms for addressing international water pollution issues on the Great Lakes and remains in effect. Among other things, the Boundary Waters Treaty created the International Joint Commission (IJC) and charged it to prevent disputes and settle questions related to rights, obligations, and interests as they pertained to boundary waters.[3] The treaty addressed pollution quite narrowly – concentrating its attention on contamination that crossed the international border and inflicted harm on the other side. Clearly, the decision to limit the definition of pollution covered by the treaty had more to do with protecting national sovereignty than with preserving the quality of water. Very little movement took place on the international water pollution control front until after World War II.

In 1956, the United States suggested to Canada a joint reference to the IJC that addressed abatement and control of water pollution in Lake Erie, Lake Ontario, and the international sections of the St Lawrence (i.e., the lower Great Lakes).[4] The initial push for this reference came from the United States, driven by complaints from the state governments of New York and Michigan over pollution of Lake Erie by Canadian cities.[5] Canada responded slowly, in part because of concerns related to cost sharing with Ontario and in part because of a lack of a sense of urgency. It took until 1963 for Canada to address this federal/provincial impasse over regulatory authority and financial responsibility.

Between the mid-1950s and the early 1970s, as Canada and the United States sought international remedies for pollution of the Great Lakes, they also struggled internally over the federal/state, federal/provincial authority and responsibility for regulating water pollution. Despite constitutional differences and against a backdrop of growing public demands for environmental regulation, both nations moved in the direction of greater federal involvement. The United States travelled much further down that path than Canada had, a journey that culminated with the passage of the federal amendments to the Federal Water Pollution Control Act in 1972.[6] Terrance Kehoe's *Cleaning up the Great Lakes* chronicles the history of state and federal water pollution control legislation, with special emphasis on the impact of shifting authority to regulate water quality in the Great Lakes. In Canada, a parallel but different story of provincial and federal efforts to regulate water pollution has received less attention from historians. Canadian federal officials

engaged in a serious debate about how much authority the national
government could assume at the expense of the provinces, while the
provinces insisted on maintaining their own constitutional and historical authority. Within Ontario and the other provinces, a parallel
struggle took place between provincial and municipal governments
over responsibility for the cost of pollution clean up and control.

Jurisdiction over water resources in Canada is divided between
the federal and provincial governments, a fact that has had a significant impact on the question of who has the authority and responsibility for regulating the environment. Canada's provincial
governments own the water resources within their borders, but legislative responsibility is divided between the provincial and federal
governments. Historically, the federal government has had jurisdiction over navigation and fisheries (management of fisheries became
the responsibility of Ontario in the late 1920s), international waters,
and the regulation of interprovincial and foreign trade. Crucial in
the case of negotiations with the United States on a water quality
agreement is the fact that under the Canadian constitutional system,
authority and responsibility for water pollution control is divided
between the federal government and the provinces. Without active
cooperation from Ontario, an agreement with the United States
would have been unenforceable. Therefore, as Canada attempted to
develop a joint strategy with the United States, it engaged in parallel
negotiations with Ontario centring on which level of government
would pay for constructing sewage treatment facilities.

Ontario is the only Canadian province that borders the Great
Lakes, and in the 1950s and 1960s, as pressure built to clean up the
lakes, the potential cost to Ontario was staggering. In the early
1950s, Ontario's premier, Leslie Frost, seemed open to cleaning
up the province's waterways. But whatever incipient commitment
Premier Frost had suggested collided with fiscal reality in the summer of 1953. In August the chair of Ontario's Pollution Control
Board, A.E. Berry, reported that pollution control would cost the
province's municipalities more than $113 million over a ten-year
period. Berry recommended that the province pay 25 percent of the
cost, or about $28 million over a decade-long period, as an incentive
to the municipalities. A handwritten notation on the bottom of
Berry's report conveyed the response of the Frost administration to
the recommendations of the Pollution Control Board: "NOT TO BE
QUOTED. PM says to let this matter stand. Province cannot embark

on any grandiose scheme of this character. Local municipalities create these problems and primarily responsible for their solution."[7]

While Premier Frost may have hoped that he had put to rest the
matter of paying for pollution control, events in 1954 placed even
greater pressure on the province. In the fall, the chair of the Canadian
section of the IJC and the attorney general for Michigan complained
that municipal pollution from Ontario cities posed a cross-border
threat.[8] Canada therefore found itself potentially in violation of the
Boundary Waters Treaty of 1909, a situation that would have required construction of expensive municipal sewage treatment plants.
The issue quickly boiled down to one question: which level of government bore the financial responsibility for constructing such facilities? Canadian federal authorities concluded in the fall of 1954 that
the financial cost of abating pollution in the Great Lakes belonged
to Ontario. Thereafter, Frost and his successor, John P. Robarts, refused to acknowledge correspondence on this subject from Ottawa.
The province held fast on this course until July 1963.[9]

During the late 1950s and early 1960s, pressure mounted for a
settlement of the impasse between Canada and Ontario. When in
1956 the United States suggested a Joint Reference to the IJC concerning abatement and control of pollution in the Lower Great Lakes,
both federal governments approved, and Canada sent it on to Ontario
for comment. Ontario remained silent. As the years dragged on,
Ontario's uncompromising position proved to be an increasing embarrassment to the Canadian government. At the same time, growing
scientific evidence documenting the degradation of the lower Great
Lakes, an emerging environmental movement, and new institutional
arrangements to address Canada's environmental problems placed
indirect pressure on Ottawa and Toronto to break the deadlock. In
1960, an amendment to Canada's National Housing Act alleviated
some of the potential financial burden faced by Ontario by making
low-cost federal loans available to the provinces for the construction
of sewage treatment plants. In 1961, the federal government sponsored
the Resources for the Future Conference, which gave environmental
issues a high national and international profile. A direct outgrowth of
that conference was the Canadian Council of Resource Ministers,
an institutional mechanism for developing federal/provincial cooperation in the area of the environment.[10]

By the early 1960s, the Canadian federal government found itself
caught between Ontario's silence and ever more insistent cries for

action from the United States and its border states that Canada approve the proposed joint reference to the IJC. Finally, in 1963, changes in the administrations of both the Canadian federal government and the province of Ontario put in place new officials who worked out a solution that allowed Ontario to approve the joint reference to the International Joint Commission.[11] The issue of which level of government should pay for sewage treatment remained unsettled until the Canada/Ontario Agreement of 1971. But with Ontario's consent, the IJC was now authorized to conduct a study of the lower Great Lakes.

In October 1964, eight years after it was initially proposed, Canada and the United States formally asked the IJC to undertake a study of pollution in the lower Great Lakes. The IJC issued three reports, in 1965, 1968, and 1970. Cumulatively, they provided considerable scientific evidence for the seriousness of the pollution of the lower Great Lakes, especially eutrophication of Lake Erie caused by phosphates found mostly in detergents that came into widespread use after World War II. (Eutrophication is an acceleration of the aging process of a lake, pond, or slow-moving stream. Excess nutrients, such as phosphates, permit explosive growth of algae and other aquatic plants. Alive they create copious amounts of "slime." In death, their decaying remains create a smothering layer of organic silt on the bottom. Decomposition decreases the amount of dissolved oxygen in the water.) The IJC's reports played a major role in creating the public constituency, political will, and momentum that produced the Canada/Ontario Agreement and the Great Lakes Water Quality Agreement. At least on the Canadian side of the border, eutrophication had become an overriding reason for concluding agreements on the Great Lakes.[12]

In 1970, Canada invited the United States and Ontario to join in discussions to work out cooperative mechanisms for restoring and protecting the water quality of the Great Lakes. At this point, the momentum and the initiative had passed from the Americans to the Canadians. From the Canadian perspective, negotiations proceeded on parallel tracks with the clear objective of completing an agreement with Ontario before concluding one with the United States.[13] The Canada/Ontario Agreement, signed in 1971, established formal mechanisms for cooperation and shared responsibility for pollution abatement, which in turn allowed the Canadian government to push hard for an international Great Lakes Water Quality Agreement. In brief, Ontario agreed to a five-year program (1971–75) of accelerated construction of municipal sewage treatment facilities and trunk sewers in the Lower Great Lakes – Ontario, Erie, their connecting channels, and the international sections of the St Lawrence River. Ontario also vowed to assist in implementing the pending agreement with the United States. For its part, under terms and conditions of the National Housing Act, the federal government promised in the central provision of the agreement to loan Ontario two-thirds of the $250 million estimated cost of this accelerated program. In addition, the federal government would forgive 25 percent of the loans if Ontario and its municipalities completed the projects within five years.[14] So, after years of standoff and struggle, Ontario got the federal funding that it sought to help defray the massive costs of water pollution control in the Great Lakes, and Canada got the cooperation from Ontario that it needed before concluding an agreement with the United States.

Although delayed when the United States reversed its position on phosphates, the Great Lakes Water Quality Agreement was finally signed on 15 April 1972.[15] The agreement committed both nations to develop common water quality objectives and regulatory standards for several pollutants and to create and implement their own national programs to achieve those goals. There were provisions for joint monitoring and for enhanced responsibilities for the IJC. The Great Lakes Water Quality Agreement is also noteworthy for the difficult issues that it left for further study: pollution of the upper lakes (Huron, Michigan, and Superior), waste discharged from vessels, and pollution from non-point sources, such as contaminated run-off from agricultural lands.[16]

On one level, the Canada/Ontario Agreement and the Great Lakes Water Quality Agreement can be understood within the larger context of the environmental histories of the United States and Canada. The two decades before 1972 had witnessed the emergence and rapid growth of the ecology-based environmental movement, which provided an important new constituency for environmental protection and remediation in both nations. Highly publicized environmental crises, such as DDT and mercury contamination, the Santa Barbara and Torry Canyon oil spills, and the "death" of Lake Erie, energized the Canadian and American environmental movements and contributed directly to the passage of landmark environmental legislation in both nations. The passion and commitment of a popular, grass-roots environmental movement provided a constituency that pushed Canada and the United States to do something about the pollution of the Great Lakes. At the same time, government officials and policy-makers had to work through the challenges presented by political and cultural boundaries and by assigning authority and responsibility for regulating the environment. In 1956, most Canadians saw water pollution as an American problem. By the mid-1960s, however, complacency had given way to a growing nationwide call for action, galvanized by concerns over degradation of the Great Lakes. In 1967, the Calgary *Albertan* declared that "the most contaminated inland water associated with Canada lies in the Great Lakes basin." The newspaper then got to the point: "It was in the Great Lakes area that Canada first received the shock which wakened it to a pollution menace in this country. To an extent, it is fortunate we shared in the Great Lakes problem. Otherwise Canadians would have gone on in the self-righteous attitude that we have nothing to worry about, at least not now, in regard to water pollution. Definitely water pollution is a growing problem in Canada."[17] In chiding Canadians for their "self-righteous attitude," the *Albertan* also highlighted the role that cultural borders have played in the environmental history of the Great Lakes.

Americans and Canadians approached the shared problems of the Great Lakes within a context characterized by similar attitudes towards nature and quite different attitudes towards one another. After adjusting for population density and industrial development, one cannot see significant differences in the way the two nations have used and abused the Great Lakes or their environments in general. Constitutional variations between the two nations have led to differences in apportionment of the authority to regulate the environment between Canada and its provinces and the United States and its states. Even so, a very good recent Canadian study of US and Canadian environmental laws suggests that when judged by results the differences are not great.[18] Despite apparent similarities, there are important cultural differences with roots that stretch back at least as far as the American Revolution.[19] As a result of historical developments, the two peoples understand one other and themselves differently, and that has had an impact on shared environmental issues such as management of the Great Lakes. In Canada, historically and in the present, the American presence has been significant. The reverse has not been true. A dispatch to the US State Department from the embassy in Ottawa reported in April 1961 that behind a decline in Canadian goodwill toward the United States "is the viewpoint and deep-rooted fear that the United States may smother 'Canada's identity.'"[20] In January 1963, a "confidential" briefing paper prepared by the US Department of State observed, "There is in most Canadian minds, never far from the surface, a latent fear that the United States will, inadvertently, engulf Canada – economically, culturally, and finally politically."[21] Prime Minister Pierre Trudeau, who signed the Great Lakes Water Quality Agreement on behalf of Canada, often described the US/Canadian relationship as similar to sleeping with an elephant, an image that resonated with his constituents then and has ever since.

While Canadians may have felt as though they were sleeping with an elephant, most Americans hardly paid attention to who they were sleeping with at all. In January 1963, an unusually insightful briefing paper prepared for senior officials of the US State Department who were bound for a meeting in Ottawa explained that most Americans "tend to be uninformed about Canada and to take for granted that Canada will automatically align itself with whatever the United States position may be. This attitude on the part of most of the US public is extremely irritating to many Canadians."[22]

In Canada, long-standing differences between Canada and the United States became incorporated into public discourse over the management, protection, and preservation of the environment. As the two nations edged towards an agreement on the Great Lakes, ambivalent feelings that many Canadians held towards the United States were injected not only into international negotiations but also into an internal, domestic debate over protecting and preserving that nation's waters. In December 1966, Senator Frank Moss of Utah, head of a Senate subcommittee on water, suggested that Canada should share its abundant supplies of fresh water. Moss's suggestion was not taken seriously by Americans in official positions, but according to the *Ottawa Citizen*, "the response in this country was swift and angry. Canadians at all levels made it known in no uncertain terms that they intended to guard jealously the water wealth of the nation."[23]

By the mid-1960s, fears that the United States had designs on Canadian water became entangled with the emerging environmental movement and growing concerns over water quality. John Turner, the parliamentary secretary to the minister of northern affairs and national resources, expressed a common theme: the United States had fouled its waters, but there was still time for Canada to act and avoid a similar fate.[24] A slightly darker but related view was that the United States had contaminated and ruined its own waters and therefore had an eye on the relatively unpolluted supplies in Canada. Or, in the case of the Great Lakes and other boundary waters, that the United States had used up its share of the capacity of those waters to absorb pollution and now had designs on what rightfully belonged to Canada.[25] Historically, the United States has contributed a much larger volume of pollution to the Great Lakes than Canada, a fact that Canadians and Americans have interpreted very differently and that has reminded Canadians of the dangers of sleeping with an elephant.

On the Canadian side of the border, a number of factors pushed the federal government and the provincial government of Ontario to address the pollution of the Great Lakes, including the eutrophication crisis in Lake Erie and the popular ecology-based environmental movement. Even so, the volume of pollution originating on the US side of the border was the single most important factor motivating the Canadian federal government to reach accommodation with Ontario and to negotiate an agreement with the United States. In October 1973, Canadian under-secretary of state A.E. Ritchie prepared a confidential assessment of the Great Lakes Water Quality Agreement that offers valuable insight into why the Canadian federal government pushed so hard for an agreement with the United States. Ritchie argued that "the Agreement, thus, is essentially achieving the purpose for which it was created, i.e., to encourage the US to give priority to abatement programs in the Great Lakes Basin."[26] Looked at from the Canadian federal perspective, the Great Lakes Water Quality Agreement was a success from the moment it was signed. The agreement satisfied an important constituency composed of Canadian citizens who were worried about environmental degradation, the fate of the Great Lakes, and the potential impact of their neighbour to the south on Canadian environmental quality. More to the point, it achieved the primary goal of the Canadian federal administration, which was to encourage the United States to assign a high priority to the Great Lakes.

In the United States, a strong and vocal environmental movement, combined with widespread citizen interest in the environment, created a powerful political constituency for pollution control. But constituency alone was not enough to translate public concern into public policy. Richard Nixon was president from 1969 to 1974, during the years preceding the signing of the Great Lakes Water Quality Agreement. Nixon was no environmentalist, yet he signed several major pieces of environmental legislation, including the National Environmental Policy Act (1970), the Clean Air Act (1970), and significant amendments to the Water Quality Act (1972). He also created the Environmental Protection Agency (EPA) by executive order in 1970 and appointed William Ruckelshaus as its first director. During the early 1970s, President Nixon was in trouble with many US voters as a result of a cluster of issues, including Vietnam, an economic downturn, unemployment, and inflation. As Jeffery Stine has shown in *Mixing the Waters: Environment, Politics, and the Building of the Tennessee-Tombigbee Waterway*, the interest of Nixon and many of his key advisors in environmental issues was highly correlated with their assessment of the impact of the president's actions on his own political fortunes.[27]

Early in 1971, William Ruckelshaus endeavored to get Nixon behind an initiative of the EPA for an accelerated Great Lakes Program. Ruckelshaus sent his blueprint for an accelerated cleanup to the White House, accompanied by a cover memo in which he presented a rationale he believed would persuade the Nixon White House to support the EPA's plan. Ruckelshaus began by stating the "problem": the president's reputation "as a strong advocate for environmental improvement had suffered." After explaining why he thought this had come to pass, Ruckelshaus noted the political implications, saying, among other things, that "the very people RMN appeals to are also vitally interested in the environment. The white middle class suburbanite (particularly women) are very concerned over this issue." And, he added, they likely would not vote for someone they believed insensitive to the environment. Ruckelshaus then offered his "remedy": take the offense. "The one area," he said, "that stands out for the environment and its degradation in the minds of the American people is the Great Lakes." In order to drive his point home, Ruckelshaus listed the eight states that touched the Great Lakes and noted that they had 180 electoral votes. Nixon, he noted, had carried only four of those states in 1968. Ruckelshaus's unambiguous message to the president was that both the environment and the Great Lakes were issues that could have a material impact on the outcome of the election in 1972.[28]

It was in this political context that President Nixon made his decision to sign the Great Lakes Water Quality Agreement. In March 1972, Russell Train, chairman of the president's Council on Environmental Quality, in a memo to Henry Kissinger, strongly recommended that President Nixon sign the Great Lakes Water Quality Agreement:

> The signing of the agreement by the President would give him personal credit for initiating a new program that has broad public support in the eight Great Lakes Basin States. Such an action would have the further advantage of enhancing the President's national environmental image at a time when environmental issues are becoming increasingly important in the political arena ... the agreement represents one of the few positive features of US-Canadian relations at this time ... Failure to sign or further postponement would surely have a negative effect on relations, particularly since there is considerable public feeling in Canada that the United States has been less than forthcoming on the agreement.[29]

Nixon's other advisors concurred, and the president ultimately made the journey to Ottawa to sign the Great Lakes Water Quality Agreement in mid-April 1972. President Nixon's public image and domestic political fortunes played a pivotal role, but relations with Canada and "public feeling" in Canada also influenced the decision. The agreement itself was little more than a promise from both nations to address the pollution problems of the Great Lakes. Its real significance in April 1972 was as a symbolic commitment and in the framework that it offered for future action. For the first time in the history of relations between Canada and the United States, an agreement had created an international, institutional mechanism that held real potential for regulating, controlling, and reducing water pollution in the Great Lakes.

The Canada-Ontario Agreement and the Great Lakes Water Quality Agreement need to be understood as signature events in an evolving and interwoven story of human and natural history on the Great Lakes. The reciprocal interplay between nature and people produced a Great Lakes environment that was a highly humanized cultural artifact – molded and shaped by the intended and unintended actions of people who themselves were motivated by attitudes and values embedded in their cultures. One dimension of culture that contributes to an understanding of the recent environmental history of the Great Lakes is to be found in the sometimes subtle but nonetheless distinct ways that Canadians and Americans understood themselves and each other. Another is the profound change in attitudes and values towards nature that developed on both sides of the border as a result of the post–World War II environmental movement. Not everyone was an "environmentalist," but the constituency generated by the ecology-based environmental movement powerfully shaped politics and policy in both nations. No other explanation accounts for Richard Nixon's support of the environment.

Together, the two agreements came about as the result of the confluence of a number of historical factors, including the development of a constituency for environmental quality and clean water in Canada and the United States. Increasingly in the years after World War II, politicians and bureaucrats had to take into account growing public concern over the environment. Without any doubt, the scientific findings of the IJC brought the plight of the Great Lakes into sharp public focus and helped create the constituency that pushed the US and Canadian governments towards the Great Lakes Water Quality Agreement. Eutrophication of Lake Erie, which, as mentioned, was bound up with the issue of phosphates in detergents, caught the public imagination. Within Canada, public pressure to do something about the lakes and the growing momentum of a pending agreement with the United States forced Ottawa and Toronto to work through the difficult negotiations that produced the Canada-Ontario Agreement. On the US side, public interest in the environment and the Great Lakes heavily influenced the decision of the Nixon administration to negotiate with Canada and to sign the Great Lakes Water Quality Agreement. In effect, scientific evidence of a serious environmental crisis in the Lower Great Lakes, combined with inflamed public opinion on both sides of the border, provided the incentive and the will for overcoming the obstacles presented by political and cultural boundaries.

When considering historical factors that produced these agreements, the Canadian concern over "sleeping with an elephant" looms large. This perspective was part of the fabric of Canadian culture and national identity that was little known or understood within the United States. Canadians worried that Americans who had dirtied and wasted their own water supplies coveted their abundant supplies of fresh water. Federal and provincial policy-makers and politicians knew that no matter what they did or how much money they spent, they could not clean up the Great Lakes by themselves. With a wary eye on the elephant, it was the Canadians who pushed hard for an international agreement. Even before the ink had dried on Richard Nixon's signature, Canada had gained its primary policy objective: persuading the United States to make the Great Lakes a priority and to devote attention and money to cleaning up the mess that had originated south of the border.

While there is much in common between the Canadian and the American environmental experiences, there are also significant differences. Those experiences are embedded in related but different histories, and perhaps more importantly, Canadians and Americans have interpreted those experiences through the prism of different memories of themselves and of each other. Coming to terms with the environmental history of the Great Lakes requires an understanding of the fact that the dynamic interplay between human and natural history has been refracted through political and cultural boundaries. The outcome of that interaction has been bent and shaped in ways that would not be evident in considering environmental issues alone.

NOTES

The author acknowledges and appreciates funding from the Indiana University Center on Philanthropy, the IUPUI Office of Faculty Development, and the IUPUI School of Liberal Arts.

1 College Reprint, University of Wisconsin, WIS-SG-74-351, reprinted from *American Scientist* 62 (July/August 1974), offers a good hydrological overview of the Great Lakes.
2 The following shed considerable light on the negotiations surrounding the Canada-Ontario Agreement and the Great Lakes Water Quality Agreement: Department of Foreign Affairs and International Trade, Historical Section, Lester B. Pearson Building, 125 Sussex Drive, Ottawa, Ontario K1A 0G2 (hereafter cited as DFAIT), File 25–5–2–Great Lakes-4, vols. 6–8, (May 1968 to May 1972). Also very helpful are documents from Government of Canada, Privy Council, Ottawa, Ontario, K1A 0A3 (hereafter cited as PC, followed by the date of the particular Cabinet meeting). Canada-Ontario Agreement: PC, 11/13/1969; PC, 2/12/70; PC, 7/30/70; PC, 12/3/70; PC, 6/7/71; and PC, 7/29/71. Great Lakes Water

Quality Agreement: PC, 6/18/70; PC, 5/27/71; PC, 3/23/72. See also Don Munton and Geoffrey Castle, "The Continental Dimension: Canada and the United States," chap. 11, in Robert Boardman, ed., *Canadian Environmental Policy: Ecosystems, Politics, and Process* (Toronto: Oxford University Press 1992), 203–23.

3 William R. Willoughby, *The Joint Organizations of Canada and the United States* (Toronto: University of Toronto Press 1979); Peter Neary, "Grey, Bryce and the Settlement of Canadian-American Differences, 1905–1911," *Canadian Historical Review* 49 (December 1968). See also *The Dawn of Conservation Diplomacy: US-Canadian Wildlife Protection Treaties in the Progressive Era* (Seattle: University of Washington Press 1998).

4 Memorandum for the Minister, "Pollution of Boundary Waters," 30 May 1963, Library and Archives Canada, Record Group 25, Records of the Department of External Affairs, vol. 5058, file 2871-40, pt. 6. (Hereafter, LAC and RG 25.)

5 "Memorandum to the Chairman: Water Pollution – IJC Involvement, 1912 and 1946 References," from D.G. Chance, Secretary, IJC, 10 January 1968, DFAIT, file 25-5-2-Great Lakes-4, vol. 5, s24

6 Terrance Kehoe, *Cleaning up the Great Lakes: From Cooperation to Confrontation* (DeKalb, IL: Northern Illinois University Press 1997). For an examination of events leading up to the passage of the federal Water Pollution Act of 1948, see Philip V. Scarpino, *Great River: An Environmental History of the Upper Mississippi, 1890–1950* (Columbia, MO: University of Missouri Press 1985), 153–63.

7 Letter, A.E. Berry, Chairman, Ontario Pollution Control Board, to Mr W.M. McIntyre, Executive Assistant to the Prime Minister, 13 August 1953, Archives of Ontario, Toronto, Record Group 3–23, Office of the Premier, Frost Administration, General Correspondence Files, 1949–1961, Box 148, file, Pollution of Border Waters,1945–53. (Hereafter, Archives of Ontario, RG 3–23, Frost, Gen. Corr.)

8 Draft, "Memorandum to the Cabinet: Pollution of Boundary Waters," from the Secretary of State for External Affairs, LAC, Record Group 89, Records of the Water Resources Branch, 1887–1982, Acc. 1988–89/059, Box 27, file 7358-1, pt.1. (Hereafter, RG 89). See also "Report of the International Joint Commission, United States and Canada, on the Pollution of Boundary Waters," 1950, Record Group 59, General Records of the Department of State, CDF60–63, Box 1242, File 611.4232–SCR/ 6–1360, National Archives and Records Administration, College Park, MD (hereafter, RG 59, CDF60–63, NARAII).

9 Letter, Louis S. St Laurent, to My dear Premier, March 24, 1955, LAC, RG 89, Acc. 1988–89/059, Box 27, file 7358-1, part 1. The story of the relations between Ottawa and Toronto in the 1950s is further described in documents contained in this same file. Also essential in understanding the relations between Ontario and Canada in the late 1950s and early 1960s are documents found in NAC, RG 25, volume 2933, file 2871-40, pt.2., f1.

10 On the amendment to the Municipal Housing Act see Memorandum, "The I.J.C. and Pollution of Boundary Waters," 29 April 1961, LAC, RG 25, vol. 6835, file 2871-40, pt. 4.1; Memorandum, to files, from USA Division/J.N. Whittaker, "Amendment to National Housing Act (1960)," 24 January 24 1961, LAC, RG 25, vol. 6835, file 2871-40, pt. 4.1. On the connection between Resources for the Future and the Canadian Council of Resource Ministers, see John N. Turner, Parliamentary Secretary to the Minister of Northern Affairs and National Resources, "Clean Water – National Priority," Notes for Keynote Speech before the First Paper Industry Conference on Water Conservation and Stream Improvement," 19 October 1965, DFAIT, file 25-5-2-Great Lakes-4, vol. 2.

11 In 1961 John Robarts was elected as premier of Ontario, replacing Leslie Frost, who had served continuously since 1949. At the federal level in 1962, the Liberal party handed the Conservatives a defeat and Lester Pearson replaced John Diefenbaker as prime minister. Memorandum from the Office of the Secretary of State for External Affairs, to U.S.A. Division, "Pollution of Boundary Waters," 19 July 1963, LAC, RG 25, vol. 5058, file 2871-40, pt. 6; Telegram, 18 July 1963, from John P. Robarts, Prime Minister of Ontario to Honorable Paul Martin, Secretary of State for External Affairs, LAC, RG 25, vol. 5058, file 2871-40, pt. 6; Memorandum for the Minister, initialed N.A.R. [N.A. Robertson, Under-Secretary of State for External Affairs], "Pollution of Boundary Waters," 8 July 1963, LAC, RG 25, vol. 5058, file 2871-40, pt. 6.

12 Memorandum to Cabinet, "Canada-United States Ministerial Meeting on Great Lakes Pollution, Ottawa, June 23," n.d., stamped "received," 15 June 1970, Doc. No. 714/40, PC, 6/18/70.

13 On Canadian strategy see Memorandum to the Cabinet, "Canada-United States Ministerial Meeting on Great Lakes Pollution, Washington, June 10," Doc. No. 536–71, PC, 5/27/71.

14 Memorandum to Cabinet, "Canada-Ontario Agreement on Great Lakes Water Quality, Doc. 896–71, PC 7/29/71; text of agreement is in PC 7/29/71. 28

15 In mid-September 1971, with negotiations on the Great Lakes Water Quality Agreement nearing completion, the US Department of Health

Education and Welfare recommended reconsideration of policies that restricted phosphates in laundry detergents and advised against the use of substitutes for phosphates. Instead, the US elected to meet phosphorous reduction requirements in the nearly completed Great Lakes Water Agreement through water treatment alone. Reaction in the Canadian press to the US announcement was swift and angry. See several clippings and related documents in DFAIT, file 68-18-Great Lakes, vol. 3.

16 "Agreement between Canada and the United States of America on Great Lakes Water Quality," PC 3/23/72; Memorandum to the Cabinet, "Agreement between Canada and the United States on Water Quality," PC 3/23/72. See also Munton and Castle, "The Continental Dimension," in Boardman, Canadian Environmental Policy, 205–9.

17 "Inland Water Research Centre," Calgary Albertan, 10 April 1967, LAC, RG 89, vol. 5, file 7340-1, part 4. A recent, comparative analysis of US. and Canadian environmental policies reinforces my conclusion about the role of the Great Lakes. See Munton and Castle, "The Continental Dimension," in Boardman, Canadian Environmental Policy, 203–23.

18 George Hoberg, "Comparing Canadian Performance in Environmental Policy," in Boardman, Canadian Environmental Policy, 246–62.

19 Seymour Martin Lipset, Continental Divide: The Values and Institutions of the United States and Canada (New York: Routledge 1990), especially chap. 1.

20 Foreign Service Dispatch no. 864, from Embassy, Ottawa, to Department of State, 5 April 1961, RG 59, CDF, 60–63, Box 1241, File 611-42/4-461, NARAII.

21 Memorandum, "Briefing Papers for Ottawa Conference of Principal Officers," 22 January 1963, NARAII, RG 59, CDF60–63, Box 1241, File 611.42/6-562.

22 Memorandum, "Briefing Papers for Ottawa Conference of Principal Officers, 22 January 1963, NARAII, RG 59, CDF60–63, Box 1241, File 611.42/6-562.

23 "Federal Authorities Make It Clear, Canada Is Not in Water-Selling Game," Citizen (Ottawa), 16 December 1966, LAC, RG 89, Vol. 5, File 7340-1, pt 3.

24 John N. Turner, Parliamentary Secretary to the Minister of Northern Affairs and National Resources, "Clean Water – National Priority," Notes for Keynote Speech before the First Paper Industry Conference on Water Conservation and Stream Improvement, 19 October 1965, DFAIT, File 25-5-2-Great Lakes-4, vol. 2.

132 Conflict and Cooperation

25 Memorandum to Cabinet, "Canada-United States Ministerial Meeting on Great Lakes Pollution, Ottawa, June 23," n.d., but stamped "received," 15 June 1970, Doc. No. 714/40, PC, 6/18/70. The memorandum explained that "the United States is in effect pre-empting the use of Canadian waters to absorb its waste, thus obliging Canada to provide additional treatment facilities."

26 Memorandum for the Minister, from A.E. Ritchie, Under-Secretary of State for External Affairs, "Great Lakes Water Quality Agreement," 18 October 1973, DFAIT, file 68-18-Great Lakes, vol. 5.

27 Jeffrey K. Stine, *Mixing the Waters: Environment, Politics, and the Building of the Tennessee-Tombigbee Waterway*(Akron, OH: University of Akron Press 1993), chap. 4.

28 Mr John C. Whitaker, from William D. Ruckelshaus, Administrator, EPA, "The President and the Environment," 11 January 11 1971, NARA II, Nixon/Whitaker, Box 135, Great Lakes Agreement, 2 of 2.

29 Memorandum to Henry A. Kissinger from Russell E. Train, Chairman, Council on Environmental Quality, "Great Lakes Agreement with Canada," NARA II, Nixon/Whitaker, Box 70, Great Lakes 1 of 2.

8

No Pushovers in Ottawa

Canadian-American Relations
As Seen through Cars and Nixon 1962–1972

BRUCE MUIRHEAD

It is common wisdom in some circles in Canada that the country "sold out" to the United States during the years of Liberal government following the end of World War II. The main reason for this development, Conservative and "nationalist" critics contend, was because of the Liberal affinity with the American way. In his misguided *The Forked Road*, historian Donald Creighton put it down to choice. The governments of William Lyon Mackenzie King, Louis St Laurent, and Lester Pearson veered off the British Empire/ Commonwealth highway Canada had been on since 1867, onto the modern US interstate system to make common cause with American political and corporate leaders.[1] Other commentators elaborated on this theme. Philosopher George Grant, with his (in)famous *Lament for a Nation: The Defeat of Canadian Nationalism,* wrote eloquently about the demise of Canada at the hands of American interlopers. He presented Conservative and British Canadian nationalist prime minister John Diefenbaker's defeat in April 1963 as coming at the hands of Liberal continentalists.[2]

In literature, as well as historical and social commentary, the 1960s and 1970s were halcyon decades for Canadian cultural and economic nationalisms. Anti-Americanism played a central role in both forms of nationalist discourse. Al Purdy's *The New Romans: Candid Canadian Opinions of the US* was a good example of cultural nationalism. Many of its contributors – such as Margaret Atwood, Peter Newman, Farley Mowat, Mordecai Richler, Larry Zolf, Louis Dudek, Robert Fulford, and Cy Gonick – constituted the elite of Canada's chattering classes. Most of them "[hit] below the belt" in their assessments of Americans.[3] For example, Atwood, in a poem entitled "Backdrop Addresses [American] Cowboy," wrote that "you are innocent as a bathtub/full of bullets ... I am the space you desecrate/as you pass through."[4] In another piece, Louis Dudek asked rhetorically, "Who owns Canada? You know who owns Canada,"[5] while the novelist Farley Mowat wrote in "Letter to My Son" that there could be "no other real choice open to a Canadian except to resist the Yanks and all their works so that we, as a people and a nation, may escape being ingested into the Eagle's gut, never to emerge again except – maybe – as a patch of excrement upon the pages of world history."[6]

Given this context, the decade gave birth to a new industry in Canadian criticism, those decrying the extent of US investment in Canada and the overwhelming proportion of Canada's trade that went south. These writers marshalled their facts and wrote polemical tracts to change minds and practices. Most often, their arguments were sound, at least when documenting the unique nature and expanding scope of American ownership of Canada's economy. Indeed, Kari Levitt's *Silent Surrender* used government-generated data from the Dominion Bureau of Statistics to support her case in a masterful example of this phenomenon.[7] Their nationalist discourse constituted the dominant paradigm for a generation, in part because of their prolific output. These nationalists uniformly denounced "sell-out" Liberal governments, but oddly, not an equally sell-out Conservative one. And Canadians as a group were so ready to distance themselves from the United States that, while they might not know the specifics of the arguments presented, they largely supported them.[8]

These economic nationalists went too far in their condemnation of federal policy and the federal government. Implicit (or explicit) in the critics' analysis was the assumption of choice. Governments with more backbone or insight into Canada's problems would have designed different policy options to secure Canadian independence from the United States, whether in issues of trade or in those relating to the development of the branch plant economy. It was, after all, or so they argued, Ottawa that had refused to set limits on US involvement in Canada's economic development or to search out alternatives to the US market. The short-term gain had been more than offset by medium- and long-term pain.

Their analyses of federal personnel and policies were, however, flawed, and their critique did not stand up. While the very conservative and overwhelmingly continentalist private sector might have been content to throw its lot in with its US counterpart, the public sector was not. Canadian officials and politicians spent a great deal of time attempting to negotiate multilateral trade deals through the General Agreement on Tariffs and Trade, as well as expressing concern about the emerging European Economic Community, especially its protectionist policies and practices. Of course, Ottawa had to be sensitive to US issues and concerns. To have been otherwise would have been irresponsible, for, as Pierre Trudeau had suggested in his first visit to the new Richard Nixon administration in March 1969, living next to the United States was like sleeping with an elephant. No matter how friendly or even-tempered the beast, Canadians were affected by every twitch and grunt.

Importantly, Ottawa politicians and senior mandarins were concerned about growing US dominance of the Canadian economy, and many were writing critical and informed analyses of Canada's apparent predicament. Many of their insights anticipated those of Abe Rotstein, James Laxer, and Melville Watkins, the three most prominent members of the social democratic "Waffle"school of economic nationalists.[9] Moreover, politicians and bureaucrats were not part of a weak comprador system. Theirs was a world of hard negotiations and tough-minded opponents. They were well aware of the limitations placed on Canada as a middle power sharing the continent with the giant United States. They were also determined to push for the best possible deal for their country and its citizens, despite the overwhelming economic power represented by Canada's southern neighbour. In the years between 1957 and 1973, official Ottawa was self-assured, deliberate, and conscious of its responsibilities. The three prime ministers and their governments of this era in Canada-US relations pursued "Canadian" policies, very often irritating and alienating their counterparts in Washington. While ever mindful of the influence that the United States exerted on Canada's economy, in certain critical situations they ignored US demands and promoted Canada's interests.

From the implicit veto given to Canada over US wheat sales to third countries, through the Autopact, which almost single-handedly helped to solve Canada's balance of payments problems, to the various exemptions from punitive American legislation that were given

over the decade, respective Canadian governments rolled the dice
with Americans and occasionally won, a not inconsiderable feat. In
the case of the Autopact, even Walter Gordon, the then minister of
finance and an implacable and unrelenting critic of US investment in
Canada, welcomed the benefits it bestowed on his country.
And while a cynic might claim that such an initiative merely enhanced continental integration to the further detriment of Canada,
that agreement was not what the United States wanted. Indeed,
Canadian political leaders stuck to their policy guns and arguably
out-negotiated the Americans, playing a kind of Russian roulette
in the process. As Brian Tomlin and Peyton Lyon have correctly
observed, not all the aces lie with the stronger power in international affairs. In certain areas Canada was able to exert its influence to bring the United States to its point of view. As they note, "the
Canadian policy community is smaller and better able to concen-
trate its main attention on relations with Canada's giant neighbour."[10]
In the final analysis, these federal successes and the continuing prosperity that they brought with them were all that mattered, at least
for the great plurality of the population, as Liberal governments
(with a brief Conservative interregnum) succeeded one other.

Looking back, it is clear that Washington adopted a relatively benign view of Canada – at least until the election of the Nixon administration – which Canadians exploited. To claim that the United
States was altruistic in many of its dealings with Canada in the
1960s might leave one open to charges of naïveté or worse, because
superpowers, we are told, have interests and not friends. But the
historian is left wondering why various US governments in the 1960s
and early 1970s treated Canada so mildly, often in the face of the
kind of provocation Walter Gordon's 1963 budget exemplified.[11]
There was, it seems clear, a special relationship that existed between
the two countries between 1945 and 15 August 1971, the date of the
announcement of the so-called Nixon shock. Among other things,
Nixon's proposed legislation imposed a 10 percent tariff on imported products from which Canada was not exempted. The unilateral
termination of Canada's special relationship came as a shock to
most Canadians, who had benefited from exemptionalism for a long
time and had taken it as a given. In response, the Trudeau government undertook what was called the Third Option policy. It was not
successful, because even the most assiduous of trade "diversifiers" in
Ottawa could not convince the Europeans, the Japanese, or other
nations to take their overtures seriously.

The discourse and activity surrounding a search for Canada's national identity in the roughly ten years following 1965, whether it be in literature, the economy, or politics, was important and played a central role in negotiations between Canada and the United States. Many Canadians were stimulated by what they saw and repelled by the excesses of the American empire. Moreover, these entreaties fell on ready ears as the first wave of baby-boomers were hitting universities, clearly unhappy with the status quo. "Don't trust anyone over thirty," or so the saying had it. Post-secondary institutions opened their doors to an increasing percentage of young Canadians, and enrollment more than doubled from 196,700 students in 1962–63 to 513,400 by 1972. More often than not, these young minds were influenced by the writings and lectures of those converts to the new orthodoxies of cultural and economic nationalisms.

This study is an attempt to begin to examine that part of the economic story that is most often left out. Much more than merely American domination of Canada's economy was at issue. This study also demonstrates that Ottawa made the best of the hand it was dealt. As Lester Pearson said in an address to the Radio Club in Ottawa in 1969 following his retirement from office, he had never realized how difficult it was to maintain his country's separate existence in North America until he became prime minister. Faced with a neighbour more than ten times its size with an economy anywhere from twelve to fifteen times larger, with a very similar culture, history, traditions, and, arguably most importantly, language, Canadians not only carved out their own successful niche on the continent but did so using a federal government and a civil service that right- and left-nationalists despised as weak and uninterested in, or incapable of, projecting, defending, and promoting Canada's economic interest vis-à-vis the United States. The Autopact was a special example of this point that benefited Canada's balance of payments condition enormously. Indeed, in some ways it was so one-sided that President Lyndon Johnson was later to tell Charles Ritchie, Canada's ambassador to the United States, that Canada had "screwed" him in its negotiation, given that Canadians had obviously prospered at the expense of, it seemed to the president, his countrymen. It began during the autumn of 1963, when the United States confronted the Canadian announcement of a new policy designed to ease the country's balance of payments problems. The automobile export incentive scheme, introduced by the government on 25 October and implemented one week later, was a logical progression for Canadian policy. It followed upon two connected issues. The first was the 1961 *Report* of the Royal Commission on the Automotive Industry, conducted by the University of Toronto's dean of arts, Vincent Bladen. It had focused on the shift in the Canadian auto industry during the late 1950s. In 1955, Canadians had bought 22,000 British and foreign cars. By 1959 the number had reached 114,000. By the beginning of the 1960s, about 32 percent of total car sales in Canada were comprised of compact models from Europe. This increase paralleled a rather startling decrease in domestic passenger car production in Canadian plants, down about 20 percent between 1955 and 1959, from 375,000 units to 300,000. Employment in the industry had also dropped, from 67,000 to 56,000.[12]

Faced with this situation, the United Auto Workers (Canada) lobbied Prime Minister John Diefenbaker on 5 July 1960, who had then responded with the Bladen Commission. As an interim measure while it awaited Bladen's report, the government announced a change in the valuation on imported cars for duty purposes which would add between Can$100 and Can$300 to each vehicle sold in Canada. When he reported, Bladen "recommended various inducements that might produce a more extended integration of the North American car industry" and thereby increase employment in the Canadian industry.[13]

While the recommendations of the report largely gathered dust, there were other developments in this area. The Conservatives had introduced a program in 1962 that covered automatic transmissions and a stated number of stripped engines and provided for a refund on duties paid on automobiles and parts imported into Canada by any firm that by itself or through independent parts manufacturers increased the export of cars and parts. One dollar of exported Canadian content would earn the remission of duties on one dollar of dutiable imports. Its objective was to increase Canada's share in the production and trade of automobiles, particularly vis-à-vis the United States and in so doing, help to ameliorate Canada's current account deficit with its southern neighbour, which ran at Can$1.116 billion in 1962 and Can$1.158 billon the following year. Autos accounted for about Can$500 million of that. The Kennedy administration had opposed the Canadian program, but did not try to end it. For the Liberal finance minister, Walter Gordon, reducing the deficit was an absolute necessity if the US capital inflow that caused him so many headaches was to be reduced. Reducing the inflow was also quietly questioned, but not opposed, by the United States. Griffith Johnson later told A.F.W. Plumptre of the Department of Finance that it broke "all accepted commercial practices."[14]

In the auto sector, the numbers were simply appalling for the finance minister. By 1963, Canada was exporting only 16,000 vehicles, down from 52,000 a decade previous. That situation did not seem likely to improve on its own, and members of Cabinet knew the figures well. Canada accounted for 9 percent of the total US/Canada population during the 1960–63 period, yet it accounted for the production of less than 7 percent of the North American consumption of passenger cars, less than 7.5 percent of the consumption of trucks and buses, and less than 6.5 percent of the use of original equipment motor vehicle parts made in Canada or the United States.[15]

As well, the Auto Pact was designed to improve the efficiency of a major Canadian industry that had to export into order to achieve lower costs. That had not been possible to date because of restrictive corporate decisions made by US parent firms. The major problem in this regard was Canada's limited domestic market, allowing Canadian producers only short production runs, which resulted in higher costs than those of volume producers in other countries. It had also meant that Canadian auto manufacturers had not been able to adopt the latest technological advances in production techniques, a problem made worse by the multiplicity of models demanded by consumers. As a result, the competitive position of the Canadian automotive industry was adversely affected in both home and export markets. The Canadian measures were designed in large part to overcome these institutional barriers to trade, to help the vehicle and parts industries compete more effectively in domestic and export markets through the economies of specialization and longer production runs. The government was clear. The industry's competitive position had to be improved through access to wider markets. That could happen only if "barriers to trade and procurement [were] relaxed so that Canadian vehicle and parts makers [had] access to world markets and automotive manufacturers in other countries [were] willing to go beyond their domestic sources of supply."[16] The Canadian measures also did not involve the payment of a subsidy. Rather, they were a plan for conditional free entry of vehicles and those parts on which there would otherwise be a duty.

To the extent that the Canadian automotive industry would become more efficient, it would displace vehicles imported from

countries other than the United States, and the net result would be a
larger market in Canada for auto parts from below the border. A
Canadian document demonstrated that that trend had been discern-
able in 1963, when US manufacturers had exported an additional
US$113 million of parts to Canada, for a total of US$545 million.[17]
The measures announced also did not take a bilateral approach.
"There were already firm indications," or so the government believed, "that a sizable portion of the exports resulting from the plan
will go to third countries." Much of this new trade was in finished
cars that, as noted above, created additional demand in Canada for
US production parts.

The scheme was discussed in both governments, and President
John F. Kennedy took a personal interest. Indeed, in October he had
instructed that all reports and negotiations with Canada were to
flow to him through William Brubeck, the White House staff officer
for Canadian affairs. A memorandum from McGeorge Bundy had
emphasized this point, noting that "all aspects of Canadian-American
relations are of intense interest and concern to the President ... The
President desires that the White House be fully informed of all significant negotiations or plans for negotiation with the Government
of Canada."[18]

Washington was not entirely unhappy with the pact's announcement in late October, but it faced some legislative hurdles that could
have resulted in legislation that would have penalized the Canadians.
A senior American delegation met with Canadians to draw their
attention to a US law dating back to 1897 and updated in the Tariff
Act of 1930 that provided for the mandatory imposition of countervailing duties on imports that enjoyed a grant or bounty from the
government of the exporting country. In mid-November, the treasury noted that it had received complaints about the Canadian plan
requesting the imposition of countervailing duties, and it was inves-
tigating whether or not that constituted a grant or bounty within the
meaning of US law. There was every indication that if satisfaction
had not been given by government, the aggrieved parties would have
taken their case to the US judicial system, where it would have been
upheld, or so Dean Rusk, the secretary of state, believed. He tele-
graphed George Ball, then in London, noting that if it unfolded as
the State Department thought it would, then "USG faced with possibility of having to impose duties whether this desirable or not as
matter of policy."[19]

Through various twists and turns of discussion and negotiation, the Canadians pushed ahead with their automotive agenda, ignoring US threats of retaliation. At the joint Canada-US Committee on Trade and Economic Affairs meeting in 1964, the policy was raised by the Americans, who were told that it was "an important corner-stone of the Government's policy to strengthen and make Canadian manufacturing industries more competitive." If it was thwarted somehow by the United States, such action would have "the most serious implications for Canada–United States relations."[20] Ottawa's delegation won the point, although both sides prepared for an extended dispute.

Although it appeared at several points as if the United States would actively oppose the program, that did not happen. Why? In part because of a letter sent by Henry Ford to President Johnson highlighting the merits of the Canadian case. As well, the anti-Canadian US ambassador in Ottawa, Walton Butterworth, had, for a change, counselled that Washington not reject the Canadian case out of hand, because they "had a special problem" in the automotive trade.[21] By late 1964, despite a pending countervail brought by the Modine Manufacturing Company of Racine, Wisconsin, the two sides came to a fruitful conclusion, although not without some hand-wringing by Americans and a claim by the Treasury's Douglas Dillon that if an agreement was not forthcoming by 1 January 1965, he would have to countervail Canadian automotive imports or "face jail."[22] The agreement was signed by the president and the prime minister on 16 January 1965 and was brought into effect by Canada on 18 January. As a result, Ottawa amended the Order-in-Council to provide that duty remissions would not be paid as a result of any exportation after 17 January. The treasury then terminated its inves-tigation on the 18th, and the District Court action filed by the Automotive Service Industry Association was dismissed on 18 May. The approval process was slightly slower in the United States, even though a Canadian document noted how "pleased" the government was "that the President and Congress gave this legislation such a high priority."[23] It was finally approved in October and made retro-active to 18 January.

By Canada's one hundredth birthday, autos and parts formed the largest single item in the country's North American trade. During the two years following 1964, US exports (the great bulk to Canada) in the sector had risen from US$660 million to US$1.3 billion. Canada's exports, mainly to the United States, had gone from US$75 million to US$900 million. Other numbers were equally encouraging. Canadian vehicle production was up by 35 percent and employment by 27 percent.[24] The Bank of Canada's 1969 *Annual Report* quietly pointed out the results: "The trade balance with the United States, which had strengthened by about $800 million in 1968, improved by a further $140 million in 1969. The change in 1969 was more than accounted for by a reduction in Canada's trade deficit on auto- motive products."[25] That was the sentiment expressed in the *Ninth Annual Report of the President to the Congress on the Operation of the Automotive Products Trade Act of 1965*, submitted to the Senate finance committee in January 1976. It was manifest, the report noted, "that the only true concessions granted in the agreement are those granted by the Government of the United States according duty free treatment to imports of automotive products manufac- tured in Canada."[26] It contained no substantive concessions, or so the report pointed out, on the part of Ottawa except those that were subject to the commitments and obligations to the government of Canada in the letters of undertaking. Despite some considerable US opposition, Ottawa had gone to the wall in pursuing its policy ob- jective and won.

The second event considered here is the so-called Nixon shock of 15 August 1971. The sharp turn of that new path, epitomized by President Nixon's New Economic Policy (NEP), announced on 15 August 1971, took American trading partners and allies by sur- prise. Some American officials who had not been informed were also stunned by this sudden and significant policy change. Peter Towe, the Canadian minister at the embassy in Washington, told Mitchell Sharp, the secretary of state for external affairs, that the "content of the package put together at Camp David seems to have come as a surprise even to senior USA officials left in Washington."[27] Most of these officials, and especially those from the State Department, would have been opposed to the Nixon plan. As the president had earlier pointed out as a rationale for excluding the State Department, "that agency [only] represented the interests of foreign govern- ments[!]"[28] At Camp David, the solitary voice of Arthur Burns, the chair of the Federal Reserve Board, had put the opposing case, ob- jecting that the type of program suggested "would squander the valuable good will of foreign governments." He even warned of re- taliation. The secretary of the treasury and author of the NEP, John

Connally, had responded: "We'll go broke getting their good will ... So other countries don't like it. So what? ... Why do we have to be 'reasonable'? Canada wasn't [when it imposed import quotas in 1962] ... Let 'em [retaliate]. What can they do?"[29]

Among the more worrisome provisions of the program from a Canadian trade point of view were a 10 percent surcharge on imports, the introduction of a 10 percent tax credit for investment in new American-produced machinery and equipment, renewed proposals for the implementation of the Domestic International Sales Corporation export incentives, and a job development investment tax credit. It was all legal under Article XII of the General Agreement on Tariffs and Trade, as long as the United States did not discriminate in favour of any country like Canada, and a new, tough US administration meant to see it through. It was draconian, and, as Peter Dobell has pointed out, "it [was] no exaggeration to suggest that the effect in Canada of these short-term measures and of the negotiations that followed their introduction produced a national catharsis."[30] The Nixon program vaulted the United States back into the center of Canadian calculations, from which it had strayed following the publication of *Foreign Policy for Canadians*. Ottawa's denunciations of the surcharge began almost immediately, but they were just as quickly rejected by Connally. Washington wanted action on the Autopact – at first its abrogation, but the administration was convinced to remove that from consideration. In the end, the White House wanted Canada to agree to the removal of the transitional safeguards and also to the removal of Ottawa's limitation on duty-free entry to bona fide car manufacturers.[31] It also wanted some changes to the Defence Production Sharing Agreement of 1959, having been alarmed over a cumulative surplus in the trade account on defence purchases of more than US$500 million in Canada's favour. As well, the newly established Michelin Tire plant in Nova Scotia drew some fire from US officials. They had focused on the government assistance provided to the French company that had resulted in its location in the Maritimes because approximately 60 percent of the tires produced at the plant were expected to be exported to the United States. Finally, Washington wanted reciprocity in tourist allowances.

Canadians continued to be perplexed as to why they did not fit into a "special" category, as they had in the past. Their economic situation vis-à-vis the United States had not changed since the 1960s. Moreover, to lump Canada in with the EEC and Japan, as was done in the NEP, was in their view ludicrous. Certainly they figured that they had done their bit. A memorandum prepared for Prime Minister Trudeau suggested that the country had met the test of good neighbour and trading partner. The Canadian dollar had been allowed to float in mid-1970, and it had appreciated in value against the American dollar by about 8 percent. As well, Canada did not maintain any discriminatory or unfair trade restrictions against US imports, and it had unilaterally accelerated the Kennedy round tariff reductions, which had helped American exports to the country. The take-no-prisoners American approach suggested that the so-called special relationship between Canada and the United States was over. Indeed, Ottawa had been very surprised to learn that it was among the primary targets of the NEP – and that was almost unthinkable.

Canadians kept the lines of communication with Washington open. They talked through meetings of the G-10 in Europe and North America, with Americans in the Canadian capital and in Washington, and with both President Nixon (where the 10 percent import surcharge against Canada was repealed), and in the basement of the Smithsonian Institution with Connally, where the G-10 (minus Canada) undertook to have their currencies appreciate in value against the greenback. That was not to say, however, that Canadians accepted the American position. Indeed, they consistently opposed it. Nowhere was that to be seen more clearly than in Washington's demand that Canada agree to the same sort of package deal as had the Europeans and the Japanese, a deal designed to help the United States out of its difficulties. In short, Canada refused in large part "because the Canadians had objected vigorously to the unilateral positions and pressure tactics of the United States, and behind this posture of objection Canada refused to participate in meaningful talks."[32] This obstinacy greatly surprised John Connally, who believed that his northern neighbours would eventually cave in.

Despite intense American pressure, the major issue on which Canada refused to budge was the third safeguard of the Autopact, which restricted the duty-free import of US-made cars. Obviously, under these circumstances agreement was impossible, and Ottawa began an evaluation of where that would leave Canada. Certainly the ramifications were very serious. As the *Globe and Mail*'s Ross Munro wrote, "The breakdown of the talks between the United States and Canada may have set the stage for the worst period of relations between the two countries in a decade."[33] He reported an important US official as saying that he thought they were "in a situation that borders on catastrophe ... These damn things [trade issues] have been discussed *ad nauseum*. There are going to be people on both sides who're going to say 'it's a waste of time.'" Connally himself believed that the negotiations were over. That, however, proved not to be the case. George Schultz became treasury secretary in May 1972 and left his self-appointed task of getting Canada to knuckle under to US pressure unfinished.

The salient fact that confronted many Canadian policy-makers and others was that Canada's hard stand against the United States had not damaged the Canadian economy. For various reasons, that crisis passed, although not without consequences for both sides. Ottawa continued more than to hold its own for the remainder of the year. No new negotiations were entered into, despite an increasing American impatience with Canada's intransigence. As Roderick Byers noted in answering the question "Why the deadlock?": "At the most general level officials agreed that Canada's international economic position had improved considerably since the mid-1960s, while the American position had experienced a sharp decline."[34]

In September 1972, perhaps reflecting the government's new-found confidence and having been pushed forcibly out of the continental nest, Mitchell Sharp articulated a new vision, the Third Option, where the objective was to diversify Canada's foreign linkages abroad, away from the United States. It was almost as if key cabinet members had re-read Claude Julien's 1965 book *Canada: Europe's Last Chance*. As Julien had then noted, "the key question for the European is ... will Canada allow itself to be colonized by the United States or will it strengthen its ties with Europe and help to balance the power of the United States?"[35] It seemed as if the country was at least exploring the latter.

As these examples from the Pearson and Trudeau governments demonstrate, Canadian decision makers were often aggressive and focused on issues of concern to Canada when dealing with their counterparts from the United States. This flies in the face of the "normal" interpretation of the decade covered here. The left-leaning nationalists have done the country a disservice with their insistence that Canada was governed by a sell-out, comprador elite that was more intent on giving in to the United States than in pursuing, with considerable skill and determination, Canadian interests and objectives.

NOTES

1 US control in some sectors was quite high: 60 percent of manufacturing, 75 percent of oil and gas, and 60 percent of mines and smelters in Canada. Donald Creighton, *The Forked Road: Canada, 1939–1957* (Toronto: McClelland and Stewart 1976).

2 George Grant, *Lament for a Nation: The Defeat of Canadian Nationalism* (Toronto: McClelland and Stewart 1970).

3 Al Purdy, *The New Romans: Candid Canadian Opinions of the US* (Edmonton: M.C. Hurtig 1968), ii.

4 Margaret Atwood, "Backdrop Addresses Cowboy," in Purdy, *The New Romans,* 10–11.

5 Louis Dudek, "O Canada," in Purdy 82.

6 Farley Mowat, "Letter to My Son," in Purdy, *The New Romans,* 1.

7 Kari Levitt, *Silent Surrender: The Multinational Corporation in Canada* (Toronto: Macmillan 1970).

8 See *Canada 1970* (Toronto: McClelland and Stewart 1969). This publication was a snapshot of Canadian attitudes compiled by a group of senior editors and writers of the Toronto *Telegram.*

9 See, for example Abraham Rotstein, ed., *The Prospect of Change* (Toronto: McGraw-Hill 1965), published under the auspices of the University League for Social Reform (ULSR); Peter Russell, ed., *Nationalism in Canada* (Toronto: McGraw-Hill 1966). This volume was also published under the auspices of the USLR and included contributors who were to make their marks in Canadian academe in the 1970s and later, among them historians Carl Berger, Craig Brown, Michel Brunet, and Kenneth McNaught, and political scientists like Stephen Clarkson and Melville Watkins, as well as Rotstein and Russell; Abraham Rotstein, *The Precarious Homestead* (Toronto: New Press 1973); Abraham Rotstein and Viv Nelles, *Nationalism or Local Control* (Toronto: New Press 1973); Abraham Rotstein and Gary Laxer, eds., *Independence: The Canadian Challenge* (Toronto: The Committee for an Independent Canada 1972); Abraham Rotstein and Gary Laxer, eds., *Getting It Back: A Program for Canadian Independence* (Toronto: Clarke, Irwin 1974); Dave Godfrey and Mel Watkins, eds., *Gordon to Watkins to You, Documentary: The Battle for Control of Our Economy* (Toronto: New Press 1970); James Laxer, *The Liberal Idea of Canada: Pierre Trudeau and the Question of Canada's Survival* (Toronto: James Lorimer 1977); Wallace Clement, *The Canadian Corporate Elite: An Analysis of Economic Power* (Toronto: McClelland and Stewart 1975); Wallace Clement, *Continental Corporate Power:*

Economic Elite Linkages between Canada and the United States (Toronto: McClelland and Stewart 1977); Walter Gordon, *Troubled Canada: The Need for New Domestic Policies* (Toronto: McClelland and Stewart 1961); *Storm Signals: New Economic Policies for Canada* (Toronto: McClelland and Stewart 1975). Many of these names would also appear in books and conference proceedings published by the Committee for an Independent Canada and in the pages of the *Canadian Forum* and *Canadian Dimension*.

10 Peyton Lyon and Brian Tomlin, *Canada as an International Actor* (Toronto: Macmillan 1979), 108.

11 For a discussion of Gordon's budget, see Bruce Muirhead, *Against the Odds: The Public Life and Times of Louis Rasminsky* (Toronto: University of Toronto Press 1995), 208–9.

12 John D. Harbron, "Business and Industry," in John Saywell, ed., *Canadian Annual Review for 1960* (Toronto: University of Toronto Press 1961), 213.

13 Robert Bothwell, Ian Drummond, and John English, *Canada since 1945: Power, Politics, and Provincialism* (Toronto: University of Toronto Press 1989), 197.

14 Library and Archives Canada, Ottawa, ON., Department of External Affairs Records (DEA-R), vol. 6057, file: 50316-8-40 (pt. 1.1), Washington, DC, to External, 12 August 1963.

15 DEA-R, vol. 6057, file: 50316-8-40 (pt. 1.1), Washington, DC, to External, 12 August 1963.

16 United States International Trade Commission Report on the United States–Canadian Automotive Agreement, "Canadian Automotive Agreement," January 1976, 111.

17 Library and Archives Canada, Department of Finance Records (DFR), vol. 3943, file 8522-U-585 (64), Joint United States–Canadian Committee on Trade and Economic Affairs, "Trade Policies and Problems," April 1964.

18 Knowlton Nash, *Kennedy and Diefenbaker: Fear and Loathing across the Undefended Border* (Toronto: McClelland and Stewart 1990), 316.

19 John F. Kennedy Presidential Library, Boston, MS., NSF, Box 19, Canada, General, 11/9/63 – 12/2/63, Rusk to Ball, 14 November 1963.

20 DFR, vol. 3943, file: 8522-U-585 (64), Joint United States – Canada Committee on Trade and Economic Affairs, "Trade Policies and Problems," April 1964.

21 For the Ford letter, see Lyndon Baines Johnson Presidential Library (LBJL), Austin, TX, NSF, Box 165, file: Country File – Canada Memos vol. 2, Henry Ford to the President, 22 September 1964. For the Butterworth intervention, see Department of State Records, Memoranda to the

Secretary July-September 1964, B. 22C-ES, Butterworth to Rusk, 25 August 1964.

22 LBJL, NSF, Box 165, file Country File – Canada Memos vol. 2, McGeorge Bundy to the President, 27 November 1964.

23 Bank of Canada Archives, Ottawa, ON, Louis Rasminsky Papers, LR76–361, Joint Canada-United States Ministerial Committee Meeting, "Canada-United States Automotive Agreement," March 1966.

24 J.L. Granatstein, *Canada, 1957–1967: The Years of Uncertainty and Innovation* (Toronto: McClelland and Stewart 1986), 207.

25 Bank of Canada, *Annual Report of the Governor to the Minister of Finance for the Year 1969*, 67.

26 United States International Trade Commission Report on the United States–Canadian Automotive Agreements, "Canadian Automobile Agreement," January 1976.

27 Rasminsky Papers, LR76–373–3, Washington, DC, to External, 15 August 1971.

28 See John S. Odell, "The US and the Emergence of Flexible Exchange Rates: An Analysis of Foreign Policy Change," *International Organization* 33 (1979): 74. For a personal account of the process leading up to Camp David and its aftermath, see Robert Solomon, *The International Monetary System, 1945–1976: An Insider's View* (New York: Harper and Row 1977), 176–215.

29 *Foreign Relations of the United States*, vol. 3, *Foreign Economic Policy, International Monetary Policy, 1969–1972* (Washington: USGPO 2001), 454.

30 Peter Dobell, "Reducing Vulnerability: The Third Option, 1970s," in Don Munton and John Kirton, eds., *Canadian Foreign Policy: Selected Cases* (Toronto: Prentice-Hall 1992), 237.

31 Rasminsky Papers, LR76–374–1, Prime Minister's Meeting with the President of the United States, "Trade Discussions," 2 December 1971.

32 Harald B. Malmgren, "The Evolving Trading System," in H. Edward English, ed., *Canada-United States Relations, Proceedings of the Academy of Political Science*, 32, no. 2 (New York 1976), 125.

33 Ross Munro, "Slump in US Relations Likely," *Globe and Mail*, 11 February 1972, 1.

34 R.B. Byers, "External Affairs and Defence," in John Saywell, ed., *Canadian Annual Review for 1972* (Toronto: University of Toronto Press 1973), 260.

35 Claude Julien, *Canada: Europe's Last Chance*, trans. Penny Williams (Toronto: Macmillan 1968), 6.

9

From Conflict to Cooperation

Canada's US Oil and Gas Policy from the 1970s to the 1980s

TAMMY NEMETH

More than thirty years after the first international energy crisis prompted by the Organization of Petroleum Exporting Countries (OPEC), the world again faces ever-increasing oil prices. With a sense of déjà vu, the United States has looked to decrease its dependence on overseas oil, and consumers in both countries have bemoaned high fuel prices. In the 1950s and 1960s, the situation was the reverse and low oil prices threatened the viability of the Canadian and American oil and gas industries. Consequently, Canada and the United States entered into an informal continental arrangement. But by the late 1960s this informal relationship began to break down, and despite numerous discussions, a more formal sectoral agreement failed to emerge. In the 1970s, but especially in the early 1980s, increased oil prices polarized and politicized debate surrounding energy policies, and Canada embarked on an economic-nationalist course, which created conflict in Canada-US relations. Successive Liberal governments led by Pierre Trudeau embraced a form of economic nationalism in oil and gas policy that entailed the phasing out of oil exports in 1974, the creation of Petro-Canada, a state oil company, and the National Energy Program of 1980, to achieve its goal of greater Canadian and federal government control over the oil and gas sector. Concurrently, Trudeau reorganized and restructured the operations of the Canadian federal bureaucracy and the Department of Energy, Mines and Resources in particular. He did so in a way that led to its politicization and created an environment that enabled the controversial and interventionist oil and gas policies to be developed and implemented.[1] Determined to improve Canada-US relations, revitalize Canada's failing economy, and constrain future governments on both sides of the border from implementing discriminatory trade policies on certain issues, Prime Minister Brian Mulroney's Progressive Conservative government rejected both informal continentalism and any form of economic nationalism, choosing instead to negotiate and ratify a formal continental trading arrangement. The importance of the energy chapter of the Free Trade Agreement (FTA, later folded into NAFTA), is that it comprised a formal continental energy agreement that has depoliticized or neutralized oil and gas as a volatile issue in Canada-US political relations.

Although there were overtures after 1958 by each country to develop a more formal accord to govern the trade of oil and natural gas at different times, it was not until 1988 that a formal and comprehensive continental agreement was reached between Canada and the United States. Over these three decades the dramatic changes occurred in three phases and were influenced by changing domestic and international circumstances, the interaction of leaders and important officials, and changes in personnel in certain departments. To understand how and why informal continentalism was accepted in the 1950s and 1960s, how and why continentalism was rejected in the 1970s and early 1980s, and how and why formal continentalism was embraced in the mid- to late 1980s requires analyzing and explaining the course of Canada-US oil and gas relations through these three distinct phases.

In the postwar period, the traditional Canadian approach to trade with the United States was a form of informal continentalism. The general strategy involved two stages: first, an exemption was secured from American policies that would normally apply to foreign countries. Then, when the exemption began to fail, a more formal sectoral or commodity agreement was negotiated, such as the Autopact. Canada-US oil policy followed this pattern, except that it failed to complete the second stage.

Pragmatism, rather than an ideological commitment to continentalism, was the spirit behind informal continentalism. As one scholar aptly describes it, "The tilt of Canada's economy toward continentalism during the 1950s had been less a matter of design than of circumstance. The markets of Europe, Latin America, and Asia had all been virtually closed to Canadian exporters in the decade after the

Second World War."[2] The US market, on the other hand, was more open, and it had investment capital "to make up for the shortage of Canadian capital and to help develop Canada's resource and manufacturing sectors."[3] The goal of any Canadian government has been to have a strong and expanding economy, and given the lack of feasible alternatives and the pull of geographic proximity, it is not surprising that increased trade with the United States and the courting of US investment has been the policy choice of successive postwar Canadian governments.

Given the importance of oil and gas to an industrial economy and the instability and uncertainty of the world market, it was better, in the view of the pragmatic informal continentalists, to have a policy that permitted flexibility if circumstances changed, instead of being constrained by formal arrangements. This view was best articulated by Mitchell Sharp. Reflecting in his memoirs on the difference between informal and formal arrangements with the United States, Sharp wrote:

> The fundamental reason why, over time, Canadian governments preferred to pursue their objectives more quietly, with less fanfare, was that results were better ... Our economic ties were extensive and very close. It did change, however, when the Free Trade Agreement between Canada and the United States came into effect at the beginning of 1989. Thereafter, economic relations between Canada and the United States were governed not by understandings but by enforceable rules that were different from the rules that governed relations between Canada and any other country. We became part of a North American trading bloc in a world of regional trading blocs ... Until then, we had done what we could to resist the overwhelming influence of the United States in our economy, our culture, and our politics. By entering into an exclusive free-trade agreement designed to integrate the economies of our two countries, we were not only abandoning our resistance, we were deliberately inviting ourselves to be overwhelmed ... Our relationship, economic and political, became very special indeed, to my regret.[4]

Sharp's view is important because he was the deputy minister of trade and commerce in the 1950s and left government during the first year of Progressive Conservative John Diefenbaker's administration. Most other senior officials within the Canadian bureaucracy embraced the informal continental approach and, as Sharp described, attempted to balance increased economic interdependence with the United States and Canadian political and economic independence. But even at this time, not everyone was convinced that this approach was working to Canada's advantage.

By the 1950s, some Canadians began to worry about the growing interdependence in Canada-US trade and investment, particularly US direct investment in Canada. People such as Walter Gordon, a member of the Liberal Party but a representative of the kind of economic nationalism that was popular in the socialist New Democrat Party (NDP), argued that the costs of such interdependence were greater than the material benefits. These costs included, in the economic nationalist view, US domination in Canada, loss of political independence, and a stifling of Canadian manufacturing potential because of an over-reliance on the export of staple products.[5] The rising rhetoric of economic nationalists, led by Gordon through the late 1950s and the 1960s, and the well-organised NDP Waffle group of the early 1970s, targeted the oil and gas industry as the most visible symbol of US economic domination in Canada.[6] This was due to the concentration of foreign (mostly American) ownership and control of the oil and gas industry.

In 1958, however, the main concern for Prime Minister John G. Diefenbaker's Progressive Conservative (PC) government with respect to the oil and gas industry was to find markets. The proposals to construct a new oil pipeline to Montreal or to extend the existing one from Sarnia were possible solutions to a problem of surplus production. Another, less expensive proposal was to increase exports to the United States. The most vocal advocates of an oil pipeline to Montreal were the Canadian independent oil producers led by R.A. Brown of Home Oil. This coalition of Canadian independent companies wanted a pipeline to Montreal so that more of their oil could be sold. They believed that under the prevailing system, the multinationals were impairing the independents' ability to sell their oil.[7] With oil prices considerably lower outside North America, the majors could endure the oil surplus mainly because they had producing fields in these outside nations. The independents could not wait, because their production was solely in Canada, where prices were high and markets constricting. They had the support of Premier Ernest Manning of Alberta. However, it should be noted that although his main interest was to increase production and sales, Manning was indifferent to the final destination. The multinationals, however, indicated that they would not voluntarily enter into contracts to purchase the oil; thus, the federal government would have to force them to do so through regulation and legislation.[8]

Diefenbaker was sympathetic to the independents' cause but was concerned about expanding government control, as well as the possibility that the federal government would have to underwrite the project or give financial guarantees the way the Liberals had with TransCanada Pipelines.[9] Therefore, he deferred the pipeline decision while he awaited the report of the Royal Commission on Energy (the Borden Commission, after its president) that he had appointed in 1957. Since it would be at least another year before the Borden Commission would issue its report, Diefenbaker decided to pursue the second option of increased exports to the United States, in order to assist all Western producers of oil and gas.

The problem for Canada was that the United States was attempting to control imports in order to protect its own domestic industry. Plentiful, cheap oil imports from Venezuela and the Middle East threatened to diminish the capacity of the US domestic industry to increase production adequately in an emergency, such as a war. Given the context of the Cold War, this type of argument resonated with President Dwight D. Eisenhower and his officials, as they sought to find a balance between encouraging trade with unstable and developing countries and being able to supply the military in case of war. Canada and Venezuela lobbied for an exemption from any import program on those grounds.[10] The State Department was split. Some advisors favoured Canada, while others supported Venezuela.

Although Eisenhower preferred to favour Canada alone, in order to mollify forceful State Department objections he signed a National Security directive at the end of 1958 that stipulated preference should be given to Western Hemisphere sources in any oil import program. Discussions were held in 1958 and early 1959 to try to arrive at a hemispheric agreement on oil, but the talks collapsed.[11] In early 1959, however, it became clear from meetings with Canadian ministers and because of a diplomatic blitz from the Canadian embassy led by Ambassador Arnold Heeney that this was an extremely important issue to Canada.[12] The dynamics in the State Department altered with the return of Livingston Merchant as assistant under-secretary of state for political affairs. Merchant, who had just served as US ambassador to Canada and who understood how much Canada wanted the exemption, brilliantly outmanoeuvred Thomas Mann, his rival in the State Department.[13] He also ensured that Eisenhower's personal directive to do something to "act in unity with Canada" and to "make this oil move look better to our neighbours to the north"[14] actually happened. The United States, despite much opposition from Venezuela, acceded to Canadian pressure for an exemption to the Mandatory Oil Import Program (MOIP). In phrasing that applied mostly to Canada, oil transported overland was spared from the import restrictions. But in granting the exemption to Canada, the United States made it clear that if a pipeline to Montreal were built, the exemption would be revoked, and Canada would have reduced access to the US market.[15]

The next task for the Canadian government was to develop its own National Oil Policy (NOP).[16] First, acting on the recommendation of the initial Borden Report, Diefenbaker created the National Energy Board (NEB), one of whose functions was to help create oil and gas policy. Then, he waited for the second report of the Borden Commission, which was on oil.[17] The report recommended that Canada give the exemption a chance and defer consideration of the Montreal pipeline. If Canadian exports did not increase significantly and more Canadian oil did not displace foreign oil in Ontario, then the Montreal pipeline should be built. This is perhaps one of the reasons why it was another two years before the NOP was announced.

The NOP of 1961 was created around the MOIP exemption and committed Canada to reliance on access to the US market for its Western crude, while continuing to import oil from Venezuela and the Middle East. It reinforced the North-South trade pattern that seemed to be more natural for the Western part of the continent. The policy called for deferral of the Montreal Pipeline for the time being and advocated a substantial increase in exports to the United States that would be equivalent to the amount of oil imported into the Montreal area.[18] As mentioned above, Eisenhower himself had pressed his officials to find a way to accommodate Canada's request for an exemption. The significance of this action on Eisenhower's part was not lost on Diefenbaker. As a result, in part, the shape of Canada's NOP honoured Eisenhower's efforts by establishing the Ottawa Valley line and postponing an oil pipeline to Montreal.

From the announcement of the NOP in 1961 until 1968, Canada's main objective was to maintain its exemption to the MOIP, while the

United States sought to ensure that Canada did not exceed the agreed-upon informal export limits. Soon after the administration of John F. Kennedy grasped the reigns of government, US officials insisted on an informal understanding to prevent oil exports from expanding too quickly into their market. The terms of the understanding were reviewed regularly and adjusted according to changes in the supply and demand structure of the import areas. The most fascinating part of this rather bureaucratic process was the Canadian success at exceeding the limits on a regular basis. However, as tensions between Diefenbaker and Kennedy increased, their relationship began to have a negative effect on Canada-US oil relations. Kennedy's officials, particularly John Kelly, the assistant secretary for mineral resources of the Interior Department, sought to reflect his disfavour with Ottawa in tangible ways.[19] In fact, Kennedy was set to revoke Canada's exemption to the MOIP to spite Diefenbaker, but after the Liberals were elected, Prime Minister Lester Pearson talked him out of it at the Hyannisport meeting in 1963.[20] This reinforced, for many officials and ministers within the government, Canada's vulnerability to US whims.

Since it was widely perceived that Canada-US relations had deteriorated significantly during the Diefenbaker years, Pearson and Kennedy decided to have a joint study written on the nature and future of the relationship. Work on the study continued under the new presidency of Lyndon B. Johnson, even after Kennedy's untimely death. The result, published on 1 July 1965, was a document titled "Canada and the US, Principles of Partnership" or what became known as the Merchant-Heeney Report. In order to assist the writing of the report, at the Joint Committee on Trade and Economic Affairs (JCTEA) meeting of April 1964, Canadian and American representatives agreed to initiate joint energy studies "to serve in essence as an analytical tool in pursuing the objective of freer movement of energy."[21] The discussions did not last long and did not result in an agreement.

Canadian oil policy during the Pearson era was to preserve the NOP, maintain the MOIP exemption, and negotiate increased exports of Canadian oil to the United States, while continuing to receive cheaper imported oil into the eastern part of Canada. The policy for natural gas continued as before. Amounts surplus to Canadian use could be exported, and exchanges of information between the NEB and the American Federal Power Commission (FPC) were encouraged in order to expedite applications, though this did not always happen. The Pearson government did not undertake an oil and gas policy review while it was in power. Nor did the Johnson administration initiate any major changes to its oil and gas policy. Studies were undertaken, but when Johnson removed oil policy from the White House, his administration's approach to oil and gas issues was in a state of suspended animation and affected by a power struggle between Secretary of the Interior Stewart Udall and Under Secretary of State for Economic Affairs Thomas Mann.[22] This meant that the MOIP stayed essentially the same, and the informal limits to Canadian exports were constantly renegotiated and culminated in a secret agreement in 1967 that formally limited Canadian exports, which the Canadians nonetheless exceeded.

Although there was some talk about the merits of a continental oil agreement in the 1960s, the support for a continental approach oscillated. Both governments were keen on increasing their continentalism between 1963 and early 1965, when Canada started to retreat from this policy and emphasis fell on the informal transgovernmental networks that tended to keep issues from escalating into major irritants. A year later, around the time that Walter Gordon was no longer in Cabinet and the NEB received word that a large new pipeline was going to be built in the United States that seemed likely to reduce Canadian access to the American market, the idea of a continental oil agreement was reintroduced by Canada. This time the United States rejected the proposal, though it was mentioned, but rejected, again in 1967. The uncertainty created by oil being removed from White House oversight and the ideological struggles within the Pearson Cabinet meant that continental economic integration during most of the 1960s stalled. The election of new governments in Canada and the United States allowed a new round of continental talks to re-enter the stage in 1969.

Under the new Liberal government of Pierre Elliott Trudeau, elected in 1968, and at the request of Secretary of State for External Affairs Mitchell Sharp, discussions of a continental energy agreement and then a scaled-down continental oil policy began in April 1969 and continued into 1973.[23] The large Alaskan oil fields discovered around Prudhoe Bay in 1968 threatened Canada's export position in the US Pacific Northwest. In addition, a new pipeline bringing oil into the Chicago area was nearing completion and would displace Canadian oil in that region as well. Even with rising

American demand, it appeared to many policy-makers that Canadian oil exports would most likely be curtailed and that it would become even more difficult to obtain US understanding (or sympathy) for ensuring Canada's share of the US market. Those, such as Sharp, who subscribed to informal continentalism realised that the first stage was no longer working. There was too much uncertainty and potential for arbitrary US action, and therefore some kind of formal sectoral arrangement would be preferable.[24]

During these discussions, however, it became clear to the US officials that the Canadian government did not want to take any action, or support any policy, that would increase prices in eastern Canada.[25] US officials insisted that, as part of any agreement, Canada should limit its exports and reduce its reliance on imported oil. But Canada refused to guarantee that it would not curtail exports to the United States in an emergency, impose export taxes, or reduce its imports into eastern Canada. Several meetings were held to try to reach a common position. The strategy of the Canadian officials, as directed by Cabinet, was to delay and distract for as long as possible. Frustrated at the diversions and delays, American officials counselled President Nixon to enact "temporary" formal restraints on Canadian oil imports as a means to motivate the Canadians to take the negotiations for a continental energy policy more seriously.[26]

Canada's immediate response was to suspend negotiations, but within a few months discussions restarted. The United States was concerned because it seemed that Canada was increasing its oil exports in order to take advantage of the higher prices, while making the Canadian market even more dependent on cheaper, but insecure, imported oil. In fact, this was the admitted intent as revealed in the Cabinet discussions of the Canadian "Oil Policy Review" of May 1969. The Cabinet understood Canadian domestic policy to be one "of buying in the cheapest market [Middle East/Venezuelan oil] and selling in the most expensive [US market]."[27] As a consequence Canadian oil was exported to the United States in record amounts in order to gain the premium price, while significantly cheaper Venezuelan and Middle Eastern oil poured into eastern Canada. Canada was also becoming increasingly dependent on imported oil for its domestic needs and was unwilling to alter that situation. Then, when pipeline capacity peaked in 1972 and it appeared that Ontario refiners would fall short of supplies because sellers received a higher price in the United States, export controls to limit the amount moving into the US market were implemented in February 1973.

When the Arab embargo on the United States appeared in October 1973, the Canadians, worried that US oil companies would divert their shipments from Canada and that Canada too might be subjected to the boycott, suddenly "seemed eager to enter into serious discussions about a 'coordinated' oil policy."[28] US officials replied that they understood from Canadian statements that oil exports to the United States would be curbed, which prompted Washington to pursue a policy of self-sufficiency.[29] A month later, Prime Minister Trudeau alluded in a letter to President Richard Nixon that oil exports were to be phased out.[30] Over the next year, Canadian officials privately served notice to US officials that oil exports would indeed be phased out, and an announcement was issued in November 1974.[31]

There were three reasons for Canadian reluctance to make a formal agreement with the United States in this period. First, Canada did not want to give up its policy of having the lowest possible energy prices in Canada while "surplus" energy would go "to export markets at optimum prices."[32] Second, by the beginning of 1972 world oil prices increased more than expected, future increases seemed likely, and overseas supplies appeared to be even more unstable than ever before. In this situation, Canada did not want to be committed to supplying the US market with specific amounts because, owing to pipeline capacity limitations, cheaper Canadian oil could not then be used to displace the more expensive imports.[33] Finally, and perhaps most importantly, the political will for such an agreement from the prime minister had never really existed. If that is true, then why did Canada initiate the talks? In 1969, when the talks began, Trudeau was only beginning his consolidation of power and was trying to balance the left and right wings of the Liberal Party. Thus, by agreeing to have Mitchell Sharp introduce the option to the United States, the more business-oriented and continentalist-minded ministers and officials would think the prime minister supported and actively considered their views and interests. The gradual politicization of EMR with appointees loyal to Trudeau, which had begun in 1970, meant that he could count on the department by 1974 to reflect rather than undermine his views of energy development in Canada; these did not include increasing trade with the United States. The era of informal continentalism was at an end.

Between 1973 and 1984, Canada-US oil and gas relations under-
went a tremendous shift, and interdependence in the shape of an
informal continental oil and gas agreement was no longer a favoured
option. More nationalistic and interventionist policies emerged, especially from Canada, as confrontation and unilateralism were employed in order to assert controversial goals. The divergence in
Canadian and American views of their oil and gas trade had more to
do with internal Canadian dynamics than with US goals, which at
this time were to expand imports from non-OPEC countries like
Canada. The politicization of the Canadian bureaucracy and the
changes to the policy-making process had a profound effect on
Canada's oil and gas policy, which had deleterious consequences for
the United States. The Americans learned from this period that they
too were vulnerable to Canadian whims and experienced the uncertainty of not having some kind of formal agreement to govern oil
and gas trade.

The Canadian policy reversal, from seeking expanded US markets
for Canadian oil to phasing out exports altogether in 1974, was
heavily influenced by Prime Minister Pierre Trudeau's politicization
of energy issues and the bureaucracy that was driven by his government's embrace of economic nationalism. Energy became politicized
during the Trudeau era, not only because prices increased dramatically but also because energy was at the center of Trudeau's economic
policy. An economically strong and united Canada, with the federal
government planning and reshaping the economy to Trudeau's vision, in line with popular left-wing thinking of the time, meant
shifting the Canadian economy's reliance on staple exports like oil,
to secondary manufacturing.[34] In practice that meant encouraging
Canadians to displace foreign investment in all industrial sectors
so that the revenue generated would accumulate in Canadian hands
and could then be reinvested in expanding manufacturing. If
Canadians were unwilling to act or act quickly enough, the federal
government itself would take an active interest through the creation
of a state petroleum company, as it did with Petro-Canada. In addition, once prices began to rise, the Trudeau government sensed an
opportunity. If Canada could have all its oil supplied internally at a
controlled price, well below the world price, then the competitive
advantage gained by Canada's industrial base, which happened to be
in Quebec and Ontario, would be guaranteed. In order to carry
out these changes, officials had to be trusted to develop the appropriate policies. Trudeau and others in his inner circle suspected that

there would be a great deal of resistance to these ideas within the bureaucracy.[35] Their solution was to restructure the bureaucracy and the policy-making process. The result was the politicization of the bureaucracy.

First, it must be said that Trudeau introduced a whole new approach to government policy- and decision-making that was intended to make the Cabinet and bureaucratic processes more rational, structured, and efficient than the ad hoc method that had marked the Pearson era.[36] Before the restructuring of the bureaucracy that began in 1968, the deputy ministers (DM) of departments were normally suggested by the clerk of the Privy Council and were drawn from the higher ranks of the civil service within that department. It was not uncommon before 1968 for officials to ascend through the ranks over time to the DM position and relatively rare for a senior level appointment outside the normal civil service ranks to occur.[37] With Trudeau, this gradually began to change. DMs were still suggested by the clerk and approved by Cabinet, but several senior bureaucrats who had worked their way up and through a particular department over several years but were expected to be uncooperative were moved or retired to make way for a younger generation from outside the normal civil service system. The replacements were individuals who were recruited to and trained in or had some connection with the Prime Minister's Office (PMO) or the Privy Council Office (PCO). Energy, Mines and Resources (EMR) was one of the departments chosen for restructuring.

The restructuring in EMR took place in two phases. The first phase of the early 1970s was gradual. Time was taken (four years) to manoeuvre, manipulate, or exclude those who would be obstacles. Those targeted in particular for removal were individuals thought to be a hindrance to the execution of Trudeau's vision. For example, Claude Isbister, the career civil servant who had worked his way up to be DM of EMR, was replaced by the outside appointment of Jack Austin. Austin was a former Liberal candidate and advocated a state role in the oil and gas industry. He was given the task of consolidating policy-making power in EMR, diverting it from the NEB. Another example is Robert Howland of the NEB, who had been with the board since its inception in 1959. In the summer of 1973, two years before the end of his seven-year term, he "retired" in the midst of a power struggle with Austin over whether or not the NEB would maintain a policy advisory function or become a rubber stamp for

EMR decisions. Marshall Crowe replaced Howland. Crowe had served in the PMO as an economic advisor to the prime minister in various positions in the PCO and had been head of the Canada Development Corporation. There is evidence that during public hearings on oil exports, the NEB under Crowe deliberately disregarded testimony and data that did not coincide with the government's goal of phasing out exports.[38] The modification of the policy-making structure of EMR and the NEB, as well as the personnel in those areas, ensured that there would be few difficulties in developing and implementing a more interventionist role for the state in Canadian oil policy. The ultimate objective of the interventionist policies was to keep oil prices for Canadian consumers at a relatively low level for as long as possible, enhance the state's role in the oil and gas industry, and increase Canadian ownership of the industry. The first step toward that larger vision of self-sufficiency was to phase out oil exports.[39]

Importantly, the idea of phasing out exports emerged before the oil crisis during the departmental policy review. When the Finance officials, led by Tommy Shoyama and George Tough, introduced the concept, some EMR officials dismissed it as absurd.[40] But Austin, with great finesse, circumvented those who opposed the policy by establishing a committee dominated by people he could trust to come up with the right treatment, like George Tough and Joel Bell. Though the energy policy review drafts did not contain the no-export option, it was surreptitiously included in the published report *An Energy Policy for Canada: Phase I – Analysis*. Those who had disagreed with the policy at the original meetings were quietly moved to other divisions with less responsibility.

In order to convince the public and deflect criticisms from Alberta, the other producing provinces, and the United States, there had to be a better reason for phasing out oil exports than industrial advantage in central and eastern Canada. The politicization of EMR and the NEB and the shift in power and policy-making capacity from the NEB to EMR were crucial to this development. The new role of the NEB, envisioned by Austin and others, was not to provide policy advice but rather to support and corroborate policies emanating from EMR. Thus, two NEB reports on supply were written and used as a justification to limit and then phase out exports.[41] In these changing circumstances, the conscientious and independent-minded Robert Howland was encouraged to take "early retirement," and was replaced by the well-connected and astute Marshall Crowe. So ended the first phase of EMR and Finance restructuring.

If politicization matters, and causes conflict, then why was the US reaction to the phasing out of oil exports in 1974 relatively mild? There is little mention of the phase-out in the archival record, except for a brief comment made during Trudeau's visit to Washington in December 1974, when President Gerald Ford expressed his disappointment with the policy.[42] There are several reasons that combined to shape the benign response. First, advanced consultations and "signals" that these changes would be taking place had warned the Nixon and Ford administrations about pending actions, hence he and his officials were not surprised, and the reaction was mild. In the early restructuring of the EMR bureaucracy interdepartmental discussions still took place with regard to policy development, and the traditional involvement of External Affairs in energy issues still existed. Thus, when it was decided to phase out oil exports to the United States, US officials were apprised of and reminded of the fact for almost a year in advance by Canadian officials from EMR, the NEB, and External Affairs.[43] In November 1973, a year before the policy was introduced, the prime minister had warned President Nixon that oil exports were to be phased out.[44] In addition, since the United States was trying to establish an International Energy Agency to counter OPEC, it did not want to send the wrong message to OPEC or the international community by responding harshly to Canadian policies. Finally, despite Canadian signals, US officials did not really believe that Canada would follow through with the phase-out and "hoped that Canada would not cut back on its export of crude."[45] Washington protested Canada's oil export fee through quiet diplomacy but seemed resigned to the Canadian policy shift on phasing out exports. The context and the dynamics were very different when the NEP was announced in 1980 and was greatly affected by the second phase of bureaucratic restructuring in the Department of Energy, Mines and Resources.

This second phase of restructuring and politicization had a different dynamic. There was a sense of urgency because the changes were not happening quickly enough, nor were they comprehensive enough. Too many compromises had been made and time was running out. A major restructuring of EMR was initiated in 1978, at the behest of Marc Lalonde, who anticipated taking over the portfolio after the next election.[46] This time a completely new policy-making division was created under the direction of Mickey Cohen, George Tough, and Ed Clark. They personally selected the new employees and reassigned those who did not meet their standards.[47] When Lalonde became minister of EMR in 1980, after the brief Tory interregnum, EMR was prepared to tackle the creation of a comprehensive program. The prospect and intellectual challenge of "redesigning an entire industry's dynamics" was exciting, as ideas could be put into action.[48] These people were motivated and buoyed by their unwavering faith in the ability of technocracy and planning to address and solve pressing and troublesome economic issues. The effect of this rapid restructuring of personnel was that since top government officials in important departments were in agreement with their political ministers, the policies were focused but narrow. Indeed, Gordon Robertson, clerk of the Privy Council during Trudeau's first term, called these people Trudeau's acolytes.[49] There was a limited conception of "acceptable" policy options or alternatives and a lack of diversity of ideas, and the few valid criticisms that did emerge were either dismissed or not taken into account. With the assistance of core Finance and PCO officials, like Ian Stewart and Michael Pitfield, and without consultation with other departments, the provinces, or the United States, the NEP was developed in great secrecy as part of the 1980 budget.[50]

The primary goal of the NEP was to achieve energy self-sufficiency in Canada by 1990 and thereby enhance national sovereignty at home and abroad. Energy security was to be achieved by increasing Canadian ownership and participation in the oil and gas industry at the expense of the mostly US owned multi-national companies, finding new sources of Canadian oil and gas, and increasing the federal share of oil and gas revenues. Canadian consumers were to be protected and Canadians were to have priority and guaranteed access to Canadian oil and gas supplies.[51] Many new taxes and regulations were introduced and the Canadian Oil and Gas Lands Administration (COGLA) was created to administer exploration and development on Canada Lands (federal lands including the Arctic and offshore areas).[52] Following exploration, any production from the Canada Lands had to be done by a firm that had a minimum of 50 percent Canadian ownership. All companies holding interests on Canada Lands had to renegotiate their exploration agreements with the COGLA and return 50 percent of their lands to the Crown without compensation. In addition, a 25 percent interest or "back-in" to be controlled by Petro-Canada or some other Crown corporation was required, without compensation, for every development, past or future on the Canada Lands.[53] Exports of natural gas to the United States were frozen at the then current rates, and exports of oil were reduced significantly, while prices were subsidized for Canadians. These measures were met with shock, dismay, and anger from different affected quarters, including the United States.

Although Alberta and the United States suspected that the revitalized Trudeau government was going to take some kind of policy action on oil and gas issues, as outlined during the 1980 election, the crisis that ensued between the federal government and Alberta and the United States was magnified because there had been little forewarning about the nature and depth of federal intervention included within the policy changes.[54] What concerned Washington the most was that the NEP and the Foreign Investment Review Agency (FIRA) were "blatantly discriminatory with reference to the operations of American companies in Canada."[55] If Canada wanted to preserve its resources for itself, the US government would be disappointed but would not object strenuously. Discrimination against US companies was a whole other matter, because it set a dangerous precedent for other countries in the world. Several accounts of the US reaction to the NEP have claimed that Washington was outraged and made heavy-handed demands.[56] This is an exaggeration. Although elements within the newly elected Reagan administration advocated retaliatory action, forceful arguments emerged with the support of the president that diplomacy should be employed instead.[57] The US government responded by holding a series of discussions with Canadian officials, but US participants began to sense that the discussions were a delaying tactic to keep them occupied while the NEP legislation made its way through the House of Commons. Once enacted, it would be difficult to convince the Canadians to alter the policies. Still, President Reagan insisted that his officials "attempt to resolve our differences with the Canadians through quiet bilateral consultations."[58] These discussions bore some fruit and some minor changes were made to the NEP.

Despite these changes, it remained mostly intact and in effect until the 1984 election. When Brian Mulroney became leader of the opposition in the spring of 1983 he appointed Patricia (Pat) Carney as opposition energy critic. Her task was to develop a Canadian energy policy that would dismantle and replace the NEP when the

Conservatives took office. After Mulroney's victory, the economic nationalist bureaucrats from the Trudeau era did not make it easy for the Mulroney government to implement its free-market energy policy. When Mulroney came to power, many of the senior officials who had created the NEP remained working for the government. By 1984, several of the most important officials, including Mickey Cohen and George Tough, had moved to Finance with Lalonde. Some of the officials who had come from the Trudeau PMO or PCO tried to undermine Carney's efforts to dismantle the NEP by secretly urging Alberta officials to deal with the Finance staff, and especially Finance Minister Michael Wilson, instead. A senior federal bureaucrat referred to in an Alberta document depicted Carney as an overwrought and uninformed minister and claimed that she had no authority from the PM.[59] Carney began to face protests from Wilson and his officials about the elements of the policies and the negotiations and reflected in her memoirs that "the stance taken by Michael Wilson and his officials did, in fact, undermine the effects of the Conservative energy policy."[60] Nevertheless, with the full backing of Prime Minister Mulroney, Carney was able to stand up to Wilson and the Finance officials and dismantle the NEP. The one compromise she had to make was to phase out one of the most controversial NEP taxes instead of eliminating them all immediately.

Based on the recommendations of various task forces or study groups assigned and coordinated by Carney while in opposition, the government under Mulroney dismantled the NEP using four separate agreements.[61] These agreements represented the different elements of Canadian energy policy and deregulated various aspects of the oil and gas industry by phasing out or eliminating all of the NEP taxes and regulations, including the controversial 25 percent "back-in." The goal was to allow market forces to prevail, but in each policy document the federal government retained a *force majeure* clause that would allow the Canadian government to protect consumers in the case of extraordinary fluctuations in world oil prices. The major impediment to smooth Canadian-American relations, the NEP, was no longer in place. And yet it would continue to play a major role in fuelling a sense of Western grievance against the federal government.

All of these policy changes did not prevent the possibility of another NEP being implemented by a future government. One option that the Mulroney government could have taken once the NEP was

dismantled was to embrace the traditional informal continentalism
approach and enter into an informal or even a sectoral agreement
with the United States on the trade of oil and gas. But the world oil
and gas market had changed remarkably since the first oil crisis. The
increase in world prices and the uncertainties of OPEC had led to an
increase in exploration and development in non-OPEC areas. By the
mid-1980s, those new supplies began to enter the market, and instead of oil shortages, there were now surpluses. World oil prices
began to decline appreciably, and the future of OPEC seemed to be in
question. Now that the Canadian policy was not to reserve Canadian
resources for Canadian use, an assured market would be needed,
and the Conservatives looked south. But protectionism in the United
States was on the rise, particularly after the mid-term congressional
elections in 1986, and many US officials and politicians still har-
boured some resentment and a great deal of mistrust towards
Canada because of the policies of the 1970s and early 1980s.[62] The
Reagan administration disliked much of the protectionism and subscribed instead to the ideology that market forces should direct the
economy, including the oil and gas industry. Less government would
allow business to operate more efficiently and profitably.[63] In addition, stung by the previous Canadian actions, US officials in the
Reagan administration wanted something more permanent than an
informal understanding or a sectoral agreement.[64]

Mulroney shared many of Reagan's economic views.[65] The Conservatives also recalled the difficulties Canada had experienced
under the informal continentalism of the 1960s and did not want to
be held hostage to possible US arbitrariness and the caprices of Congress. A sectoral agreement was also ruled out because of the greater
chance for either country to disregard it in a crisis. Both sides rejected informal continentalism. Furthermore, fearful that a future
government could reinstate the NEP in some form, the Mulroney
government, in a dramatic departure from traditional Canadian
policy and with the full backing of the Alberta government, agreed
to include energy in the negotiations for a comprehensive free trade
agreement with the United States, in part to preserve a free-market
approach to the discovery, extraction, and distribution of Canada's
oil and gas reserves. A continental energy arrangement became chapter 9 of the 1988 Canada-US FTA, which was a binding treaty.[66]
Such an arrangement cannot be undone or dismantled without dis-
solving the entire agreement.

The consequences of a continental energy policy in this case are many, and they demonstrated a dramatic departure from traditional Canadian trade and foreign policy. Since the energy provisions affected both Canada and the United States, the implications for both countries were significant. Future Canadian and US governments were committed to freer trade in oil and natural gas and limited in their policy options unless the energy provisions in the FTA were renegotiated or the entire agreement was abrogated. Neither country could impose price controls on oil and natural gas or impose import or export charges without levying the same amount on domestic consumers. Neither country could establish a two-tiered pricing system, as both countries had during the 1970s and early 1980s. Both countries could continue to provide government incentives for oil and gas exploration and development, but investors had to be treated fairly in both countries.[67] Regulatory changes affecting the other country had to be discussed by both countries before being implemented. This provision was meant to limit the regulatory powers of the US FERC and the Canadian NEB and discouraged discriminatory regulations. Canada gained access to Alaskan oil, which was forbidden from export to any other country. Both countries agreed to limit the regulatory actions available to them through the proportional-sharing arrangement so that neither country could arbitrarily cut off exports to the other country in a time of crisis or conservation. The reduction had to maintain the same proportion of export to supply as averaged over the previous thirty-six months. Since Canada exports more oil and natural gas than it imports from the United States, this provision is often considered to be more favourable for the United States than for Canada.[68]

Debate surrounding the energy provisions in the FTA is now usually centred on the proportional-sharing clause and the import and export pricing restrictions, because they do limit Canada's policy options and sovereignty to some degree. Why would Canada agree to measures that compromised its independence? Energy crises are uncommon, whereas more general fluctuations in the market are not. Policy-makers believed it was more prudent for Canada at this time to secure guaranteed access to the large US market, even if it meant the remote possibility that Canada's sovereignty would be constrained in a time of crisis. Through their membership in the IEA, Canada and the United States are committed to share resources in a time of crisis. The inclusion of the proportional sharing clause confirmed this obligation and further limited the potential regulatory actions available to both countries in a crisis. Canada's agreement to the energy provisions within the FTA could be interpreted as an attempt to guarantee the long-term economic stability of oil and natural gas exports to the large US market, while both sides would be constrained from imposing protectionist discriminatory taxes and regulations as they had often done in the past.

By 1988, both Canada and the United States believed that market rather than protectionist forces should prevail, and they sought a comprehensive bilateral agreement to ensure that the deregulation of the oil and gas industry would be difficult to reverse. Even though by the time the FTA was being negotiated both countries had undertaken initiatives to deregulate their respective oil and gas policies, the energy chapter within the FTA served to ensure that discriminatory taxes and regulations could not be implemented by future governments, nor could energy be used as a bargaining lever for other trade disputes without renegotiating or terminating the agreement. In exchange for the inclusion of a dispute settlement mechanism in the FTA, the Mulroney government limited Canada's economic policy options as they pertained to oil and gas trade, in the pursuit of wholesale continental integration in the energy field. This was a profound shift in established Canadian energy policy.

The established approach and priority for Canadian oil and gas policy throughout the 1950s and into the early 1970s was to secure guaranteed access to the US market for increased oil and gas production that was surplus to Canadian use. The informal continental approach succeeded in the 1950s and 1960s for a number of reasons. There was a surplus of cheap oil on the world market, Canada was keen to develop its fledgling industry, the United States wanted to treat its main cold war ally favourably, and most importantly, the personal relationships between leaders and important officials across the border reinforced the understanding of the benefits of an informal relationship.

This changed in the 1970s and early 1980s when oil prices increased dramatically, Middle East oil supplies became less stable, OPEC became more militant, and the leadership changed in Canada and the United States. The restructuring of the bureaucracy in Canada also happened to coincide with reorganisation in the United States, which meant that the informal networks of officials deteriorated. By 1980, the traditional lines of communication between

Canadian and US officials were either ignored or no longer existed, and the stronger the US reaction, the more the Canadians believed they had taken the right action. In addition, the politicization of civil service positions under the Trudeau government meant that these people were dedicated to Trudeau and his vision, and this vision did not endorse increased trade in oil and gas with the United States. The goal was to reconstruct or refashion the Canadian oil system; hence the decisions to phase out oil exports, create a state oil company, and introduce the NEP.

As time wore on, changes were made to the NEP that addressed some US complaints. Yet many of the interventionist aspects of the NEP remained. These would change after the election of the Mulroney government, which moved to dismantle the NEP. That accomplished, the possibility of another NEP remained. That was, in part, one of the reasons why the Mulroney government agreed to include the energy chapter within the Free Trade Agreement with the United States.

Although the informal continentalist approach was relatively successful in the 1950s and 1960s, the world economy had changed by the 1980s. The FTA as a whole reflected the international trend toward large formalized trading blocs. Attempts in the 1970s and early 1980s to increase trade with Europe and Japan and decrease dependence on access to the US market, did not succeed. By rejecting the other policy alternatives of economic nationalism, especially informal continentalism, and embracing formal continentalism in the energy chapter of the FTA, the Conservatives initiated a profound alteration of traditional Canada-US oil and gas relations.

NOTES

1 Politicization here has a dual meaning. First, it denotes a high level of attention given to a particular issue among cabinet ministers and the prime minister. Second, it means the appointment into civil service positions of specific recruits who were either linked with the leader of the ruling political party or were of similar ideological persuasion; the purpose here was to develop and implement policies that would otherwise not likely have emerged.

2 Michael Hart, *A Trading Nation: Canadian Trade Policy from Colonialism to Globalization*, (Vancouver: UBC Press 2002), 171.

3 Ibid.

4 Mitchell Sharp, *Which Reminds Me...* (Toronto: University of Toronto Press 1994), 180–1, 183, 185.

5 Walter Gordon was the most vocal proponent of this view in the Liberal Party. See Walter Gordon, *A Choice for Canada: Independence or Coloni-al Status* (Toronto: McClelland & Stewart 1966). See also Greg Donaghy, *Tolerant Allies: Canada & the United States, 1963–1968* (Montreal and Kingston: McGill-Queen's University Press 2002); Stephen Azzi, *Walter Gordon and the Rise of Canadian Nationalism* (Montreal and Kingston: McGill-Queen's University Press 1999), and Denis Smith, *Gentle Patriot: A Political Biography of Walter Gordon* (Edmonton: Hurtig Publishers 1973). For studies of the problem of the "Americanization" of Canada, see *Close the 49th Parallel etc.: The Americanization of Canada*, ed. Ian Lumsden (Toronto: University of Toronto Press 1970); John Richards and Larry Pratt, *Prairie Capitalism*; Melissa Clark-Jones, *A Staple State: Canadian Industrial Resources in the Cold War* (Toronto: University of Toronto Press 1987); and anything by Gordon Laxer in this period, such as *Canada's Energy Crisis* (Toronto: James Lewis & Samuel 1974).

6 The term Waffle arose "because its members demanded that the New Democrat Party 'waffle' to the left, away from the political center." John Herd Thompson and Stephen J. Randall, *Canada and the United States: Ambivalent Allies* (Montreal and Kingston: McGill-Queen's University Press 1994), 253. See also Gwyn, *49th Paradox*, 76–80.

7 Bruce Doern and Glen Toner, *The Politics of Energy: The Development and Implementation of the NEP* (Toronto: Methuen 1985), 78.

8 Canada, Royal Commission on Energy, "Submission to the Royal Commission on Energy, Imperial Oil Limited," May 1958, 39–45. See also Library and Archives Canada (LAC) MG 32 B9, Gordon Churchill Fonds, vol. 37, file, Oil and Gas Committee Meeting, 25 1960 (MTL), "Meeting in Montreal – July 25, 1960 Summary by Ian McKinnon," 2–7; and "Notes on Meeting with Executives of the Oil Industry in Montreal – 25 July 1960, Summary by James A. Roberts, Deputy Minister of Trade and Commerce."

9 John N. McDougall, *Fuels and the National Policy* (Toronto: Butterworth 1982). See also Doern and Toner, *Politics of Energy*, 72–4; Robert Bothwell and William Kilbourn, *C.D. Howe: A Biography* (Toronto: McClelland and Stewart 1979), 287–90. The great Pipeline Debate took place through May and June 1956. The company was half-owned by US interests. In 1956 the Liberal Government in Ottawa announced it would advance a loan for up to 90 percent of the $80 million cost of the Western portion of

the line. The line was completed to Montreal in 1958, all loans were repaid, and controlling interests in the company were sold back to Canadians.

10 In 1955, for defense reasons the first phase of the VOIP exempted Canada and Venezuela as reliable suppliers during World War Two and the Korean War. However, the first phase unravelled because some companies chose not to comply, so after 1957 no exemptions were granted. See William J. Barber, "The Eisenhower Energy Policy: Reluctant Intervention," in *Energy Policy in Perspective*, ed. Craufurd Goodwin (Washington, DC: Brookings Institution 1981), 229–51.

11 LAC, RG 25, vol. 3175, File Oil and Gas (2) 1958–1972, Memorandum of Conversation, Oil Import Problem, Meeting with Venezuelans Monday, 19 January 1959.

12 USNA, RG 59, State Department, Bureau of Economic Affairs, Office of British Commonwealth and North European Affairs (BNA), Alpha-Numeric Files Relating to Canadian Affairs, 1957–63, 6-D-3.17, box 3, file Oil Quotas, Memorandum to Mr Mann (E) from Mr Merchant (EUR), Subject: Restrictions on Oil Imports, 16 January 1959, 1–2. See also an account of Heeney's meeting with Eisenhower, DDEL, WHO, OSS, International Series, box 2, file Canada (1) [May 1958–August 1959], Telegram 671 from Ottawa to Secretary of State, Reference Embassy Telegram 669, 10 March 1959.

13 For Merchant's position see USNA, RG 59, General Records of the Department of State, Alpha-Numeric Files Relating to Canadian Affairs, 1957–1963, box 3, file Oil Quotas, Memorandum to Mr Mann from Mr Merchant, Subject: Restrictions on Oil Imports, 16 January 1959.

14 "Act in unity" – DDEL, DDEP, PPUS 1953–1961, AWF, Cabinet Series, box 13, file Cabinet Meeting 6 March 1959, Minutes of Cabinet Meeting, 6 March 1959, 5. "Make Oil Move Look Better" – DDEL, D.A. Quarles Papers, Box 3, File Daily Diaries 1/2/59–5/17/59c3, Diary Donald A. Quarles, Monday, 9 March 1959, 2. Fifteen minutes after Quarles' phone call with Mueller regarding the president's wishes on the Canadian exemption, Quarles phoned Mr Loftus Becker from the State Department and arranged an immediate meeting to discuss the matter.

15 DDEL, DDEP, PPUS 1953–61, AWF, Diary Series, box 40, file *Staff Notes – April 1959 (1)*, "Memorandum for Mrs Whitman from Don Paarlberg, April 27, 1959."

16 See also Tammy Nemeth, "Consolidating the Continental Drift: American Influence on Diefenbakers' National Oil Policy," *Journal of the Canadian Historical Association* 13 (2002): 191–215.

17 Diefenbaker asked Borden to delay the release of the report until it was known whether Canada had received an exemption to the MOIP.

18 LAC, MG 31 E83, H.B. Robinson Fonds, vol. 4, file 4.2, February 1961, "Notes on the New Canadian Oil Policy, February 17, 1961." The NOP was created and considered within the Cabinet Committee on Oil and Gas. The Committee was given specific terms of reference in 1960 by the Cabinet to explore the recommendations of the Borden Commission's second report and the newly formed National Energy Board's (NEB) study on the oil pipeline question. Recommendations for the policy were then brought before and debated within the full Cabinet.

19 Charles Ritchie, *Storm Signals: More Undiplomatic Diaries, 1962–1971* (Toronto: Macmillan of Canada 1983), 2–3. Ritchie comments, "For an embassy to be in disfavour with the White House at a time when the office of President was at the height of its power and influence was a disconcerting experience. The word had swiftly percolated down into every department of the United States Administration"(2). See also USNA, RG 59 Alpha-Numeric files Relating to Canadian Affairs, 1957–63, box 3, file Oil Quotas 1957–1961, "Memorandum to George Ball from Philip Trezise, Subject: Canadian Oil, 2 November 1961. A few senior officials, such as Livingston Merchant, Ivan White, Ball, Trezise, and Ed Martin supported Canada's exemption. Some, such as Thomas Mann and Mr Alexander, preferred to see Canada's exemption retracted and seemed to undermine Canada to the secretary of state and the presidential advisors. See ibid., box 2, file Oil Import Program Jan-June 1961, "Memorandum to Mr Ball from Mr Mann, Subject: Canadian Oil Problem, 25 January 1961."

20 See, for example, John F. Kennedy Library (JFKL), Papers of President Kennedy (PPK), National Security Files (NSF), Countries, box 19A, file Canada – Subject Pearson Visit, 5/63, Memorandum of Conversation, No. 7 of 10, Subject: Canadian Oil Exports, 10 May 1963; USNA, RG 59, Records Relating to Venezuela, 1960–63, Box 4, File Petroleum 17–2 US Import Program May-June 1963, Memorandum to Governor Harriman from Philip Trezise, Subject: US Position in 27 May Meeting with Canadian Oil Delegation, 21 May 1963, 1–2; NA, RG 99, vol. 67, file 23, Future Discussions with the US Regarding Canadian Exports of Oil, 6 May 1963, 17; LAC, RG 2, vol. 6253, file 1963 Cabinet Conclusions 3–25 June, Cabinet Conclusions, 11 June 1963, 12–13.

21 LAC, RG 99, NEB, vol. 72, file 53, JCTEA Meeting of 29–30 April 1963, Item 3A (iv): Energy Relations, Joint Energy Studies. See also, ibid., Memorandum to Mr I.N. McKinnon from Grey Hamilton, Subject: Joint Energy Studies, 3 June 1964.

22 For Johnson removing oil from the White House, see Lyndon B. Johnson
Library (LBJL), White House Central Files (WHCF), Subject File TA-6,
box 19, file TA6/Oil 1/1/65–5/31/65, Memorandum to President from Jack
Valenti, 29 April 1965. For his designation of Udall as "oil czar" see
USNA, RG 59, CFPF, 1964–66, Subject Numeric-Petroleum, box 1382, file
PET 10 Resource Oil Fields CAN 1.1.64, Memorandum to the Secretary
from Mr. Johnson [Assistant Secretary Economic Affairs], Subject: Senator
Humphrey and Canadian Oil, 30 January 1964, 2. See also, LBJL, WHCF,
Subject Files TA-6, box 19, file TA-6/Oil 1/1/65–5/31/65, Memorandum to
the President from Lee C. White, 30 March 1965, Subject: Residual Oil
Import Program. See also Drew Pearson, "Oil Sticky Problem for LBJ,"
Washington Post, 31 May 1965, B37. For the competing positions be-
tween Udall and Mann regarding Canadian oil see LBJL, NSF, Country
files, box 166, File Canada-Memos vol. III 3/65–12 [2 of 2], Memoran-
dum of Conversation, Subject: Canadian Oil Imports and Venezuelan
Charges of Discrimination, 2 April 1965. On political instability in
Venezuela and the role of the MOIP see LBJL, Conference files, box 92,
file TA-6/Oil-Tariff-Imports, Note to Leigh White from George Jacobs
[State Department], Influence of US-Venezuelan Oil Trade on Venezuelan
Political Stability, 1 June 1965; LBJL, WHCF, Subject Files TA-6, box 19,
file TA-6/Oil 6/1/65–8/30/65, Memorandum to the President from Lee C.
White, Subject: Proposed Adjustment in Crude Oil Import Program, 4 June
1965, 2. For Udall lobbying on Canada's behalf see, for example, LBJL,
WHCF, Subject File, box 6, file CM/O, Memorandum to Joseph Califano
from Stewart Udall, Subject: Oil Price Stability, 23 November 1965.
23 USNA, RG 59, E-1613, CFPF, Subject-Numeric – Economic 1967–1969,
box 1350, file PET 17–2 CAN 1/1/67, Memorandum of Conversation,
Subject: Canadian Oil, 25 March 1969, 1–2. See also idem, box 1349,
file "PET 11–2 CAN 1/1/69," Telegram 031468 from State Department
to American Embassy Ottawa, Subject: Canadian Oil, 28 February
1969.
24 USNA, RG 59, E-1613, CFPF, Subject-Numeric – Economic 1967–1969,
box 1349, file "PET 11–2 CAN 1/1/69," Telegram 023543 to American
Embassy Ottawa from Department of State [Secretary Rogers], no subject,
13 February 1969. Norm Chappell, the Canadian Embassy's energy counsellor, was reported to have assured Interior and State Department officials that "Canada intended to live up to the 1967 understanding, but he
pointed out that it could be modified by joint consultations and GOC was
anxious to embark on such talks as soon as certain key positions in State
and Interior were filled."

25 USNA, RG 434, Oil Import Administration, box 100, file Oil Import
Administration, *Canada* (Gen Corres w/Companies See file on Dept of
Defense Prod.), Resume of Canadian Talks at Ottawa February 10–12,
1970, 3.

26 USNA, RG 396, Office of Emergency Preparedness (OEP), Subject Files Oil
Policy Committee 1969–1973, box 46, file "Oil Policy Committee – Gen-
eral 2 of 4," Memorandum to Peter Flanigan from G.A. Lincoln [director,
OEP], 3 March 1970; USNA, Nixon Project, WHCF, Subject Files TA Tariff-
Imports, Box 26, File "[EX] TA4–CM Tariff-Imports [7 of 12 Oil March
1970], Memorandum to the President from Peter Flanigan, 9 March 1970.

27 LAC, RG 2, vol. 6347, file "512–69," Memorandum to the Cabinet, Oil
Policy Review, 15 May 1969.

28 Lafayette College, William Simon Papers, Series IIIA, Subject Files (Deputy
Secretary), drawer 12 Administration Miscellany – Federal Budget, folder
12:17 "Canada: 1973–74," Memorandum for William E. Simon from
William A. Johnson, Subject: Discussion with Canadian Energy Officials
on October 23, 24 October 1973, 1.

29 Ibid., 2–3.

30 USNA, RG 59, E-1613, Subject-Numeric – Economic 1970–1973, box
1490, file "PET 1 CAN 6/1/70," Letter to the President from Prime Minister
Trudeau, 7 November 1973.

31 Gerald R. Ford Library (GRFL), WHCF, CO 28, box 11, file "CO 28
Canada, 12/1/74–12/31/74 (Executive)," Briefing Memorandum for the
President from Henry A. Kissinger, Meeting with Pierre Elliott Trudeau,
Prime Minister of Canada, Wednesday, 4 December 1974, 4.

32 USDOE, Job 1009, box 1, folder 3 "US/5/417 Canada Vol. 1," Airgram
A-323 from American Embassy Ottawa to Department of State, Subject:
Oil and Gas: Address by Deputy Minister of Energy, Mines and Resources
Jack Austin," 11 May 1971, 17, and ibid., Briefing document, Canada:
Oil, Gas and General Energy Questions [no date].

33 USNA, RG 396, Office of Emergency Preparedness, Subject Files Oil Policy
Committee 1969–1973, box 60, file "Oil and Energy Canada,"
Memorandum of Meeting on 18 April 1972, Subject: Call by Canadian
Oil and Energy Officials, 20 April 1973. The Canadian representatives
were from Ontario and accompanied by embassy officials including
Norman Chappell, the energy counsellor. They told the US officials,
"Ontario fears the great US 'thirst' for oil and gas and is most anxious
that its [Ontario's] own needs be met from secure Canadian sources in the
future" (2).

34 Pierre Elliot Trudeau, *Memoirs* (Toronto: McClelland & Stewart 1993),
   164, 203–5. Pierre Elliott Trudeau, "The Values of a Just Society," in
   Towards a Just Society: The Trudeau Years, ed. Thomas S. Axworthy and
   Pierre Elliott Trudeau (Markham, ON: Viking 1990), 361. For Trudeau's
   intellectual development up to 1968, his left-wing ideas, and his preference for associating with left-wing intellectuals see John English, *Citizen
   of the World: The Life of Pierre Elliott Trudeau* (Toronto: Knopf Canada
   2006), 296–7, 307, 312–14, 325–6, 331–4, 361. More on Trudeau as a
   "left liberal" is in Ramsay Cook, *The Teeth of Time: Remembering Pierre
   Elliott Trudeau* (Montreal and Kingston: McGill-Queen's University Press
   2006), 97. See also, John Erik Fossum, *Oil, The State and Federalism: The
   Rise and Demise of Petro-Canada as a Statist Impulse* (Toronto:
   University of Toronto Press 1997), 186.
35 Members of Trudeau's inner circle included Marc Lalonde, Michael
   Pitfield, Allan MacEachen, Jean Marchand, and Gerard Pelletier. One of
   the five conditions Trudeau stipulated to Jim Davey before he would run
   for the Liberal Party leadership concerned the civil service. Davey reported
   to Ramsay Cook in 1968 that Trudeau "had to be sure that the Ottawa
   bureaucracy would work with him. He implied that this might mean some
   changes at the top in the civil service." Cook, *Teeth of Time*, 55.
36 For Trudeau's reorganization of the Cabinet committee system and
   bureaucracy see LAC, RG 2, vol. 6338, file 22 May to 17 July 1968,
   Cabinet Conclusions, 8 July 1968, Cabinet Procedures and Structure and
   Composition of Cabinet Committees. Colin Campbell and George J.
   Szablowski, *The Superbureaucrats: Structure and Behaviour in Central
   Agencies* (Toronto: Macmillan of Canada 1979); Michael Pitfield, "The
   Shape of Government in the 1980s: Techniques and Instruments for Policy
   Formulation at the Federal Level," *Canadian Public Administration* 19,1
   (1976): 13–14.
37 See Donald J. Savoie, *Governing from the Centre* (Toronto: University of
   Toronto Press 1999), for example, and Stephen Clarkson and Christina
   McCall, *Trudeau and Our Times*, vol. 2 (Toronto: McClelland & Stewart
   1994), 280–2, and Christina McCall-Newman, *Grits: An Intimate Portrait
   of the Liberal Party* (Toronto: Macmillan of Canada 1982).
38 US DOE, Job 1418, box 1, folder 11 "Johnson, Bill Memos and Bass,"
   Memorandum to William E. Simon, John C. Sawhill, Gerald L. Parsky
   from William C. Calkins through William A. Johnson, Subject: Oil Policy
   Review in Canada – A Trip Report, 12 April 1974. See also, Gray, *Forty
   Years in the Public Interest*, 58.

39 See also Tammy Nemeth, "Continental Drift: Canada-US Oil and Gas Relations, 1958–1974," PHD diss., University of British Columbia, 2007, chap. 4.

40 LAC, RG 99, vol. 77, file "57S – EP12 – NEB Notes – Feb '73," Memo to Dr Dickie from D.M. Fraser, Subject: E.P.R., 28 February 1973. Energy, Mines and Resources, *An Energy Policy for Canada: Phase 1 – Analysis, Summary of Analysis* (Ottawa: Energy Mines and Resources 1973), 16–17.

41 John Bridger Robinson, "Pendulum Policy: Natural Gas Forecasts and Canadian Energy Policy, 1969–1981," *Canadian Journal of Political Science* 16, 2 (June 1983): 299–301.

42 GRFL, WHCF, CO 28, box 11, file "CO 28 Canada, 12/1/74–12/31/74 (Executive)," Briefing Memorandum for the President from Henry A. Kissinger, Meeting with Pierre Elliott Trudeau, Prime Minister of Canada, Wednesday, 4 December 1974, 4.

43 See for example, USNA, RG 59, CFPF, Subject-Numeric – Economic 1970–1973, box 1055, file "FT CAN-US 1/1/70," Telegram 1110 from Amembassy Ottawa to SecState WashDC, Subject: Policy: US Oil Import Policy and Canada's Role in US Supply, 20 June 1972; USDOE, Job 1009, box 10, folder 8 "US/8/111 Canada – Oil, Gas, etc. Vol. I," Memorandum to Deputy Secretary Simon from D. R. Ligon, Subject: Canadian Oil Export Controls, 27 February 1973.

44 USNA, RG 59, E-1613, Subject-Numeric – Economic 1970–1973, box 1490, file "PET 1 CAN 6/1/70," Letter to the President from Prime Minister Trudeau, 7 November 1973.

45 USDOE, Job 1401, box 2, folder 6 Canada, Memorandum to ERD/IEA Task Force from Robert G. Sands, Subject: Northern Tier Refineries Dependency upon Canadian Crude, 13 December 1974, 2.

46 Clarkson and McCall, in *Trudeau and Our Times*, vol. 1 (Toronto: McClelland & Stewart 1990), suggest that the 1978 bureaucratic shuffle was motivated by the anticipation of an election in 1978, delayed until 1979 (138–9). See also McCall-Newman, *Grits*, 318–19.

47 James A. Desveaux, *Designing Bureaucracies* (Stanford: Stanford University Press 1995), 78–80.

48 Clarkson and McCall, *Trudeau and Our Times*, vol. 2, 199.

49 Gordon Robertson, *Memoirs of a Very Civil Servant* (Toronto: University of Toronto Press 2000), 256.

50 For Lalonde on these issues see LAC, RG 2, PCO, Cabinet Discussions, 17 January 1974, "Oil and Natural Gas Pricing, Taxing and Revenue Sharing," 14.

51 Robert N. McRae, "Canadian Energy Development," *Current History*, March 1988, 117.
52 New taxes included the Petroleum Compensation Charge (PCC), the Oil Import Compensation Program (OICP), the Natural Gas and Gas Liquids Tax (NGGLT), the Petroleum and Gas Revenue Tax (PGRT), and the Canadian Ownership Charge (COC).
53 Government of Canada, Department of Energy, Mines and Resources, *The National Energy Program* (Ottawa: Supply and Services 1980).
54 See also Bruce G. Pollard, "Canadian Energy Policy in 1985: Towards a Renewed Federalism?" *Publius* 35 (spring 1991), 166. See also Kenneth Norrie, "Energy, Canadian Federalism, and the West," *Publius* 14 (winter 1984), 88; Tammy Nemeth, "Duel of the Decade," in Michael Payne et al., eds., *Alberta Formed, Alberta Transformed* (Edmonton: University of Alberta Press 2006), 413–49. For Alberta's suspicion of unilateral federal action see Provincial Archives of Alberta (PAA), Peter Lougheed Papers, Accession 85.401, Box 28, file 463, Alberta's "Energy Package" Proposal Including Commitments for Canadian Energy Self-Sufficiency.
55 Ronald Reagan Library (RRL), WHORM, Subject Files, FG010–02, box 15, file FG 010–02 (018919CA), National Security Council, Memorandum for Richard V. Allen from Norman A. Bailey, Subject: Cabinet Council on Economic Affairs Meeting of 29 July 1981, 30 July 1981.
56 See for example, Stephen Clarkson, *Canada and the Reagan Challenge* (Toronto: James Lorimer 1985), 33–45; Clarkson and McCall, *Trudeau and Our Times*, vol. 2, chap. 6, "Hurricane Ronnie: American Retaliation"; and J.L. Granatstein and Robert Bothwell, *Pirouette: Pierre Trudeau and Canadian Foreign Policy* (Toronto: University of Toronto Press 1990), 325–6.
57 RRL, WHORM, Subject Files, FG010–02, box 15, file FG 010–02 (018919CA), National Security Council, Memorandum for Richard V. Allen from Norman A. Bailey, Subject: Cabinet Council on Economic Affairs Meeting of 29 July 1981, 30 July 1981. The US Trade Representative remarked at the meeting that he "intend[ed] to take a measured, quiet and non-demagogic approach to the issue."
58 RRL, WHORM, Subject Files, FG010–02, box 17, file FG010–02 (018975CA) [1 of 2], Memorandum to the President from William E. Brock [US Trade Representative], Subject: Status of US-Canada Bilateral Trade and Investment Issues, 30 October 1981, 2. Brock also conveyed a warning to the president: "We cannot allow these discussions to become a further delaying device, as has happened in the past" (2).

59 PAA, Energy and Natural Resources, Accession (Acc.) 93.337, No Author, "Issues Surrounding Federal/Provincial Energy Negotiations," 26 October 1984.

60 Pat Carney, *Trade Secrets* (Toronto: Key Porter 2000), 223.

·61 The four agreements were the *Atlantic Accord*, the *Western Accord*, the *Frontier Policy* and the *Agreement on Natural Gas Markets and Pricing*. For Conservative energy policy-making in 1983 and 1986, see Tammy Nemeth, "Pat Carney and the Dismantling of the National Energy Program," MA thesis, University of Alberta, 1997. The task forces and study groups were mostly composed of industry representatives from both the majors and independents. A few meetings were also held with consumer interest groups.

62 See, for example, Allan Gotlieb, *The Washington Diaries* (Toronto: McClelland & Stewart 2006), 414, 415. At a briefing for the prime minister, the Canadian ambassador to the US, Allan Gotlieb, told him, "The news was also worrying on the energy front; we will face an assault on our oil, gas, and electricity exports" (415). The day before his briefing of Mulroney, Gotlieb had met with Lloyd Bentsen, a Democratic senator from Texas and chairman of the Senate Finance Committee from 1986. Bentsen let Gotlieb know that he "was also completely in favour of an oil import tax. Texas, he said, is going through a depression, not a recession" (414).

63 One of the first announcements made when Reagan assumed office in January 1981 was that of a complete decontrol of oil prices. Later Reagan announced the National Energy Policy Plan, which promoted a reduction in federal interference in energy markets. The Reagan administration's efforts to deregulate the natural gas industry were less successful. Department of Energy, *The United States Department of Energy, 1977–1994: A Summary History* (Oak Ridge: Office of Science and Technical Information 1994), 34, points out that by June 1984 American oil consumption was down 10 percent, oil imports had decreased by 33 percent, and 3 percent of oil imports were from the Middle East (40).

64 At a 1999 conference assessing ten years of the FTA, Clayton Yeutter, the US trade representative during the negotiations, noted that Canada had kept energy off the table because with the dismantling of the NEP, energy trade was mostly free and fair. Canada included the energy chapter, however, in exchange for US acceptance of the dispute settlement provisions. There is some evidence to suggest this is true, because the energy sections of the International Trade Advisory Committee (ITAC) and the Sectoral Advisory Groups on International Trade (SAGIT) were among the last to

be established. See also, Bruce Doern and Brian Tomlin, *Faith and Fear: The Free Trade Story* (Toronto: Stoddart 1991), 82.

65 John Herd Thompson and Stephen J. Randall, *Canada and the United States: Ambivalent Allies* (Montreal: McGill-Queen's University Press 1994), 274, 277.

66 Bruce W. Wilkinson, "Trade Liberalization, the Market Ideology, and Morality: Have We a Sustainable System?" in Ricardo Grinspun and Maxwell A. Cameron, eds., *Political Economy of North American Free Trade* (Montreal: McGill-Queen's University Press 1993), 27, where Wilkinson states that the Canada-US FTA "stress[es] the importance of market forces and market objectives."

67 As a direct result of the NEP's 25 percent "back-in" with no compensation, articles 1602 and 1605 ensured that US companies would be treated the same as Canadian companies and receive fair remuneration based on market value for any expropriated assets.

68 Government of Canada, Department of Foreign Affairs and International Trade, *The Canada-US Free Trade Agreement* (Ottawa: Supply and Services 1988), 233–7, chap. 9, "Energy," and chap. 16, "Trade and Investment." The energy chapter also recognizes other agreements or arrangements, such as the IEA (sec. 908), provides a clearer definition of national security (sec. 907), and establishes a formal dispute settlement or grievance board (sec. 905). Five years later when the North American Free Trade Agreement (NAFTA) was negotiated, the energy chapter of the FTA as it applied to Canada and the United States was transplanted completely to NAFTA under chapter 6, "Energy and Basic Petrochemicals." The text may be found at a number of different websites, as well as in the library. For example, the Canadian Department of Foreign Affairs and International Trade has the full agreement on its website: http://www.dfait_maeci.gc.ca/nafta_alena/agree_e.asp (last accessed 23 April 2004).

PART FOUR

Security in North America

10

A North American Peace?

Canada–United States Security Relations since 1867

STÉPHANE ROUSSEL

Any model that attempts to understand the evolution and dynamics of Canadian-American security relations must respond to two questions: how to explain the "long peace" that occurred between the two states since 1867, if not since 1814, and how to explain the fact that the two states developed a relationship of cooperation much more "egalitarian" than one would expect.

The answer to these questions poses problems when one considers the principal characteristic of Canadian-American relations, that is, the considerable asymmetry in military, economic, and demographic power between the two partners. The nature of the relations between Canada and the United States suggests, in effect, traits unlike those that characterize the majority of great-power/small-power dyads, where relations are often marked by either the recurring use of force or the imposition of forced cooperation.

With difficulty one could explain the dynamic of Canada-US relations simply by examining the distribution of power between the two states: the complete domination of Canada by the United States, as predicted by an approach based exclusively on power politics, would not approximate reality – quite the opposite. Not only are coercive measures, pressure tactics, and unilateral decisions rare, but ties of cooperation have tended to develop along the lines of rules of consultation, transparency, "collegiality," shared responsibility, and respect for sovereignty. In this sense, the relationship of cooperation has been more "egalitarian" (without necessarily being "equal") than a single reading of power indicators would lead us to believe.

Policy-makers and commentators recognized early on the distinct character of this relationship and described it with the help of terms such as "exceptionalism" or "North Americanism."[1] These terms have taken on a meaning much more political or normative than explanatory. In an attempt to understand the dynamics of the relationship, international relations theories offer conceptual tools that are more precise. The variables employed by realists (power, alliance, threats) and liberals (interdependence, institutional factors, transgovernmental relations) describe the essentials of the manifestation of the phenomena, such the "long peace" or "egalitarian cooperation." But they generally tend to leave certain matters in the dark, and above all, they have trouble explaining *simultaneously* the two phenomena.

There is another explanatory factor that, curiously, has been neglected by scholars interested in this topic – the fact that the two states are liberal democracies. No author seems interested in focusing on the impact of values and the institutions specifically *associated with this type of regime* (elected representation, the separation of powers, the existence of legal opposition to the governing authorities such as the rule of law, the protection of private property and personal liberty, and freedom of the market)[2] on the dynamic of conflict and cooperation between the United States and Canada.

The variable of democracy offers the advantage of applying to the phenomena both of the long peace and of egalitarian cooperation. On the one hand, the theory of "democratic peace," according to which "democracies do not go to war against each other,"[3] explains the absence of armed conflict since 1867. The United States, Britain, and Canada can, in effect, be considered among the oldest liberal democracies, a status they earned respectively in 1776, 1832, and 1867.[4] Various hypotheses have also been advanced to explain the correlation between the existence of democratic regimes and the maintenance of peaceful relations.[5] Dyadic variants of the theory propose that democratic peace is a product of the interaction between democratic states, and notably, of a process of the internationalisation of liberal values and norms. This approach aims most of all to explain why democracies sustain peaceful relations *between themselves,* while still remaining as aggressive as any other state when entering into relations with non-democratic states.

Thomas Risse borrows this last hypothesis, reinserts it into a constructivist framework, and then utilizes it to explain the capacity of

European states to influence the politics of security of the United States. He sees the explanation of the phenomenon as existing within an ensemble of norms that structure the decision-making process: the "shared values of the democratic security community will be reflected in the rules and decision-making procedures of the institution. Norms of regular consultation, of joint consensus-building and non-hierarchy should legitimize and enable allied influence. These norms serve as key obligations translating the domestic decision-making rules of democracies into the international arena. The obligation to regularly consult each other can then be regarded as the functional equivalent to domestic norms regulating the publicity of the political process, its constitutionality, and the equality of the participants."[6]

The privileged relationship maintained by democratic states will manifest itself through the application of norms related to the peaceful settlement of disputes, regular consultation, the pursuit of consensus, and the equality of actors. In other words, the leaders of these states will apply the functional equivalent of norms that guide their actions at the internal level to the relations they share with each other. This model not only aims to explain *the absence of war* between democratic states but also the dynamic of their *cooperative relations*.

Canada-US relations of the nineteenth century cannot be described as harmonious. From 1776 to 1814, the two states engaged in essentially conflictual relations that gave rise to two armed conflicts (the War of Independence and the War of 1812–14). It was thus through recourse to war that they attempted to solve their early quarrels. But paradoxically, if the differential in power was accentuated during the period 1814–1936, it appeared not to have had a significant impact. Even though resorting to war was considered a viable option, the differences between the countries were numerous, and the asymmetrical nature of the distribution of power was so pronounced that the stronger of the two parties was virtually assured of being able to swiftly crush its adversary. Consequently, war was never waged in North America after the war of 1812. There are numerous indications that the United States posed a military threat during the nineteenth century, such as tension between Washington and London during the US Civil War, transboundary raids led by groups in conflict with each other or governments (survivors of the Canadian revolts of 1837, the Confederates at St Albans in 1864, and the Fenians in 1866), and rumours of Anglo-American war that arose during the Venezuelan crisis (1895–96). Until the 1930s, the British, Canadian, and American military forces devised plans of attack or defense for eventual use in the event of conflict between the United States and the British Empire.[7]

Despite all that and despite periodic rumours of war, a "long peace" developed between Canada and the United States. This situation, which has persisted for close to two centuries, presents an interesting puzzle, especially if one compares the relations between Canada and the United States with other relations between large and small powers in the nineteenth century – for example, between the United States and Mexico. How to explain the maintenance of this pacific relationship in a context in which the large power did not hide its continental ambitions? The war with Mexico in 1848 and the US expeditions in 1914 and 1916–17 bore witness that resorting to arms was not excluded as a possible means of satisfying these ambitions. Even if the tension between the two states was not uncorked in armed conflict, how is one to explain how Canada was able to escape pressures, blackmail, or interventionist threats, that negotiation permitting the settlement of contentious issues did not systematically turn in disfavour of the weaker of the two states?

At the level of cooperative relations, most authors have not perceived in the rapport between Canada and the United States for the period 1814–1936 anything else but a form of "pacific coexistence" coloured by indifference as much as by fear and suspicion. This impression, which probably follows from observing the absence of formal and institutionalized ties, does not take into consideration the informal and ad hoc interactions that multiplied after the 1870s, when the gradual disengagement of the British began to favour the emergence of relations that were properly bilateral. The contention that cooperation and institutions in the domain of security were absent before 1940 is both true and false. If one searches for norms and institutions that are both formal and explicit, this affirmation seems true. If, by contrast, one searches for recurring behaviour and practices that permitted actors to predict each other's behaviour in their mutual future relations, the picture instantly becomes more nuanced. The history of Canadian-American relations before 1940 is dotted with examples of ad hoc cooperation in the security area.

The settlement of disputes regarding the drawing of borders constitutes a first example. On the one hand, from 1817 to 1903, no less than nine frontier quarrels, each producing situations at times highly strained, were settled by treaty on the basis of a compromise, symbolized by the forty-ninth parallel. On the other hand, and a fact less known, the United Kingdom, Canada, and the United States were among the only states in the nineteenth century to define and put in place effective arms control measures. The Rush-Bagot Accord of 1817 had clauses relating to the number, tonnage, and armament of ships that could be deployed on the Great Lakes. With the exception of one period of a few months in 1864 (during the tension created by the raid on St Albans), the accord was constantly in effect and is so still today. Even if it has taken on a symbolic value, and despite several manifest violations, Washington and Ottawa have judged it wise to maintain and modify it formally when their military activities have threatened the terms of the accord, as was the case in 1939, 1940, and 1946.[8]

Since the end of the 1930s, war has disappeared from the tools employed by both states to solve conflict between them. Instead, the two states now engage in a process of formal cooperation. Curiously, it is with the establishment of these cooperative relations in matters of defence that the manifestations of the differences in power have become more apparent. During a brief period between 1940 and 1946, Canada was submitted, to one degree or another, to the inconveniences of a cooperative relationship marked by an unequal distribution of power.

The process that led to the establishment of formal bilateral Canada-US relations for the defense of North America began at the close of the 1930s with the declarations of Chautauqua (1936) and of Kingston (1938), when US president Franklin D. Roosevelt and Canadian prime minister W.L. Mackenzie King recognized the bond of interdependence that united the security of the two states. German victories in the spring of 1940 and the possibility of seeing the United Kingdom succumb, in turn, incited both North American governments to establish mechanisms of consultation that extended from joint maritime and air defence to the production of armaments and the standardization of equipment. The Declaration of Ogdensburg (1940) marked the creation of the Permanent Joint Board of Defence (PJBD), while that of Hyde Park (1941) dealt with military production. The work of the PJBD has, among other matters, permitted the elaboration of joint defence plans, the construction of infrastructures necessary for their realization (bases, routes, weather stations), and the formulation of guidelines for combined military operations.

   Problems have nevertheless kept surfacing, demonstrating to
Ottawa that cooperation with the United States is not without risk
for Canadian sovereignty. The unequal nature of the Canadian-
American relationship was reflected in the plans for defence discussed during the first meetings of the PJBD, which conferred
"strategic direction" of Canadian forces to the United States,
under certain conditions, should Britain be invaded (*Basic Plan 1*).[9]
However, Canada refused to agree to this measure in *Basic Plan 2*
(or *Plan ABC-22*), which was to apply "if the United States entered
into war on the side of the allies." After negotiations that were at
times very difficult, the Americans accepted that relations be established on the basis of cooperation: "Coordination of the military
effort of the United States and Canada shall be affected by mutual
co-operation and by assignment to the forces of each nation of tasks
for which they shall be primarily responsible ... Each nation shall
retain the strategic direction and command of its own forces, except
as hereinunder provided."[10]
   The situation worsened after the bombing of Pearl Harbor.
Officials in Ottawa worried about the rate at which their neighbours
undertook "joint" ventures, as well as their offhand manner in doing
so. Several were undertaken by Washington (the Alaskan highway,
radio stations, and air defence installations) before the terms were
finalized between the two countries, as though Canada had been just
another American territory:[11] "The American authorities tend to
consider us not as a foreign nation at all, but as one of themselves ...
They make sudden demands on us, for some concession or cooperation which they consider to be required by the war emergency, and
they do not understand why we should not respond, as a Governor
of a State would."[12] These worries escalated once the Canadian government, following a series of reports by the British high commissioner Malcolm Macdonald, became fully aware of the extent of the
US military presence on its territory. In June 1943, thirty-three thousand Americans in northern Canada were involved in the construction, maintenance, or operation of a set of installations in that
region. Moreover, they were openly describing themselves as an
"Army of Occupation."[13] The problem, according to Ottawa, was
that these precedents would pose risks to the sovereignty of Canada
in the North after the war, such that the United States would be able
to invoke "acquired rights" so as to remain in place and to use the
installations and the territory as they saw fit.

In 1943, the Canadian government attempted to develop formulas that would permit US installations on Canadian territory for the war period but that would also allow Canada to preserve its rights once the war was over. One of these formulas, which consisted of reimbursing expenses incurred by the United States for permanent installations,[14] would serve as the basis for postwar politics between the two countries. Canada would not authorize the United States to conduct its activities or to establish new installations unless it assisted in their financing and development, thus ensuring a degree of control by Ottawa over the activities. Between 1943 and 1944, a series of bilateral negotiations enabled some of Ottawa's problems to be solved. Specifically, US installations would be placed under the authority of the federal or provincial governments at the war's end.[15]

After the war, the government in Ottawa recognized that the security of Canada and the United States were inexorably linked. The decision to maintain the activities of the PJBD and to create the Canadian-United States Military Cooperation Committee (MCC) in 1946 reflected the direction in which they wished to head. The crucial step came in February 1947 with the "Joint Statement for Defence Collaboration," which formalized Canada's pursuit of cooperation with the United States in times of peace. Moreover, it marked the beginning of the integration process of the Canadian and American aerial defence system. The other important initiative was the creation of the North American Air Defence Command (NORAD) in 1957–58, which established a joint air command. These different accords spawned a number of agreements and co-defence projects: detection procedures, identification and interception of objects entering into the air space of North America, construction of radar lines (the Pine Tree, Mid-Canada, and DEW lines), weather bases and stations, information exchanges, training, and exercises.[16]

The process of integration and, in particular, the creation of NORAD caused a number of Canadian critics to raise their voices, even though they benefited in terms of security. For them, increased security translated into a loss of sovereignty. Confining ties of cooperation with the United States, it is true, reduced the decision-making autonomy of the Canadian government in matters of defence and, in particular, the government's ability to define what constituted a military threat, as well as the strategy and the means to respond to such a threats. "In the face of a Pentagon that defined unilaterally the nature of threats, Canada essentially attempted to limit US ambitions, while aiming to preserve the friendliness of their exchanges."[17]

Without entirely placing in question the interpretation that has largely dominated the literature since the beginning of the 1960s,[18] we should consider another possible perspective. If the process just described is seen as largely inevitable for strategic reasons, it would seem fitting to focus on the way in which events unfolded. In fact, the worst fears of Canadian critics never materialized. Quite the opposite: the major inconveniences observed during World War II gradually receded, and then disappeared completely. Even if relations between Canada and the United States were, more than ever before, marked by an extreme disparity in power, they developed along egalitarian lines. Canada was able to effectively circumvent problems that might have manifested themselves in an asymmetrical relationship. It is therefore possible to conclude that certain factors attenuated the effects of the distribution of power.

Numerous models have been employed to study the dynamic of relations between the United States and Canada, some convincing, others faring less well. None is applicable to the entire period from the War of 1812 to the creation of NORAD. None has succeeded in explaining simultaneously the "long peace" and "egalitarian cooperation." An approach based on realist postulates may be relevant. The model that has gained the greatest currency to explain the long peace is that of a *regional balance of power*.[19] In keeping with this model, it is said that from 1776 to 1940, Canada's security was guaranteed by virtue of Canada belonging to the British Empire. This hypothesis leaves important evidence unaccounted for, however, particularly if one narrows one's scrutiny to the period of 1871 to 1939. After the signing of the Washington Treaty (1871), Britain – for budgetary reasons – ordered the retreat of the majority of its troops stationed in Canada, a process completed in 1906.[20] One of the ways in which the hypothesis of a security guarantee could be salvaged, however, is by considering the balance of power on the continent of North America in virtual, rather than actual, terms. Thus, it was not the physical presence of British troops in Canada that guaranteed stability but the fact that one could depend on London to send the Royal Navy into battle should the need arise. But this argument is less persuasive for the period of 1898 to 1939. At the turn of the century, and particularly after World War I, the British fleet saw its supremacy challenged by the Germans, Japanese, and, above all, the Americans. British Admiral Fisher recognized this reality as early as 1897 when he stated, "the defence of Canada is absolutely hopeless."[21]

This counterweight hypothesis explains even less well the dynamic of cooperative relations. Bilateral relations between Canada and the United States not only grew in frequency after the retreat, but they *improved*. In truth, the British contributed much more than arms. Most of the friction between Canada and the United States was in some way caused by Britain. Awareness of this reality is particularly embarrassing for realists, since their logic prescribes that a change in equilibrium will produce instability and conflict. The opposite was observed. Canada and the United States arrived at solutions to the majority of their differences through peaceful negotiation and compromise.

The balance of power theory was reformatted to make sense of state behaviour with the creation of the North Atlantic Treaty Organization (NATO). It was hypothesized that by engaging in a process of multilateralism, Canada hoped to dilute American influence in a wider setting than North America and to work towards building a common front with other states that would be able to counter the unilateralism of the United States in areas that would affect its security. It was assumed that the desire to build a counterbalance in Europe was a key motivation behind the Canadian decision to join the Atlantic alliance in 1948–49. This type of hypothesis is probably among the older and the most popular in the literature dealing with small states in alliance.[22] One finds this argument on the behaviour of small powers in alliances in a large number of texts, to the point that it has become a recurring theme in the literature on Canadian foreign policy. The notion nevertheless contains two flaws. The first is that only a small portion of bilateral issues between Canada and the United States could be transferred to the multilateral level. The second is that despite its popularity, this hypothesis has never been systematically tested.[23]

Two sets of liberal ideas have also dominated thinking about the relationship: *complex interdependence* and the *security community*. Theorists of interdependence account for the long peace by pointing to the expansion of commercial and financial exchanges between Canada, the United States, and Britain during the nineteenth century. From an a priori standpoint, the will to preserve an arrangement like this one could very well be interpreted as the reason why the trio of governments resisted going to war. Without a doubt, the theory brings to the table another element of explanation, but it also contains several weaknesses.

First, the worry that a war would disrupt systems of exchange, however profitable, has not always been a sufficient deterrent in the past, particularly during the twentieth century, as the glaring example of World War I demonstrates. The "cult of the offensive" and the well-accepted idea that wars would be short and thus cause little damage to commercial networks explained the optimism of economic leaders on the eve of conflicts.[24] Second, commercial relations between the two countries, however important, were never perfectly harmonious. The industrial development of the two states was more accurately the outgrowth of protectionist policies than of open trade. And if interdependence is tinged by feelings of mistrust, strong elements of protectionism, and a lack of confidence in the process by state leaders (low trade expectations), that can itself become a reason for war.[25] Third, although it is frequently asserted today that commerce and liberalism favour peace, the opposite perception was dominant in the United States during the nineteenth century.[26] War was not necessarily synonymous with hard times, economically speaking, and resorting to war to advance economic interests was not necessarily an abominable suggestion. The war against Spain and the many interventions by the United States in Latin America to protect regional interests (for example, Mexico during World War I) illustrate the point. A priori, there was no real reason to believe that this medicine might not have been administered to Canada.

The theory of *complex interdependence*[27] has for a long time been one of the leading models used to explain the dynamic of the peculiar nature of cooperative relations between the two unequal powers. Unfortunately, a major criticism has led to the marginalization of this approach, because the phenomenon of interdependence is not contextualized. Transnationalists do not specify why actors abandon the option of war to solve their differences, nor do they specify what conditions favour the development of transnational and transgovernmental relations.

The other liberal-inspired theory that may help to explain the long peace and egalitarian cooperation is that of the security community.[28] Long ago abandoned, it has recently resurfaced in the work of Emanuel Adler and Michael Barnett.[29] A security community exists when the members of a group, bounded by a sense of belonging to a community, believe that it is possible to resolve their conflicts by pacific means. The authors are interested in the objective conditions under which a pluralist security community forms and in which war is banished as an option: a community of values, predictability of behaviour, and responsiveness. This line of thinking could readily help to explain the long peace and may also further understanding of the enigma of relations between unequal partners like Canada and the United States. As Karl Deutsch and his co-authors point out, "Several of these pluralistic security-communities comprised states of markedly unequal power, but their existence always implied acceptance by both parties of a political situation between them which neither side expected to change by force. Small states in a pluralistic security-community did not have to expect an attack by the larger ones, nor did large states have to fear that their smaller neighbours were merely biding their time while preparing to join their enemies in some future military crisis."[30] For Deutsch et al., Canada and the United States form a pluralist security community whose origins date back to 1819 but which seems to have more firmly established itself in the years 1870–71.[31] This idea has also been used by authors such as Sean Shore.[32] However, as is the case with the theory of complex interdependence, the question of how and why the three conditions that characterize a security community can emerge remains unanswered. Nevertheless, in spite of its weaknesses, the concept of a security community has the advantage of focusing attention on variables that are too often neglected by specialists, notably the notion of "responsiveness" and that of "shared values and ideas." These notions naturally lead to the examination of democracy and liberalism as sources of specific ideas and values that are liable to be shared by a significant number of actors.

Employing the variable of democracy to explain the dynamic of Canada-United States relations offers two important advantages. The first is that it applies to the length of the observed period (1867–2000). Second, it permits one to contextualize and explain the development of phenomena such as interdependence and the security community, and thus to deflect certain criticisms that might be launched one's way. For example, a large number of irritants in a situation of interdependence tend to disappear when one considers only the relationship of two liberal states, just as the same phenomenon is at times a source of conflict between non-liberal states.[33]

Moreover, liberalism permits the development of transnational bonds that facilitate accommodation and compromise.[34]

Canada and the United States count among the oldest liberal democracies, and their relations figure among the longest-standing examples of the democratic peace. A priori, the link between democracy and peace seems in this instance a fair one, but it remains to prove it, and a methodological problem makes proof difficult. At what point does one consider a state a democracy? The problem is particularly pernicious when one considers the colonial, and then the semi-colonial status of Canada. Most of the conflicts that threatened to escalate into war between 1814 and 1939 in fact pitted England against the United States. This point has been made by authors who have sought to apply or to challenge the hypothesis of the democratic peace in studying Anglo-American crises that have affected Canadian security (the *Trent* affair, the Venezuelan crisis). The historical study of the Canadian-American democratic peace has been overshadowed by the study of the Anglo-American democratic peace.

Of relevance here is the argument put forward by John Owen. He argues that the mechanisms required to maintain a democratic peace are workable only if the two states *perceive* each other as democracies ("liberals must consider the other state democratic").[35] It is safe to conclude that Americans and Britons recognized each others' "liberal democratic status" throughout the nineteenth century,[36] but what is known about the mutual perceptions of Canada and the United States? The Grant administration appeared to show little sympathy for the newly formed Dominion of Canada, which was viewed in 1867 as merely "a colonial authority" and a "semi-independent but irresponsible agent [that] has exercised its delegated power [from Britain] in an unfriendly way."[37] During the period leading up to the signing of Confederation, American reactions ranged from contempt to a conviction that this event would only accelerate the inevitable peaceful absorption of Canada by the United States. Many of these reactions were specific responses to the perceived nature of the Canadian political regime. Those that were hostile were in part fuelled by the rumour that Canada was to become a monarchy under the direction of Queen's Victoria's son, Prince Arthur. Less hostile, and even delighted, commentary focused on the fact (again drawn from false impressions) that "while the British people pretend to despise our form of government and to regard it as a failure ... they have themselves consummated an almost similar one in their own colonies."[38] At the same time, it is worth noting that these attitudes did not represent the American public at large, in the sense that most members of the population had no opinion at all! In one observer's words, "Confederation and the gradual expansion of the Dominion of Canada no longer disturbed the average American; indeed, he generally ignored the fact that a colony was disappearing and a nation was rising in its place."[39] General disinterest in Canada aside, at what point was the distinction made in the United States between London and Ottawa? We know that the distinction was quite obviously apparent in the eyes of American leaders once Canada began to slowly emancipate itself from imperial tutelage after the First World War (a process completed in 1931 with the Statute of Westminster). But as we will see below, other subtle signs lead one to believe that liberal ideas structured relations between the two entities as early as Confederation in 1867.

Another problem that is addressed here, because it potentially undermines the explanatory strength of the democratic long peace, is the argument that very few contentious issues arose between the two states that were acute enough to *warrant* violence, regardless of whether or not violent settlements were seen as viable by both countries. However, this assertion is weakened when one recalls the dozen or so disputes over the drawing of borders (the most delicate of issues, as borders touch on the fundamental question of sovereignty) in the nineteenth century, each time causing the governments to go head to head. As well, the dynamic of the cooperative relationship itself risked producing tensions that might have erupted into confrontation. In the early 1940s (and several times afterwards), Canadians were afraid that the US government would adopt measures – unilaterally – to defend Canada even if Canada could not or was not willing to adopt similar measures.[40] But with the exception of these few isolated incidents in 1942–43 and with the damage repaired afterwards, this type of dilemma never repeated itself as seriously, even in the darkest hours of the Cold War. With hindsight, this episode can be interpreted as a turbulent phase in a larger process of learning and of the internationalization of norms, rather than a period typical of relations between the two states.

When examining Canadian-American interactions between 1867 and 1957, one finds elements that coincide with the notions of the democratic peace and of cooperation among democracies, notably, the absence of recourse to violence, the seeking of compromise, and the practice of consultation and of equality. These elements represent values associated with liberalism writ large, that is, at the international level. It can be expected, in other words, that the practices, norms, and formal institutions of the two states will reflect these values.

Many of the quarrels between the United States and Canada were sporadic and resulted from factors escaping the control of the governments in power (in particular, the activities of "rebel" groups like the French Canadian Patriotes or the Confederates). These conflicts generally dissolved on their own without London, Ottawa, or Washington having to intervene. Other conflicts that directly implicated the Canadian and American governments and that therefore threatened to become militarized (such as the conflicts over borderlines and fishing zones) assume, here, greater significance because they permit us to gauge the attitude of the governments towards each other. From this point of view, two particulars need to be underlined: not only were these conflicts effectively *solved* by negotiation and compromise – in contrast to conflicts simply set aside for want of a solution or an unwillingness to find one, or forcibly solved by unilateral decision – but these settlements were consistently reached through like *procedures*. It would seem, then, that there is a *pattern* in how conflicts were solved, a pattern that corresponds with the norms of resolution of conflicts in a democratic society: the banishment of force and the solving of conflicts by procedure, as well as by institutionalized mechanisms.

Until the 1940s, relations between Canada and the United States in the realm of security functioned largely without formal institutions. This is not to say that identifiable practices did not exist. They did exist, and they were important in that they permitted "habits of cooperation" to form and other recurring behaviours to take hold – they would later serve as the foundation upon which institutionalized cooperation was built. Without markers, actors often look to the past for points of reference to orient their behaviour. It is reasonable to expect that the ad hoc experiences with cooperation would influence the approaches taken by the Canadian and American governments when it came time in 1940 to enter into a more formal process of cooperation.

The series of treaties that aimed to solve boundary line disputes illustrate this pattern. These treaties enabled parties to establish the basis for future relations, in addition to offering decisive solutions to the conflicts. The Washington Treaty (1871) recognized the borders of the status quo (and with that the existence of Canada was recognized by the United States), while conferring the authority for arbitration and negotiation on a commission as part of the conflict-solving process.[41] Arbitration measures handled by "third party" representatives (members of other governments and international jurists) was one practice that gained in currency and was used mostly to solve disputes over fishing zones and boundary waters.[42] The convening of commissions of experts and government officials, like the one that settled the Washington Treaty,[43] was another practice that would in time be transformed into a more elaborate, a more formal, and above all, a more permanent feature of Canada-US relations at the turn of century and onwards. The establishment of the International Boundary Commission (1908, made permanent in 1925) and the International Joint Commission (IJC) on Boundary Waters (1909) secured in place a mechanism of peaceful resolution of conflict on border questions. The PJBD, formed in 1940, owes its appearance less to innovation than to the legacy of this practice.[44]

The process that led to the development of norms in the relationship between Canada and the United States experienced its share of stops and starts, of infractions and of temporary setbacks, problems that were in general no more numerous or severe than one would expect from any evolutionary process. Some verbalized intentions by the players of the time went so far as to contradict the very notion of "norms," such as President Theodore Roosevelt's threat to use his "big stick" to solve the differences over the borders of Alaska.

But it is important to recognize that despite these difficulties, a process of norm-building was indeed at play, as the following three considerations make clear. First, the balance of power could no longer be invoked to explain the creation and dynamic of formal institutions once Canadian-American relations began to assume, more and more, a strictly bilateral identity (as early as 1871 to 1909). At this point, the Canadians forged an approach that would permanently brand their foreign policy. The norms and the functioning of these international institutions would serve to shape and to equalize an asymmetrical power relationship with the United

States. The approach is exemplified by the creation of the International Joint Commission.[45] Kenneth Curtis and John Carroll similarly explain that "the smaller of the two nations ... opted for a strong treaty with strong methods of implementation, a natural position for the smaller power, which gains from any formula equalizing sovereign powers."[46] Thus, the use of a unique "brand" of foreign policy appears to have denied or subverted the usual effects of the balance of power.

Second, since the end of the nineteenth century, problems between the two states have more often than not been solved by technical experts and bureaucrats, rather than diplomats. Geometricians and other specialists had an equal hand in the negotiations on frontier lines and on the management of boundary waters. What has resulted from this tendency is a depoliticization of conflicts – the pursuit of solutions that are purely technical or scientific.[47] In this way, the two most problematic and sensitive of questions – decisions on boundary lines and differences over fishing rights – were conferred on commissions composed to a greater extent of experts than of diplomats. The phenomenon, in many respects, foreshadows the emergence of transgovernmental relations, to which analysts would later devote so much attention.

Third, institutions like the IJC or the PJBD devoted themselves to the principle of equality. Donald Barry makes the following observation about the IJC: "it was both endowed with potentially broad powers of investigation and decisions and structures on the basis of Canada-US equality. Canada enjoyed legal and operational parity with the US so that the actual disparity between the two countries did not become an issue in the Commission's operation. Consequently, a potentially fractious issue area in the relationship was effectively defused. As such the IJC marked an innovative departure not only in Canada-US relations but also in world politics more generally."[48] The PJBD, also functioning on the basis of parity, brings together a like number of representatives from the two governments (mainly military) and requires that decisions be passed unanimously.

It remains difficult to observe a diffuse phenomenon such as the democratic peace at work. Nevertheless, there are a sufficient number of elements pointing in this direction to consider the variable of "democracy" as a central one in the dynamic of Canada-US relations. Contrary to most observations, the two states engaged in cooperative practices in the security domain before formal rapprochement in 1940. Moreover, it is possible to associate these practices, like the formal institutions that were created after World War II, with certain liberal values.

NOTES

1 Donald Barry, "The Politics of 'Exceptionalism': Canada and the United States as a Distinctive International Relationship," *Dalhousie Review* 60, no. 10 (spring 1980); Sean M. Shore, "No Fences Make Good Neighbors: The Development of the Canadian-American Security Community, 1871–1940," in Emanuel Alder and Michael Barnett, eds., *Security Communities* (Cambridge: Cambridge University Press 1998), 333–67.
2 Phillipe C. Schmitter and Terry Lynn Karl, "What Democracy Is ... and Is Not," *Journal of Democracy* 2, no. 3 (summer 1991): 75–88.
3 Michael W. Doyle, "Liberalism and World Politics," *American Political Science Review* 80, no. 4 (December 1986); Bruce Russett, *Grasping the Democratic Peace: Principles for a Post-Cold War World* (Princeton: Princeton University Press 1993).
4 Michael W. Doyle, "Kant, Liberal Legacies, and Foreign Affairs," *Philosophy and Public Affairs* 12, no. 3 (summer 1983): 209–10.
5 Nils Petter Gleditsch and Harvard Hegre, "Peace and Democracy: Three Levels of Analysis," *Journal of Conflict Resolution* 41, no. 2 (April 1997): 283–310; John M. Owen, "How Liberalism Produces Democratic Peace," *International Security* 19, no. 2 (fall 1994): 90–1.
6 Thomas Risse-Kapen, *Cooperation among Democracies: The European Influence on US Foreign Policy* (Princeton: Princeton University Press 1995), 34–5. See also Thomas Risse Kapen, "Collective Identity in a Democratic Community: The Case of NATO," in Peter J. Katzenstein, ed., *The Culture of National Security: Norms and Identity in World Politics* (New York: Columbia 1996): 357–99.
7 C.P. Stacey, *La frontière sans défens: Le mythe et la réalité* (Ottawa: Société historique du Canada 1973), 7–12; Richard A. Preston, *The Defence of the Undefended Border: Planning for War in North America, 1867–1939* (Montreal: McGill-Queen's University Press 1977).
8 Stacey, *La Frontiere*, 4–6, 11–12; John Herd Thompson and Stephen J. Randall, *Canada and the United States: Ambivalent Allies* (Montreal: McGill-Queen's University Press 1994), 23, 25, 30, 77.
9 A.D.P. Heeney, 27 May 1941, *Documents on Canadian External Relations* (hereinafter *DCER/ 8*) (Ottawa: Department of Foreign Affairs), 215.

10 Maurice Pope, 5 June 1941, *DCER/8*, 222; Percy Nelles, H.D.G. Crerar, and L.S. Breadner, 22 April 1941, *DCER/8*, 192–6.

11 Shelagh D. Grant, *Sovereignty or Security: Government Policy in the Canadian North (1936–1950)* (Vancouver: University of British Columbia Press 1988). See also H.L. Keenleyside, 27 December 1941, *DCER/ 9*, 1131–6.

12 "Memorandum from Minister-Counsellor, Legation in United States, to Minister in United States. Certain Developments in Canada-United States Relations," 18 March 1943, *DCER/9*, 1138.

13 Malcom MacDonald , 6 April 1943, *DCER/9*, 1570; Grant, *Sovereignity or Security*, 123 and appendix D, 257–85); James Eayrs, *In Defence of Canada*, vol. 3, *Peacemaking and Deterrence* (Toronto: University of Toronto Press 1972), 349.

14 "Memorandum from Department of External Affairs to Cabinet War Committee," 5 April 1943, *DCER/9*, 1256–8.

15 Grant, *Sovereignity or Security*, 129–37.

16 See, among others, Jack L. Granatstein, "The American Influence on the Canadian Military, 1939–1963," in B.D. Hunt and R.G. Haycock, ed., *Canada's Defence: Perspectives on Policy in Twentieth Century* (Toronto: Copp, Clark, Pitman 1993), 129–39; Joseph T. Jockel, "The Canada-United States Military Co-Operation Committee and Continental Air Defence, 1946," *Canadian Historical Review* 64, no. 3 (1983): 352–77; Joseph T. Jockel, *No Boundaries Upstairs: Canada, the United States, and the Origins of North American Air Defence, 1945–1958* (Vancouver: University of British Columbia Press 1987); John English and Norman Hillmer, "Canada's Alliance," *Revue internationale d'histoire militaire* 54 (1982): 31–52.

17 Paul Letourneau and Michel Fortmann, "La politique de défense et de sécurité du Canada," in Paul Letourneau and Harold P. Klepak, eds., *Défense et sécurité: onze approches nationales* (Montreal: Méridien – CQRI 1990), 22.

18 Serge Bernier, "La perception du NORAD par divers commentateurs du Canada," *Revue internationale d'histoire militaire* 54 (1982): 246–72; Denholm Crosby, "A Middle-Power Military in Alliance: Canada and NORAD," *Journal of Peace Research* 34, no.1 (February 1997): 37–52.

19 Kenneth Bourne, *Britain and the Balance of Power in North America* (London: Longmans Green 1967); Donald Barry, "Politics of 'Exceptionalism,'" 116, 118; J.L. Granatstein, *How Britain's Weakness Forced Canada into the Arms of the United States* (Toronto: University of Toronto Press 1989); Thompson and Randall, *Ambivalent Allies*, 14, 28; C. P. Stacey, *La frontière*, 3–4.

20 Samuel F. Wells, "British Strategic Withdrawal from the Western Hemisphere, 1904–1906," *Canadian Historical Review* 49, no. 4 (December 1968): 335–56.

21 Quoted in Aaron L. Friedberg, *The Weary Titan: Britain and the Experience of Relative Decline, 1895–1905* (Princeton: Princeton University Press 1988), 197.

22 Robert L. Rothstein, *Alliances and Small Powers* (New York: Columbia University Press 1968), 61, 124–7; Allen Sens, "The Security of Small States in Post-Cold War Europe," in David G. Haglund, ed., *From Euphoria to Hysteria: Western European Security after the Cold War* (Boulder: Westview Press 1993).

23 See David G. Haglund and Stéphane Roussel, "Escott Reid, the North Atlantic Treaty, and Canadian Strategic Culture," in Greg Donaghy and Stéphane Roussel, eds., *Escott Reid, Diplomat and Scholar* (Montreal: McGill-Queen's University Press 2004), 53.

24 John Mueller, *Retreat from Doomsday: The Obsolescence of Major War* (New York: Basic Books 1989), 32, 38–51; Jack Snyder, *The Ideology of the Offensive: Military Decision Making and the Disaster of 1914* (Ithaca: Cornell University Press 1984).

25 Dale C. Copeland, "Economic Interdependence and War: A Theory of Trade Expectations" *International Security* 20, no. 4 (spring 1996): 5–41.

26 Edward Mead Earle, "Adam Smith, Alexander Hamilton, Friedrich List: The Economic Foundations of Military Power," in Peter Paret, ed., *Makers of Modern Strategy from Machiavelli to the Nuclear Age* (Princeton: Princeton University Press 1986), 217–61. See also Mueller, *Retreat from Doomsday*, 27–8.

27 Robert O. Keohane and Joseph S. Nye, *Transnational Relations and World Politics* (1971); Robert O. Keohane and Joseph S. Nye, *Power and Interdependence: World Politics in Transition* (Boston, Little Brown 1977).

28 Karl W. Deutsch et al., *Political Community and the North Atlantic Area: International Organization in the Light of Historical Experience* (Princeton: Princeton University Press 1957).

29 Emanuel Adler and Michael N. Barnett, "Governing Anarchy: A Research Agenda for the Study of Security Communities," *Ethics & International Affairs* 10 (1996): 66–7, 74–5.

30 Deutsch et al., *Political Community*, 65–6.

31 Ibid., 6, 29, 35, 64.

32 Shore, "Good Neighbors."

33 Doyle, "Kant," 231–2, 327.

34 Doyle, "Liberalism," 1161.

35 Owen, "Liberalism," 90.

36 Ibid., 110–19; Stacey, *La frontière*, 15.

37 Quoted by D.M.L. Farr, "Britain, Canada, the United States and Confederation: The Politics of Nation-Building during the Turbulent Years," in *Reflections from the Past: Perpectives on Canada and on the Canada-US. Relationship* (Plattsburg: Center for the Study of Canada – State University of New York 1991 (1967)), 57; Thompson and Randall, *Ambivalent Allies*, 39.

38 *New York Herald*, 22 October 1864, quoted by Lester Burrell Shippee, *Canadian-American Relations, 1849–1874* (New York: Russell & Russell 1970 (1939)), 188.

39 Ibid., 476.

40 Claude Beauregard, "La coopération militaire et les relations canado-américaines vues par un groupe d'éminents canadiens en 1940," *Canadian Defence Quarterly* 21, no. 6 (summer 1992): 33–6.

41 "The Washington Treaty [...] reaffirmed arbitration as guiding recourse in the reconciliation of conflicting claims." D.M.L. Farr, "Britain, Canada," 61.

42 According to Dixon, democracies are more open than other states to this kind of process. William J. Dixon, "Democracy and the Management of International Conflict," *Journal of Conflict Resolution* 37, no. 1 (March 1993): 42–68.

43 See Shippee, *Canadian-American Relations*.

44 Thompson and Randall, *Ambivalent Allies*, 72–6; Barry, "Politics of Exceptionalism," 117–19;

45 Allan O. Gibbons, "Sir George Gibbons and the Boundary Waters Treaty of 1909," *Canadian Historical Review* 34, no. 2 (June 1953), 124–38. See also Kim Richard Nossal, "Institutionalization and the Pacific Settlement of Interstate Conflict: The Case of Canada and the International Joint Commission," *Journal of Canadian Studies* 18 (winter 1983–84): 75–87.

46 Kenneth M. Curtis and John E. Carroll, *Canadian-American Relation: The Promise and the Challenge* (Lexington: Lexington Books 1983), 52.

47 Thompson and Randall, *Ambivalent Allies*, 72, 76, 78.

48 Barry, "Politics of 'Exceptionalism,'" 119.

11

The Myth of "Obsequious Rex"

Mackenzie King, Franklin D. Roosevelt, and Canada–US Security, 1935–1940

GALEN ROGER PERRAS

William Lyon Mackenzie King, Canada's longest-serving prime minister, is not normally remembered as an emotive Canadian nationalist. Not only did his contemporary political foes paint King as "American" thanks to his extensive personal and political ties to the United States, a consensus once common among historians contended that King's relationship with US president Franklin Roosevelt was entirely lopsided in FDR's favour, much to Canada's detriment. C.P. Stacey cited Roosevelt's habit of calling King "Mackenzie" to prove that FDR held the prime minister in slight regard, since King's truly close friends called him "Rex." Denis Smith described King's relationship with Roosevelt as "obsequious," Donald Creighton called him an American "puppet," and King's overtly pro-American policies, W.L. Morton fulminated, led to a Canada "so irradiated by the American presence that it sickens and threatens to dissolve in cancerous slime."[1] Yet when a freer trade pact with the United States was negotiated in 1948, King throttled the initiative because it had been "the secret aim of every American leader, including Franklin Roosevelt, to dominate Canada and ultimately to possess the country."[2] Close examination of the documentary record of the King-FDR interaction reveals that the idea that King was Roosevelt's lapdog is simply wrong. The evidence shows that King consistently resisted attempts to draw Canada into America's military orbit. He carefully qualified Roosevelt's declarations about continental security, resisted FDR's repeated requests to construct a military highway to Alaska, and pushed for Canadian rearmament to prevent Canada's security dependence on the United States and to discourage US military intervention in Canada in the event of war with Japan. After September 1939, when Canada fought alongside Britain while the United States remained officially neutral, King never contemplated a formal military alliance until after the fall of France in June 1940. When he did begin to negotiate such an alliance, he guided Roosevelt to make a politically accept- able offer but consistently declined to unquestioningly accept US strategic direction thereafter.

King's massive and fascinating diary documents fully his side of the relationship but unfortunately a secretive Roosevelt kept no diary and even forbade note taking during Cabinet meetings. Thus, any as- sessment must be based on an extensive canvass of US and Canadian archives and exploration of the contexts in which the president and the prime minister interacted. United States–Canada relations were neither warm nor close when Roosevelt took office in March 1933. The United States and the British Dominion of Canada had exchanged diplomatic missions only in 1927, while the State Department viewed Canada as an international entity "only in a limited sense." Few for- mal military ties of any substance existed. As Richard Preston has commented, the Canadian and US armies spent more effort planning to meet on the battlefield than to cooperate.[3]

How did Roosevelt conceive of security cooperation with Canada when he took office? His first formal reference to Canadian security came angrily in November 1934, when Britain was considering granting key concessions about the size of Japan's battle fleet. The president warned that if "Great Britain is even suspected of prefer- ring to play with Japan to playing with us," he would "be compelled in the interest of American security, to approach public sentiment in Canada, Australia, New Zealand and South Africa in a definite way as to make these dominions understand clearly that their future security is linked with us in the United States." American historian James MacGregor Burns has described Roosevelt's threat to detach Britain's dominions as nothing less than "astonishing." But British officials concluded that Roosevelt simply was pursuing a long- standing US policy to decouple Canada from the British Empire.[4] FDR's gambit worked; Britain abandoned the concessions to Japan.

Questions about Canada's willingness to side with the United States against Japan had long preceded Roosevelt's presidency. At the Imperial Conference of 1921, a strident Canada had successfully opposed Britain's renewal of the Anglo-Japanese Alliance to avoid possible conflict with the United States. Two years later, air power advocate General Billy Mitchell had argued that a military alliance with Canada directed against Japan was "a perfectly logical and sensible thing" because Canada was "as much exposed to this danger [Japanese attack] as we are ourselves and Canada looks to this country for protection in an eventuality of this kind, rather than to Great Britain."[5] Mitchell's goal, shared by his service successors, was to obtain Canadian permission and logistical support for US Army Air Corps flights to Alaska over Canadian territory. In 1934, when the US Army Air Corps proposed to fly twelve bombers across western Canada "to further friendly diplomatic relations with Canada and to conduct a goodwill flight to Alaska," Canadian under-secretary of state for external affairs O.D. Skelton concluded that one overflight was unlikely to commit Canada to a more permanent arrangement. Conservative prime minister R.B. Bennett thus granted the request, though Skelton regretted the decision when an American newspaper declared the mission was designed to test America's ability to reinforce Alaska quickly during wartime.[6]

Shocking transcripts from the House of Representatives' Committee of Military Affairs were released in early 1935. In connection with an Air Corps desire for airfields near the Canadian border, one American officer testified about the possibility of having to bomb Toronto and Montreal if Britain and America went to war. Another officer commented that if Canada could not prevent its territory from being used by other countries intending to attack the United States, "we would have to do so, I imagine." Appalled, Canadian chief of general staff General Andrew McNaughton cautioned that failing to safeguard Canada's neutrality could lead the United States to occupy British Columbia and could possibly lead to "the disintegration of the structure set up by the Fathers of Confederation."[7] Accused by the *Washington Post* of hypocrisy for proclaiming a "good neighbor" policy while his generals were planning to assault Canada, the president acted decisively to allay Canadian fears. While the State Department reassured Canada that Roosevelt did not approve of the military's "provocative references to Canada," Roosevelt publicly repudiating the hearings and compelled the committee's chastened chair and the secretary of war to apologize.[8]

Canadian security would not be raised again in Washington until King's Liberal Party defeated R.B. Bennett's Conservatives in a

general election of October 1935. King visited the White House in
November to discuss reciprocal trade, but Roosevelt, mentioning
Adolf Hitler's increasingly aggressive behaviour, suggested using an
air and land blockade to curb Germany. King, sidestepping the
blockade notion, turned the discussion back to trade.[9] Security returned to the agenda when Roosevelt and King next met in Quebec
City on 31 July 1936. After issuing publicly the customary platitudes
about sharing the world's longest undefended border to an apprecia-
tive crowd, behind closed doors the president told King that a road
through Canada would be vital to transport US troops to Alaska in
a crisis. Roosevelt also warned that some US senators advocated
intervening militarily if Japan invaded British Columbia. In case the
normally acutely sensitive King had missed the point, two weeks
later Roosevelt announced that "our closest neighbors are good
neighbors. If there are remoter nations that wish us not good but ill,
they know we are strong; they know that we can and will defend
ourselves and defend our neighborhood."[10]

Roosevelt likely intended to nudge King to enhance Canada's defensive capabilities; a formal military alliance was impossible, as the
president feared American isolationists would accuse him of forging
a dangerous offensive military alliance with Britain if Canada joined
an American-led hemispheric system.[11] King was further motivated
to strengthen Canada's defences by a memorandum from Colonel
Harry Crerar that confirmed that American interest in an Alaskan
route and requests to overfly Canada were "distinct portents of a
trend to come." If America and Japan came to blows, Canada could
side with the United States regardless of Britain's attitude, join an
Anglo-American coalition, or remain neutral. King and his officers
preferred the first option. Neutrality seemed impossible because
"should Canada give the United States real reason to complain of
Japanese infringement of Canadian neutrality owing to the lack of
adequate armed supervision by Canada of its territorial waters,
territory, or the air supervening, American public opinion will demand ... what would amount to the military occupation of British
Columbia by US forces." Because Canada's military considered itself
incapable of defending British Columbia, it sought to obtain six warships, two mechanized divisions, and four hundred airplanes at a
cost of $200 million over five years, most of which had not been
acquired by war's onset in 1939.[12]

Crerar's memorandum staggered King's Cabinet when it convened on 9–10 September 1936 to contemplate a rearmament program. King fretted that "British protection means less & less" but understood that "US protection [meant a] danger of losing our independence." As tight Depression-era budgets dictated that there was only enough money for proper defences on just one of Canada's coasts, because Britain's fleet was strong in the Atlantic, "virtually without discussion, the government and military agreed" to strengthen Canada's Pacific coast, the weakness that most invited US intervention.[13] King also handled Roosevelt's Alaska Highway notion gingerly. Major General E.C. Ashton, McNaughton's successor, advised that Canada "would be more than foolish" to create such a valuable military asset for the Americans. But neither senior Canadian bureaucrats nor Prime Minister King ever said this candidly to any US official, especially not to Roosevelt. In October 1936, when American Legation official Ely Palmer approached Loring Christie of the Department of External Affairs (DEA) about an Alaskan road, Christie maintained the primary problem was the project's cost.[14]

Alaska figured prominently when King next ventured to the White House in March 1937. This was not what King had gone to Washington to discuss, for the prime minister had accepted Roosevelt's invitation because he felt there was "a chance of being of some real service in the world situation." Skelton and Christie had warned him to avoid discussing security collaboration, and King did not disappoint them. Evading talk of an Alaskan highway's military utility, he emphasized the project's inordinate cost as the chief obstacle to construction. Further, while some Canadians believed the Monroe Doctrine protected Canada from attack, King told the president that "no self-respecting Government could countenance such a view." Roosevelt assured King that he would welcome just a few Canadian patrol boats operating on British Columbia's coast and some "effective" fortifications at Vancouver.[15]

Relieved that Roosevelt had discussed Canada's defences in such "a nice way and without in any way suggesting how Canada should handle her own affairs," King rejected the assertion of Canada's minister in Washington, Herbert Marler, that Canada and the United States shared a common North American point of view. Such thinking "was all right to a certain point" but could not "run counter to the advantages" Canada received from its imperial ties. King wanted Canada to be a bridge linking Britain to the United States, while pursuing a modest Canadian rearmament program.[16] When an exasperated Roosevelt told Secretary of State Cordell Hull on 4 August 1937 that he wanted an Alaskan highway completed quickly, Hull replied that Canada had shown "little inclination" to discuss the matter. The president's brief stopover in Victoria, British Columbia, on 30 September was intended to demonstrate solidarity "between our own northwest and the stretch of territory separating Alaska from the continental United States." While Roosevelt met with an enthusiastic public reception,[17] King, through Christie and Skelton, evaded a serious discussion of the Alaska highway, pleading again Ottawa's tight finances.[18] As Roosevelt's visit had convinced him that Canada's Pacific Coast defences were "almost non-existent," the president suggested a coordinated security plan for the territory stretching from Washington State to Alaska. But Roosevelt's proposal to covertly despatch an officer to Ottawa to broach the matter was blocked by Norman Armour (the US minister to Canada) and Assistant Secretary of State Sumner Welles on the grounds that it was politically dangerous.[19]

Roosevelt had his own balancing act to perform. Overt connections with Canada were ties to the British Empire, connections that were fraught with political danger given powerful isolationist elements in the United States. Roosevelt asked King and his senior officers to come to the White House to meet the US service commanders.[20] King replied evasively, arguing disingenuously that his presence in Washington might injure sensitive Anglo-American trade negotiations. Armour visited King at his residence to persuade the prime minister to visit Washington, but a reluctant King agreed only to send two officers and made very clear that their visit bound Canada to no commitments.[21] Did King shun this meeting for fear that Roosevelt might offer him a politically dangerous alliance? The evidence is not clear, but Skelton, who favoured talking to the Americans, certainly disliked the formal arrangements, noting his concern that "technical defence officials" lacking diplomatic guidance would be conducting the deliberations.[22]

Major General Ashton and Commodore Percy W. Nelles met with General Malin Craig and Admiral William Leahy at the Canadian Legation in Washington on 18 January. At Roosevelt's direct order, his commanders did not record the discussions.

Fortunately for historians, the Canadian officers laboured under no such restrictions. Craig astounded the Canadians by offering to incorporate British Columbia into the American army's regional command system. But when Ashton evaded a direct answer by embarking on a broad discussion of the strategic scenarios Canada might face in a Pacific war, Craig left his surprising offer in abeyance, to the Canadians' palpable relief.[23] If Roosevelt had orchestrated this meeting to test Canadian reactions, his strategy clearly had backfired. A concerned Ashton ordered his staff to draft a new Defence Scheme No. 2, to ensure Canada remained neutral in any war between America and Japan that did not involve Britain as a US ally. Although willing to exchange intelligence data with Washington, Canada's military, sharing King's emphasis on ties to Britain, recommended that Canada "offer no military commitments in advance of an actual crisis developing." King's diary surprisingly says nothing about the Legation discussions, though he had pushed a reluctant Cabinet on 11 January to purchase two destroyers exclusively for West Coast duty.[24]

Hemispheric defence nevertheless remained on the US agenda. In late January, after telling a parsimonious Congress that more resources were needed to keep aggressors from threatening North America, Roosevelt "heartily" approved forming a Standing Liaison Committee to fashion military cooperation with Latin American republics. Canada would be the last piece of the hemispheric puzzle. In April, the New York Sunday News advocated a mutual defence treaty with Canada, while in July, John Simmons of the US Legation in Ottawa reported that Canada, "obviously not militarily strong enough to go its own way," was displaying "a more definite leaning" towards America "than has been the case in the past."[25] Perhaps emboldened by such reports, on 18 August Roosevelt delivered an electrifying speech at Queen's University in Kingston, Ontario. Acknowledging that Canada was "part of the sisterhood of the British Empire," Roosevelt boldly promised, "The people of the United States will not stand idly by if domination of Canadian soil is threatened by any other Empire." On 31 August Roosevelt told Canada's governor general Lord Tweedsmuir that he hoped his speech would have "some small effect in Berlin."[26]

While Canadian newspapers heartily welcomed the northward extension of the Monroe Doctrine and hoped that Roosevelt would join with Britain and France to firmly oppose Germany,[27] a troubled

King described the president's speech as "most significant." But on
20 August, King publicly promised to make Canada as immune from
attack as "we can reasonably make it," so that "enemy forces should
not be able to pursue their way, either by land, sea, or air, to the
United States over Canadian territory." Canada allocated $60 mil-
lion in the next fiscal year to defence, to that point the largest peacetime military outlay in the Dominion's history.[28]

At a 15 November 1938 press conference, Roosevelt mused about
devising a new hemispheric strategy to defend the Americas "from
Canada to Tierra del Fuego." He also toyed with a grandiose notion
to build thousands of American-designed planes to strengthen the
French air force against Germany. To circumvent stringent US neutrality laws, the planes would be put together in Canadian border
communities using American workers and raw materials.[29] King,
who had already warned Skelton that Canada had to avoid dependence on America, since a "change of leaders there might lead to a
vassalage as far as our Dominion was concerned," found Roosevelt's
initiatives both "amazing" and disquieting. King promised, however,
not to hinder the plane-building project, likely because he already
knew that US secretary of the treasury Henry Morgenthau and
British prime minister Neville Chamberlain already had judged
the idea impracticable and unlikely to gain French approval.[30] In
January 1939, as King's Cabinet hotly debated the $60 million de-
fence allocation, King reminded his colleagues that Roosevelt had
not promised to "defend Canada against an attack" in August 1938.
Rather, the president "would not allow Canada to be dominated by
any other Empire or country." Unless Canada could properly defend
itself, King cautioned, "Canada would become part of America."[31]

The US military did covet bases in Canada. In March 1939, at
Roosevelt's instigation, Admiral Leahy listed naval bases whose ac-
quisition would surely enhance American security, including ports in
Newfoundland and Nova Scotia. Through Robert Lindsay, Britain's
ambassador in Washington, Roosevelt gained Britain's pledge that
US warships could now utilize Britain's North Atlantic bases.[32] King,
however, would not make the same promise, informing a visiting
British official on 19 July that permitting American warships to use
Halifax would depend "on developments." Roosevelt made another
personal tour, cruising Canadian East Coast waters on the U.S.S.
Tuscaloosa. At Halifax on 15 August, Roosevelt publicly discussed
local harbour defences and worried that German submarines might

hide along Labrador's rugged coastline. The international context of August 1939 meant that Roosevelt's visit to Nova Scotia had a much greater impact than his 1937 trip to British Columbia. Canada agreed in late August to let US forces use Halifax as an advanced air station on a limited basis.[33]

Hitler's unprovoked 1 September assault on Poland profoundly transformed the context in which King and Roosevelt negotiated North American security. Britain and France declared war on Germany two days later. Keeping his promise that "Parliament will decide" Canada's participation in the war with Germany, King summoned legislators to Ottawa to reach a foregone conclusion. Roosevelt announced on 3 September that while he could not "ask that every American remain neutral in thought," America would remain neutral. King had listened to this address with "an almost profound disgust" for America was keeping out of the "great issue" and "professing to do so in the name of peace when everything on which peace is based is threatened."[34] Yet Roosevelt clearly sought to aid Canada and the Allies in any way that he reasonably could. US neutrality laws dictated that American companies could not sell weapons to belligerents, but quite astonishingly no one in Washington knew if Canada was constitutionally committed to war by the formal British declaration. Perplexed that his officials could offer him no authoritative answer, Roosevelt telephoned King on 5 September to ask if Canada was at war. When King explained that no decision had been made, the president promptly deleted Canada from the list of proscribed states until Parliament voted to declare war on 10 September.[35]

The president told a journalist on 12 September that his 1938 pledge to defend Canada still stood. Polls taken in January 1940 revealed that three-quarters of the US public agreed with Roosevelt.[36] The military stalemate of the "phoney war" over the winter of 1939–40 seemed to render the matter moot. When King visited Roosevelt at Warm Springs, Georgia, in late April 1940, a "disgusted" President confided to Morgenthau that it had taken "two or three days to get Mackenzie King talking about the war." Roosevelt chastened King for Canada's weak defences, with King responding that Canada was doing the best that it could under the circumstances.[37] A massive German offensive on 10 May 1940 sent British troops reeling to the sea for evacuation, while a surprisingly fragile French army came utterly undone. As Canada stripped itself bare militarily to buttress a beleaguered Britain, the new British prime minister, Winston Churchill, told King that his personal appeal to Roosevelt "would be very welcome to us."[38] King dispatched Hugh Keenleyside of the DEA to Washington on 19 May to speak directly to the president. France's desperate situation concerned Roosevelt, but he had no immediate plans to aid the Allies. Roosevelt asked that King visit soon to discuss "certain possible eventualities which could not possibly be mentioned aloud" for fear of being branded a "defeatist." Lest King did not understand the implication, Roosevelt asked Keenleyside to mention the words "British Fleet" to him.[39]

Roosevelt wanted Churchill and the Royal Navy to move to Canada immediately, but certain that he could not put this contentious case directly to a prickly Churchill, Roosevelt asked King to raise that difficult question. Aghast that his self-proclaimed role of Anglo-American linchpin had thrust him into this awful situation, King felt the Americans were using Canada "to protect themselves in urging a course that would spare them immediate assistance to Britain and bring their own assistance too late to save the day for the British as well as themselves." Roosevelt complained that frequent British demands for US military assistance carried "almost an explicit threat" that if aid were not forthcoming, "we will let the Germans have the Fleet and you can go to hell." If King would lobby Churchill about the fleet's disposition, Roosevelt promised to defend the Pacific status quo and to blockade Europe.[40]

King sorrowfully relayed Roosevelt's request to London on 30 May. Five days later, Churchill famously pledged that Britain would fight on the beaches, in the streets, and in the hills, and would "never surrender." Were Britain "subjugated and starving," Churchill continued, "then our Empire beyond the seas, armed and guarded by the British Fleet, would carry on the struggle, until, in God's good time, the New World, with all its power and might, steps forth to the rescue and the liberation of the Old." But Churchill's significantly more pointed private communication to King on 5 June warned him against allowing Roosevelt to think the United States would get the Royal Navy if Britain collapsed. Only if America entered the war and Britain were "conquered locally" could such a transfer possibly occur. But if America remained neutral "and we were overpowered," Churchill would not speculate "what policy might be adopted by a pro-German administration such as would undoubtedly be set up."[41]

Asked by Roosevelt to press the matter once more, King complied, and Churchill repeated his refusal.[42] Facing an impasse, King asked the new US minister to Canada, Jay Pierrepont Moffat, to "feel out the situation" for staff talks between the Canadian and US militaries. Roosevelt had ordered Moffat "constantly to emphasize" two things while in Ottawa: that "for its own sake" Canada must ensure that the Royal Navy was not surrendered to Germany and that a neutral America could offer nearly as much military aid to Britain and Canada as a belligerent United States.[43] Moffat told King that the president could do much "short of actually declaring war" and relayed King's proposal to Washington.[44]

The US War Department was eager to talk to its Canadian counterparts, and closer bonds with Canada also had strong political support in Washington.[45] Buoyed by polls showing 80 percent of Americans backed the provision of military aid to the Allies (a 23 percent increase in just one week), Roosevelt had released 143 warplanes to France on 7 June. Three days later, when Italy attacked France, an enraged president attacked his nation's isolationism as a "delusion" and announced his determination to help the Allies. On 17 June, Roosevelt declared his desire for military staff talks with Britain. Two days later, he appointed interventionist Republicans Henry Stimson and Frank Knox to head the War and Navy Departments respectively. Roosevelt had as yet said nothing about discussions with Canada, however.[46] Conversations between Moffat and two of King's ministers with defence portfolios, C.G. Power and J.L. Ralston, prepared the way for three Canadian officers to journey to Washington on 11 July to discuss American bases in Newfoundland, industrial production programs, and Canada's adoption of American military equipment.[47] "Far from pessimistic about the outcome" of the war, the Canadians wanted no material aid if that meant depriving Britain of vital items. But despite extensive bilateral deliberations, a US official historian rightly has judged that the "inconclusive" discussions had little effect on formal US military planning. Canada would remain solely responsible for defending its eastern coast plus Newfoundland, although America might assume responsibility for Newfoundland if it entered the war. After the talks ended, Admiral Ernest J. King listed Canadian security just fifth on the American navy's list of Western Hemisphere priorities.[48]

Pressure mounted for a more formal understanding. On 19 June the isolationist *Chicago Tribune* proposed a military alliance with

Canada, soon echoed by the *New York Herald Tribune* and the *Montreal Standard*. The American Legation also reported that on 22 June the Toronto magazine *Saturday Night* had suggested that US protection of Canada would allow Ottawa to better aid Britain[49] Cooperation in hemispheric defence dominated a Canadian Institute of International Affairs (CIIA) conference held in Ottawa in mid-July. It produced "A Programme of Immediate Canadian Action" that argued that Canada risked losing its national identity by ignoring the implications of greater cooperation with America. North America's geostrategic indivisibility demanded a substantial Canadian military contribution through "a new board of strategy in connection with the present general staff." If that happened, "a political agreement with the United States would be necessary, in order to determine the extent of Canada's zone of defence and her function in the strategic sense."[50] Given Keenleyside's intimate involvement with the conference, one can be certain that Prime Minister King had carefully monitored the CIIA's efforts. King also had heard from Loring Christie, Canada's minister in Washington, that Roosevelt wished to discuss a common North American defence plan.[51] On 2 August Roosevelt offered Britain fifty old US destroyers in return for leases on various British facilities in the Caribbean, Bermuda, and Newfoundland. Desperate need and the hope that the exchange would initiate America's entry into the war overcame Churchill's initial opposition, and the "destroyers-for-bases" deal became reality on 2 September.[52]

Although there was now broad support in Canada for an American alliance, spurred by a desire to obtain US aid for Britain and by fear of Britain's defeat, King hesitated to be the first to propose such a thing. After meeting with the prime minister, Moffat therefore urged the president to take the initiative. Roosevelt telephoned to ask King to meet him on 17 August 1940 at Ogdensburg, New York, to consider the "mutual defence of our coasts on the Atlantic."[53] King quickly agreed, and they met in a private rail car. After outlining the ongoing talks with Britain, the president proposed a Permanent Joint Board on Defence [PJBD], comprised of military and civilian officials to formulate defensive plans for the northern half of the Western Hemisphere. King was "perfectly delighted with the whole thing," Stimson recorded in his diary, accepting the board's creation "almost with tears in his eyes." Indeed, greatly pleased that his nation's dire security needs seemed to have been assured, King wholeheartedly agreed with Roosevelt that the new agency should not be a stopgap measure but rather a step towards securing the continent "for the future." However, King insisted that Canada had as much right as Britain or America to defend Newfoundland. Moreover, the Dominion "would not wish to sell or lease any sites in Canada but would be ready to work out matters of facilities." The president then displayed what historian J.L. Granatstein calls "a Rooseveltian iron fist draped in the velvet of warmest good fellowship." Roosevelt admitted that he had told Churchill that in the event the United States went to war with Germany, and in the absence of a pact with Britain, that Washington would seize any British bases in the Western Hemisphere that it regarded as necessary for US security. That is why, the President said, "it was much better to have a friendly agreement in advance."[54]

The new board found immediate public acceptance in both countries. In the United States, where 87 percent of poll respondents supported defending Canada, the PJBD was seen as "opening the way for an eventual defensive alliance" and an acknowledgment of the need for advanced planning. A Canadian poll taken in November found 83.8 percent of the public approved of the PJBD, and only 5.2 percent were opposed.[55] Stimson believed he had witnessed "the turning point in the tide of the war," while Skelton called the PJBD's creation "the best day's work for many a year" and "the inevitable sequence of public policies and personal relationships, based upon the realization of the imperative necessity of close understanding between the English-speaking peoples."[56] But in Britain, Dominions Office secretary Lord Cranborne peevishly objected that the agreement constituted a defensive alliance between a British Dominion and a foreign country "without any reference to or consultation with us." An irate Churchill icily responded that if Germany did not best Britain militarily, "all these transactions will be judged in a mood different to that while the issue still stands in the balance." Disappointed by Churchill's harsh reaction, when King presented the Ogdensburg Agreement to Parliament in November 1940, he claimed to have kept Britain "duly informed of what was taking place." The agreement enhanced "defence of the British commonwealth of nations as a whole," because Canada could funnel resources to Britain, secure in the knowledge the United States would protect the Western Hemisphere.[57]

When Roosevelt telephoned King on 22 August to plan the PJBD's first meeting, however, aid to Britain was conspicuously absent from his agenda. Instead, the president wanted the board to discuss Newfoundland, Canadian coastal defence, and material procurement.[58] At its first meeting on 26–27 August, the PJBD decided to reinforce Newfoundland, to improve defences in Canada's eastern provinces, and to prepare "at once a detailed plan for the joint defence of Canada and the United States."[59] If Roosevelt was less forthcoming with military aid to Britain than King had hoped, King never acceded to Roosevelt's requests for Canadian bases. Though Ottawa would allow American warships to use Nova Scotian installations, it made clear that under no circumstances would Canada surrender territorial sovereignty to the United States.

As any good leader should, King had consistently placed Canada's interests first vis-à-vis Roosevelt and the United States. Before the crisis of 1940, King had acted cautiously when confronted by Roosevelt's strategic prodding and pushing. He had acted to safeguard Canadian security when he thought action was clearly necessary, and he had avoided action when it did not. He managed this delicate balancing act with considerable skill. When it had become clear that much more was needed following France's collapse and a feared imminent German invasion of Great Britain, King wisely chose to secure Canada's (and the British Empire's) defence by seeking the protection of a much larger and more powerful United States. To have done any less would have been to shirk his clear duties as Canada's prime minister. This did not mean, however, that King had ever abandoned his innate caution regarding Roosevelt and the United States. Indeed, a cursory examination of Canadian-American military relations after August 1940 clearly demonstrates this. In July 1941 Canada and the United States ratified ABC-22, the joint strategic plan for defending North America. But in the preceding months King and his representatives had repeatedly rejected US demands to surrender strategic control of its home defence forces, even under heavy pressure to do so. The Americans reluctantly accepted Canada's proposition that such a command arrangement was acceptable only under the direst of circumstances. Then, when America demanded strategic control of Canadian forces in British Columbia after the Japanese attack on 7 December 1941, Canada again successfully resisted the notion of automatic unity of command directed by Washington.[60] Throughout his lengthy ongoing dialogue with Franklin Roosevelt about North American security, the wily King never forgot that Canada's security and sovereignty were inseparable. The historians' myth of "obsequious Rex," the documents tell us, is indeed a myth.

NOTES

1 C.P. Stacey, *Canada and the Age of Conflict*, vol. 2, *The Age of Mackenzie King, 1921–1948* (Toronto: University of Toronto Press 1984), 230–1; Denis Smith, *Diplomacy of Fear: Canada and the Cold War, 1941–1948* (Toronto: University of Toronto Press 1988), 13; Donald Creighton, *The Forked Road: Canada 1939–1957* (Toronto: McClelland and Stewart 1976), 43–4; and W.L. Morton, "Review of *William Lyon Mackenzie King*, vol. 2, *The Lonely Heights, 1924–1932*," in *Canadian Historical Review* 45 (December 1964): 320–1.

2 J.W. Pickersgill, "Mackenzie King's Political Attitudes and Public Policies: A Personal Impression," in John English and J.O. Stubbs, ed., *Mackenzie King: Widening the Debate* (Toronto: Macmillan 1977), 15–18.

3 See Richard Preston, *The Defence of the Undefended Border: Planning for War in North America 1867–1939* (Montreal: McGill-Queen's University Press 1977).

4 Franklin Roosevelt to Norman Davis, 9 November 1934, Franklin Roosevelt Papers, President's Secretary's Files [PSF], file London Naval Conference, Franklin Delano Roosevelt Presidential Library [FDRL]; James MacGregor Burns, *Roosevelt: The Lion and the Fox* (New York: Harcourt Brace and Company 1956), 250; D.C. Watt, *Succeeding John Bull: America in Britain's Place, 1900–1975* (Cambridge: Cambridge University Press 1984), 78.

5 "Report of Inspection of Brig. General Wm. Mitchell, Assistant Chief of Air Service during Winter – 1923," William Mitchell Papers, United States Air Force Academy Archives; and "Col. William Mitchell's Opening Statement before the President's Board of Aeronautic Inquiry on Conditions Governing Our National Defense and the Place of Air Power Beside Sea Power and Land Power," 1925, Mitchell Papers, box 20, file Statements from Gen. Mitchell's Desk 1925, Library of Congress [LC].

6 O.D. Skelton to L.B. LaFleche, 12 and 13 June 1934, Department of External Affairs Records, RG 25, vol. 1684, file 53-AB, Library and Archives Canada [LAC]; Skelton to Prime Minister R.B. Bennett, 15 June 1934, ibid.

7 United States Congress, *Hearings before the Committee on Military Affairs House of Representatives, Seventy-Fourth Congress, First Session on H.R. 6621 and H.R. 4130, February 11–13, 1935*, testimony by General F.M. Andrews and Lieutenant Colonel J.D. Reardon, 11–12 February 1935, 60–1 and 72; and McNaughton, "The Defence of Canada (A Review of the Present Situation)," 28 May 1935, file 74/256,

vol. 2, Directorate of History and Heritage, Department of National Defence [DHH].

8 "The Good Neighbor?" *Washington Post*, 2 May 1935; Hume Wrong to W.L.M. King, 29 April 1935, RG 25, vol. 1746, file 408, LAC; and Roosevelt to John McSwain, 29 April 1935, John J. McSwain Papers, box 11, file Correspondence 1935: April 22–Aug., Duke University Archives.

9 Diary, 8 November 1935, W.L.M. King Papers, Diaries, LAC.

10 Pierre de la Boal memorandum, 18 March 1936, Sumner Welles Papers, box 25, file 7, FDRL; C.P. Stacey, *Canada and the Age of Conflict*, vol. 2, 83; diary, 31 July 1936, King Papers, LAC; and Stanley W. Dziuban, *Military Relations between the United States and Canada, 1939–1945* (Washington, DC: Department of the Army 1959), 3.

11 Sumner Welles to Norman Armour, 24 February 1935, Welles Papers, box 25, file 7, FDRL.

12 Joint Services Committee, "An Appreciation of the Defence Problems Confronting Canada with Recommendations for the Development of the Armed Forces," 5 September 1936, file 74/256, vol. 1, DHH.

13 James Eayrs, *In Defence of Canada: Appeasement and Rearmament* (Toronto: University of Toronto Press 1965), 138; diary, 9 and 10 September 1936, King Papers, LAC; and Roger Sarty, *The Maritime Defence of Canada* (Toronto: The Canadian Institute of Strategic Studies 1996), 99.

14 A.G.L. McNaughton to General Montgomery-Massingberd, 31 January 1935, Department of National Defence Records, RG 24, reel C4975, file HQS3367, LAC; Ashton to Skelton, 14 September 1935, in Alex L. Inglis, ed., *Documents on Canadian External Relations* [DCER] vol. 5, 267; and Ely Palmer memorandum, 19 October 1936, State Department Post Records, Canada, RG 84, Series 2195A, file 815.4 Alaska Highway, National Archives Records Administration [NARA].

15 Diary, 24 February 1937, King Papers, LAC; Loring Christie, "Monroe Doctrine," 16 February 1937, in John A. Munro, ed., DCER, vol. 6, 1936–1939 (Ottawa: Department of External Affairs 1972), 177; Skelton memorandum, February 1937, O.D. Skelton Papers, vol. 27, file 9, LAC; and Military Intelligence Division, "Canada: Political Estimate," 1 June 1937, RG 59, Decimal File 1930–39, file 842.00/504, NARA; and diary, 5 March 1937, King Papers, LAC.

16 Diary, 10 May 1937 and 12 August 1937, King Papers, LAC .

17 Roosevelt to Cordell Hull, 4 August 1937, Roosevelt Papers, PSF, file Hull, Cordell 1933–37, FDRL; and Hull to Roosevelt, 5 August 1937, ibid.

18 Armour to King, 14 September 1937, RG 25, vol. 1739, file 221, LAC; Skelton to Christie, 16 September 1937, ibid.; and Christie memorandum, 12 November 1937, ibid.

19 Armour memorandum, 9 November 1937, Armour to Welles, 17 November 1937, Armour to Welles, 10 December 1937, and Welles to Armour, 29 November 1937, Welles Papers, box 161, file Canada, FDRL.

20 Roosevelt to King, 21 December 1937, W.L.M. King Papers, Correspondence, reel C3729, 207146, LAC.

21 King to Roosevelt, 30 December 1937, King Papers, Correspondence, reel C3729, 207148–49, LAC; and Armour to Welles, 8 January 1938, RG 59, Decimal File 1930–39, file 842.20/68, NARA.

22 Skelton, "Conversations on West Coast Defence," 10 January 1938, RG 25, vol. 2959, file B-80, LAC.

23 Ashton to Ian Mackenzie, "Conversations held in Washington, DC, on the 19th and 20th January, 1938," 26 January 1938, file 112.3M2009 (D22), DHH; and P.W. Nelles to Mackenzie, "Conversations held in Washington, DC, on the 19th and 20th January, 1938," 22 January 1938, King Papers, Memoranda, vol. 157, file F1411, LAC. See also Galen Roger Perras, "'Future plays will depend on how the next one works': Franklin Roosevelt and the Canadian Legation Discussions of January 1938," *Journal of Military and Strategic Studies* 9, no. 2 (winter 2006–7): 1–31.

24 "Defence Scheme No. 2 Plan for the Maintenance of Canadian Neutrality in the Event of a War between the United States and Japan," 11 April 1938, file 322.016 (D12), DHH; Joint Services Committee to Mackenzie, 14 April 1938, ibid.; and diary, 11 January and 12 March 1938, King Papers, LAC.

25 Roosevelt to Congress, 28 January 1938, in Department of State, *Peace and War: United States Foreign Policy, 1931–1941* (Washington, DC: Government Printing Office 1943), 405; Robert Dallek, *Franklin D. Roosevelt and American Foreign Policy, 1932–1945* (New York: Oxford University Press 1979), 176; "US-Canadian Defense," *New York Sunday News*, 17 April 1938; and John Simmons to Hull, 21 July 1938, RG 59, Decimal File 1930–39, file 842.22741/1, NARA.

26 Roosevelt, "Reciprocity in Defense," 18 August 1938, Skelton Papers, vol. 5, file 5–6, LAC; and Roosevelt to Lord Tweedsmuir, 31 August 1938, John Buchan Papers, box 10, file Correspondence July – August 1938, Queen's University Archives [QUA].

27 F. H. Soward, *Canada in World Affairs: The Pre-War Years* (Toronto 1941), 107–11.

28 Diary, 18 and 20 August 1938, King Papers, LAC; and King, "Reciprocity in Defence," 20 August 1938, Skelton Papers, vol. 5, file 5–6, LAC.

29 Roosevelt press conference, 15 November 1938, in Samuel I. Rosenman, ed., *The Public Papers and Addresses of Franklin D. Roosevelt, vol. 6, The Continuing Struggle for Liberalism* (New York: Macmillan 1941), 598–600; Major General H.H. Arnold, White House meeting notes, 14 November 1938, Roosevelt Papers, OF, file OF25t, FDRL; and Dallek, *Roosevelt and American Foreign Policy*, 17.

30 Diary, 24 October 15 and 17 November 1938, King Papers, LAC; Henry Morgenthau, "Proposal that the French Government Establish in Canada Airplane Plants Capable of Constructing Several Thousand Planes a Year," October 1938, Roosevelt Papers, PSF, file Treasury: Morgenthau Henry Jr., FDRL; and Mark M. Lowenthal, *Leadership and Indecision: American War Planning and Policy 1937–1942* (New York: Garland Publishing 1988), 89–90.

31 Diary, 27 January 1939, King Papers, LAC.

32 David Beatty, "The 'Canadian Corollary' to the Monroe Doctrine and the Ogdensburg Agreement of 1940," *The McNaughton Papers*, vol. 5 (1994), 32–3; William Leahy to Welles, 24 March 1939, RG 59, Decimal File 1930–39, file 811.34500/301/4, NARA; diary, 10 June 1939, King Papers, LAC; and Robert Lindsay to the Foreign Office, 30 June 1939 and 8 July 1939, FO371/23902 and FO371/23903, National Archives of the United Kingdom [NAUK].

33 Diary, 23 March 1939, King Papers, LAC; diary, 19 July 1939, ibid.; Commander H.E. Reid to the Naval Secretary DND, 16 August 1939, RG 25, vol. 829, file 4, LAC; Lt Commander H.N. Lay, "Conversation between the President of the United States in USS Tuscaloosa and Officers of the Guard," 15 August 1939, ibid.; and Skelton, "United States Halifax Proposal," 31 August 1939, RG 25, vol. 2453, file Secret 1939, LAC.

34 Dallek, *Roosevelt and American Foreign Policy*, 197–9; and diary, 3 September 1939, King Papers, LAC.

35 Diary, 2, 3, and 5 September 1939, Jay Pierrepont Moffat Papers, vol. 33, Houghton Library, Harvard University [HL]; and diary, 5 September 1939, King Papers, LAC.

36 Felix Belai, Jr., "Pledge to Defend Canada Stands, Says President As It Enters War," *New York Times*, 13 September 1939; and Wilfrid Hardy Callcott, *The Western Hemisphere: Its Influence on United States Policies to the End of World War II* (Austin: University of Texas Press 1968), 384.

37 Diary, 29 April 1940, Henry Morgenthau Papers, fiche 5, FDRL.

38 Winston Churchill to King, 24 May 1940, King Papers, Memoranda and Notes, reel H1558, C281481–82, LAC.

39 Diary, 18 May 1940, King Papers, LAC; Hugh L. Keenleyside, *Memoirs of Hugh L. Keenleyside*, vol. 2, *On the Bridge of Time* (Toronto: McClelland and Stewart 1982), 30–1; and Keenleyside to King, "Report of Discussion with President Roosevelt," 23 May 1940, King Papers, Memoranda and Notes, reel H1558, C282902–04, LAC.

40 Keenleyside, "Report of a Discussion of Possible Eventualities," 26 May 1940, LAC, King Papers, Memoranda and Notes, reel H1558, C281907–10, LAC; diary, 26 May 1940, King Papers, LAC; Keenleyside, "Discussion of Possible Eventualities," 29 May 1940, King Papers, Memoranda and Notes, reel H1558, C281914–19, LAC; and Keenleyside, *On the Bridge of Time*, 36–7.

41 Diary, 27 May 1940, King Papers, LAC; and King to Churchill, 30 May 1940, RG 25, vol. 779, file 381, LAC; Winston Churchill, *The Second World War: Their Finest Hour*, vol. 2 (Boston: Houghton Mifflin 1949), 118; and Churchill to King, 5 June 1940, in David R. Murray, *DCER: 1939–1941*, part 3, vol. 8 (Ottawa: Department of External Relations 1976), 85–6.

42 Keenleyside, "Report of a Discussion Held on the 7th of June 1940," 8 June 1940, in Murray, *DCER*, vol. 8, 95–7; diary, 17 June 1940, King Papers, LAC; King to Churchill, 17 June 1940, RG 25, vol. 779, file 381, LAC; and Churchill to King, 24 June RG 25, vol. 819, file 674, ibid.

43 Moffat memorandum of conversation with King, 14 June 1940, RG 84, file 711, 1940 Memoranda of Conversations, NARA; and diary, 10 June 1940, Moffat Papers, vol. 46, HL.

44 Moffat to Welles, 26 June 1940, Welles Papers, box 63, file 2, FDRL; diary, 14 June 1940, King Papers, LAC; Moffat to Hull, 16 June 1940, RG 59, Decimal File 1940–44, 711.42/194, NARA; and diary, 3 May 1940, Moffat Papers, vol. 45, HL.

45 Major J.S. Gullet, "Notes on Canadian Defense–Atlantic Sector," RG 165, MID Correspondence, file 2694-72/1, NARA.

46 Dallek, *Roosevelt and American Foreign Policy*, 228 and 232; Lord Lothian to the Foreign Office, 17 June 1940, FO371/24240, NAUK; and JPC, "Views on Questions Propounded by the President on the War Situation," 26 June 1940, RG 165, Entry 281, file WPD 4250-3, NARA.

47 Diary, 27 June 1940, King Papers, LAC; C.G. Power, "Memorandum of Conversation with the American Minister, Mr. Moffat, June 29th 1940," 30 June 1940, C.G. Power Papers, box 69, file D-2018, QUA; and

Keenleyside, "Summary of Points Suggested for Discussion with the United States," 30 June 1940, RG 25, vol. 2789, file 703–40 pt. 1, LAC.

48 Dziuban, *Military Relations*, 17; General Kenneth Stuart, "Report of Conversations in Washington, DC," 15 July 1940, RG 25, vol. 2459, file C-10, LAC; Moffat to Welles, 26 July 1940, Welles Papers, box 63, file 2, FDRL; and Admiral Ernest King, "Control of Western Hemisphere," 15 July 1940, Ernest King Papers, box 21, file General Board 1940, LAC.

49 "Defensive Alliance with Canada," *Chicago Tribune*, 19 June 1949; "In Defense of the United States," *New York Herald Tribune*, 7 August 1940; "A Treaty with the US," *Montreal Standard*, 3 August 1940; and *Saturday Night,* quoted in Simmons to Hull, 3 July 1940, RG 59, Decimal File 1940–44, 842.00P.R./181, NARA.

50 John R. Baldwin to Escott Reid, 5 July 1940, Escott Reid Papers, vol. 27, file 8, LAC; and "A Programme of Immediate Canadian Action Drawn Up by a Group of Twenty Canadians, Meeting at the Chateau Laurier, Ottawa, on July 17–18, 1940," King Papers, Correspondence, vol. 286, file Church to Colquhoun, LAC.

51 Diary, 13 and 26 July 1940, King Papers, LAC; and Cabinet War Committee minutes, 26 July 1940, RG 27C, vol. 2, Privy Council Records, LAC.

52 Roosevelt memorandum, 2 August 1940, Roosevelt PSF, file Navy: Destroyers & Naval Bases, FDRL; and David Reynolds, *The Creation of the Anglo-American Alliance, 1937–41: A Study in Competitive Co-operation* (Chapel Hill: The University of North Carolina Press 1982), 125–32.

53 Moffat to Welles, 26 July 1940, Welles Papers, box 63, file 2, FDRL; Moffat to Hull, 1 August 1940, RG 84, Entry 2195A, file 711 1940 Canada's War Effort, NARA; Moffat to Hull, 8 August 1940, Edward R. Stettinius Papers, box 631, file Canada, University of Virginia Archives; Christie to King, 15 August 1940, in Murray, DCER, vol. 8, 129; and diary, 16 August 1940, King Papers, LAC.

54 Diary, 17 August 1940, vol. 30, Henry Stimson Papers, Sterling Memorial Library, Yale University [YU]; J.L. Granatstein, "Mackenzie King and Canada at Ogdensburg, August 1940," in Joel J. Sokolsky and Joseph T. Jockel, eds., *Fifty Years of Canada–United States Defense Cooperation: The Road from Ogdensburg* (Lewiston: The Edwin Mellen Press 1992), 21; and diary, 17 August 1940, King Papers, LAC.

55 "Says Defense Plan Opens Way to Pact," *New York Times*, 19 August 1940; and Dziuban, *Military Cooperation*, 25.

56 Diary, 17 August 1940, vol. 30, Stimson Papers, vol. 30, YU; and Skelton to King, 19 August 1940, King Papers, Memoranda and Notes, reel H1516, C220892–94, LAC.

57 Lord Cranborne to Churchill, 6 March 1941, Prime Minister's Papers, PREM4/43A/12, NAUK; King to Churchill, 18 August 1940, King Papers, Memoranda and Notes, vol. 428, file Ogdensburg Agreement 1940, LAC; Churchill to King, 22 August 1940, ibid., reel H1558, C282290, LAC; and King statement, 12 November 1940, *Debates*, House of Commons, 54–9.

58 Diary, 22 August 1940, King Papers, LAC.

59 Diary, 24 August 1940, vol. 30, Stimson Papers, vol. 30, YU; and PJBD, "Journal of Discussions and Decisions," 26–27 August 1940, King Papers, Memoranda and Notes, reel H1516, C220909–17, LAC.

60 See Galen Roger Perras, "Who Will Defend British Columbia? Unity of Command on the West Coast, 1934–1942," *Pacific Northwest Quarterly*, 88 (spring 1997), 59–69.

12

The Clayton Knight Committee

Clandestine Recruiting of Americans for the Royal Canadian Air Force, 1940–1941

RACHEL LEA HEIDE

When World War II began in September 1939, the British Common-wealth Air Training Plan (BCATP) became Prime Minister W.L.M. King's preferred form of military contribution. King hoped that train-ing Commonwealth aircrew would allow Canada to avoid another conscription crisis like that of World War I, when Canada's primary military contribution had been half a million infantrymen in Flanders. With the BCATP, Canadians were expected to remain in Canada to train Australians, New Zealanders, and Britons. Members of the Royal Canadian Air Force (RCAF) who wanted to fight overseas would do so as volunteers. War in the air, according to accepted air force doctrine, would cause far fewer casualties than the bloody in-fantry struggles of 1914–18. By spring 1940, air training schools were ready to train pilots, observers, gunners, wireless operators, bombers, navigators, and flight engineers. At air bases built in all of Canada's provinces, men from the British Commonwealth and re-cruits who had escaped from the German-occupied nations of Europe joined Canadians as aircrew trainees. Ultimately, a total of 131,533 air force personnel graduated from the BCATP.

Although not, of course, a signatory to the BCATP Agreement,[1] the neutral United States of America made a significant contribution to the successful operation of the air training plan. After Germany con-quered most of Western Europe in the spring of 1940, American pilots worked as instructors and staff pilots in the Canadian air training schools. Later, in 1941, when the number of recruits in Canada decreased, the Franklin D. Roosevelt administration allowed

American men interested in training to be aircrew for the RCAF or the Royal Air Force (RAF) to come to Canada. Canada recruited these American pilots and aircrew trainees surreptitiously, through a clandestine committee named after its most prominent member, Clayton Knight. The Clayton Knight Committee did its work despite US neutrality and despite US laws against recruiting American citizens for foreign armed services. The committee's success speaks volumes about Canada-United States relations during the first stage of the World War II crisis. The story of the Clayton Knight Committee is one of American tolerance, and even covert encouragement, as the Canadian government and the RCAF balanced accommodating American diplomatic concerns with a determination to keep a steady flow of American airmen coming into the BCATP, even if this had to be accomplished through clandestine means.

William Avery "Billy" Bishop, Canada's flying ace of World War I fame, came up with the idea for the Clayton Knight Committee. Based on the experience of that war, Bishop assumed that many American airmen would be eager once again to participate in combat, their country's neutrality notwithstanding. To spare such Americans expensive and possibly fruitless trips across the border to visit RCAF recruiting offices, Bishop wanted to create an organization in the United States that could counsel airmen about openings available with the RCAF, explain the minimum qualifications demanded of the volunteers, and make clear the necessary paperwork applicants should bring with them. Bishop secured the cooperation of Homer Smith, a Canadian World War I flyer living in the United States and an heir to his family's Imperial Oil fortune. Smith had been commissioned into the RCAF as a wing commander and put on the reserve list by Minister of Defence Ian Mackenzie on 9 September 1939. Smith's collaborator in the semi-covert operation and the man whose name became attached to the committee was Clayton Knight, an American First World War aviator, a well-known aviation author and illustrator, and the creator of the syndicated aviation comic strip *Ace Drummond*. Knight's background and multiple careers meant that he had extensive ties to aviation circles in the United States.[2]

The Canadian government and the RCAF embraced the Clayton Knight Committee in May 1940 after German armies swept across Europe and the Luftwaffe rained bombs on the British Isles. When Great Britain called for more help in the air to resist and strike back,

Canada accelerated BCATP training and graduated more aircrew
each month than had been originally planned. This expansion of
training demanded more instructors, but the source of pilots with
sufficient experience to teach or to serve as staff pilots in the schools
for observers, bombers, gunners, and navigators had already been
exhausted.[3] In May 1940, the RCAF's Air Council met representatives of the major airlines to determine how many more experienced
pilots could be brought into the expanding BCATP. Homer Smith
and Clayton Knight attended as well and listened as the airline executives told the air force that fewer than twenty-five pilots could be
spared for work in the BCATP. Knight seized the moment to gain the
RCAF's support for the idea of a special committee to recruit
American pilots. After the war, Knight reminisced, "in the heavy silence that followed this grim evaluation, heads were turned curiously in my direction when I stated, 'Homer Smith and I have an
initial list of slightly over three hundred pilots who are willing to
come up to help.'"[4]

Despite initial skepticism, the RCAF agreed to use the organization
that Bishop, Knight, and Smith had already set up on their own
initiative to tap into this desperately needed source of pilots. On
31 May 1940, Wing Commander W.A. Curtis sent a proposal to the
air member for personnel requesting permission to have Homer
Smith recruit one hundred pilots in the United States. Smith would
oversee the organization to "interview pilots and issue them, where
necessary, with railway fare and travelling expenses to headquarters
in Ottawa." Curtis also proposed advancing Smith five thousand
dollars to help with expenses.[5] The following day the chief of air
staff, Air Commodore L.S. Breadner, forwarded this proposal to the
deputy minister for air.[6]

The Canadian government authorized the Clayton Knight Committee to provide information to American pilots who wanted to
help Canada and Britain's war effort. The committee would ensure
that these men had all the requisite documents before they crossed
the border into Canada. Officially, the committee was trying to fill
civilian-instructor and staff pilot vacancies at the BCATP's Air Observer Schools and Elementary Flying Training Schools. Because
these positions did not require the pilots to be members of the RCAF,
the US government could not accuse the Canadians of recruiting
Americans into a foreign armed service. Nonetheless, the committee
made information available about the air force, and committee

members, as well as the Canadian and American governments, knew that pilots, once in Canada, would often opt for the glamour of the RCAF uniform instead of serving as civilians. In such cases, they would instruct at a Service Flying Training School or become staff pilots flying non-pilot aircrew trainees at a Bombing and Gunnery School. American pilots could also help the RAF by ferrying planes from North American manufacturers across the Atlantic or from British factories to squadrons in the theatre of war.[7]

Canadian officials conscientiously made sure American authorities were aware of the committee's actions and intentions in recruiting American pilots. The Canadian government even put specific measures in place to ensure that American concerns over recruitment laws and oaths of allegiance were accommodated. Members of the Clayton Knight Committee discussed their plans in advance with Major General H.H. "Hap" Arnold, chief of the US Army Air Corps, and Rear Admiral J.H. Towers, head of the Navy Bureau of Aeronautics, as early as March 1940. Both men supported the committee's efforts. They felt that there was no need for the American services to feel threatened, because there was indeed a large pool of talented would-be military flyers that had failed to meet the very strict standards required of US Army and Navy pilots. Major General Arnold told Knight that many good pilots had been released from the Army Air Corps for what he considered "technicalities": they had gotten drunk, done some low stunt flying, or turned out to be married (US pilots had to be single). In addition to pointing Knight to these available men, Arnold also offered to provide the committee with a list of failed candidates. Knight's courteous inquiries met with generous and reassuring support.[8]

To gauge the US government's reaction to the plan, the Canadian Department of External Affairs contacted the US State Department. On 18 May 1940, Loring Christie, Canada's minister to the United States, assured O.D. Skelton, under secretary for external affairs, that the "highest quarters"[9] in Washington believed that "United States authorities will not be embarrassed by the enlistment in Canada of United States citizens who proceed to Canada for that purpose." The State Department's only request was that American citizens not be required to take an oath of allegiance to Canada's head of state, King George VI, for this would cost the airmen their American citizenship. The oath of allegiance was thus replaced by an oath of obedience to superior officers.[10]

The Clayton Knight Committee had been set up as a private information agency for the express purpose of making sure that the Department of National Defence was not directly involved in recruiting American nationals for Canada's air force. Although US authorities knew that the Clayton Knight Committee was helping the RCAF, this diplomatic fiction was tolerated because it gave the appearance that the Canadian government was keeping to the letter of American law. The first problems came in November 1940, when the State Department learned that committee members had become too blatant in their advertisements of the committee. The State Department had also discovered that the Federal Bureau of Investigation was making inquiries into committee activities, that Homer Smith was an RCAF reservist being paid by the Canadian government, and that the committee was paying candidates' travel expenses to Canada. The State Department raised its concerns with Canada's Department of External Affairs, but it did so not to rein in the committee but to ensure that the committee continued to function unimpeded.[11]

The State Department's John Hickerson (assistant chief of the European Affairs Division) admitted that the newly uncovered circumstances surrounding the Clayton Knight Committee had put the US government "in a somewhat embarrassing position." Providing funds for individuals to join a foreign armed service violated the US law against recruiting Americans. As an RCAF wing commander, Homer Smith was violating the US law that required agents working for foreign governments to register with the State Department. Hickerson worried that "these features would not jibe well with the ostensible picture that Messrs Knight and Smith are simply public-spirited or patriotic private persons doing what they can to help Canada and the Allied cause." A further complication arose from the fact that the committee was very "close to advertising the organization's existence and purposes." The volume of correspondence between the committee and possible applicants was ever increasing, and the committee had even asked aviation organizations to direct potential applicants to it and to its jobs for the Canadian war effort.[12]

Despite these egregious violations of US laws, the State Department never demanded that the committee terminate its operations. Instead, Hickerson clearly intended his actions and advice to keep the committee from being closed down by other US government agencies. In his meeting with Loring Christie, the Canadian minister to the United States, Hickerson made clear that no memorandum of their conversation would be made for State Department records. Hickerson also intervened on behalf of the committee in the matter of registering Homer Smith as an agent of a foreign government. In direct contradiction to the evidence, Hickerson assured the branch of the State Department that handled registration that "Knight and Smith ... are acting as private persons and not as agents of the Canadian government." Hickerson advised Christie that the committee should employ "a wide-awake practical lawyer who could constantly advise them about what risks they were running of violating the laws." He promised the Canadian minister that his department had no intention of prosecuting or closing down the Committee but merely sought to caution Knight and Smith to "slow down and pull in their horns."[13]

On 12 November, a legal adviser for the Canadian government wrote Prime Minister Mackenzie King confirming that the Clayton Knight Committee was obviously financed by Canada's government. Despite the technical breach of American neutrality laws, the legal adviser did not consider this to be a very serious matter. The committee's accomplishments were great. It had found American airmen to fly bombers across the Atlantic for the RAF and furnished instructors for the BCATP. This success fueled the air force's determination to keep the scheme alive. If US public opinion did eventually sour, then the legal adviser proposed that "it should be possible to dissolve the committee and start again, if necessary, in a different way and under a different name."[14]

Despite the legal adviser's nonchalant approach to the matter, on 19 November the War Committee of the Canadian Cabinet reacted more vigorously to the State Department's communications than the State Department had intended them to respond. Prime Minister King and his ministers did not want to embarrass the US government. King reminded the War Cabinet that President Roosevelt had told him "that recruiting in the United States would constitute a serious embarrassment to the administration." King had promised that Canada would not undertake recruiting missions within the borders of its neutral neighbour. Nevertheless, much to the dismay of King's Cabinet, "recruiting was, in fact, being carried on, and ... such activities could not be regarded as in keeping with his [King's] understanding with the President." Because the Canadian government did not want to support, either directly or indirectly, recruiting in the United States, the Cabinet War Committee directed C.G. Power, the minister of national defence for air "to see to the immediate discontinuance of the activities of the Clayton Knight Committee."[15]

The acting deputy minister for air, J.S. Duncan, wasted no time reacting to the proposed disbandment. He sprang to the committee's defence and stressed the importance of its recruitment of pilots for the BCATP. As of 21 November 1940, over three hundred American pilots had contributed to the air-training plan. They were experienced aviators who required only short refresher courses, and they would be very difficult to replace: "securing these men had been an essential factor in the speeding up of the whole scheme, and further recruits from this source had been counted on for continued development." Duncan challenged the decision to terminate the committee. American newspapers had made no adverse comments, so why was such remedial action being taken, especially given that the Federal Bureau of Investigation, through its inaction, had deemed the committee's activities acceptable?[16] The concerns of Deputy Minister Duncan and members of the RCAF were brought to the attention of the Cabinet War Committee on 22 November. The ministers heard that the US Army and Navy had no objections to Canada's securing American pilots for the war effort; the United Kingdom was openly recruiting Americans, and US citizens were even being trained in army schools for service with the RAF. The Cabinet War Committee agreed to approach the State Department and ask directly "whether the US government had any objection to the activities such as those of the Clayton Knight Committee."[17]

Under Secretary of State Skelton wrote to the Canadian Legation in Washington on 25 November requesting that the importance of the Clayton Knight Committee be impressed upon the US State Department. Skelton wanted the legation to ask "if there are any special phases of the past or present operations of the Clayton Knight group as to which special difficulty is felt."[18] The Canadian chargé d'affaires, Hume Wrong, reported back on 27 November. When approached, John Hickerson had replied openly that "the Administration does not want to say that the activities should be terminated and has never asked that they should be terminated." Hickerson then reiterated the actions that the State Department had taken in surreptitious support of the committee. The State Department had not requested that the committee be registered as an agent of the Canadian government. Any enquiries from private

US citizens about the committee's activities had been "given a good meaningless bureaucratic answer." Hickerson then advised that a critical examination of the committee's conduct be done and that this study be reviewed by a US legal adviser. He recommended Dean Acheson.[19]

Hickerson understood that the committee's activities crossed not only the US-Canada border but also the borders of legality. He hinted that the committee should "get rid of a certain amount of its incriminating correspondence in case its files are investigated," and he feigned ignorance as to the exact workings of the committee. "The Department of State," he concluded, "does not know much about the inner workings of the committee, and they do not want to know more than they at present know." Nonetheless, Hickerson knew enough about the committee to advise that it cease lending travel money to potential recruits. He also advised that the advertising be discontinued. The committee needed to be more circumspect in its conduct.[20] Hickerson advised that the committee should get "the advice of a friendly United States lawyer with the 'instinct of an ambulance chaser' ... [someone] who would be able to stretch the law a little." Canada's scheme to secure American pilots for Canadian service had been accepted; the State Department simply wanted the committee to be less "careless."[21]

To further remove itself from the activities of the Clayton Knight Committee, on 31 January 1941 the Canadian government created the Dominion Aeronautical Association Limited, a Crown corporation that would keep the RCAF one step removed from the committee's activities. Theoretically, the Dominion Aeronautical Association was a private corporation in search of pilots to fill flying jobs in Canada that were related to the war effort. Acting as an agent for the Dominion Aeronautical Association, the committee would now seek airmen for civilian positions with the BCATP. Consequently, because the official focus was on civilian employment, it could be argued that the committee was not breaking American laws. Conveniently, though, the Dominion Aeronautical Association office in Ottawa was situated next door to the RCAF headquarters. Hence, if civilian jobs happened to be "unavailable," Dominion Aeronautical Association officials simply advised applicants to go next door to see what might be open in the RCAF.[22]

Canadian determination to stretch the law and American support for the Clayton Knight Committee's activities continued as the organization moved in a new direction to secure American air-crew for training in the BCATP. The number of experienced pilots available in the United States was decreasing for two reasons. The RCAF was no longer in desperate need of instructors and staff pilots for its air-training program, so the air force set higher standards for American candidates to meet. Furthermore, as the war continued and the likelihood of American participation seemed more probable, the demand in the United States for this same group of airmen increased as well. In February 1941, Group Captain de Niverville, director of air force manning, suggested that the Clayton Knight Committee might begin looking for American men who could be sent through the BCATP as aircrew trainees. The minister of defence for air, C.G. Power, did not approve of this new mandate, since he felt that there were still a large number of Canadians waiting to enter the RCAF and commence training. As summer arrived, Stuart Armour (managing director of the Dominion Aeronautical Association) noted the dwindling numbers passing through the committee, and he decided to pursue another approach. When Knight and Smith predicted that their committee would be able to produce no more than five or six experienced pilots a week for the RCAF, Armour decided to raise the possibility with air force officials of recruiting trainees again. At his request of Armour, Air Commodore Robert Leckie, acting chief of the air staff, assembled RCAF officers on 9 July 1941 to discuss the issue.[23] When Armour suggested that the Clayton Knight Committee could now assist the Canadian war effort by finding Americans for aircrew, the RCAF officers agreed to seek the minister's approval for a target of twenty-five hundred American aircrew by 1 September 1941. Air Minister Power did not consent to the new change outright, but he did agree to send Armour to Washington to explore the American government's reaction to this new plan.[24]

On 11 July, Frederick King, the legal adviser, discussed the aircrew scheme with members of the Dominion Aeronautical Association. He advised extreme caution in making sure that nothing was done that would be contrary to US laws. Recruiting aircrew trainees was different from offering employment to already-trained pilots. President Roosevelt had announced on 24 June 1941 "that any man wanting to join the Canadian or British armed forces had a perfect right to do so," but had added the phrase "subject to the limitations of certain statutes with regard to oaths of allegiance to foreign rulers and to recruiting for foreign armed services in [the United States]."[25]

The constraint of US isolationist sentiment still had to be taken into consideration. Even though Knight and other members of his committee declared their willingness to face the consequences of American law, the legal adviser stressed that "they should not place themselves in jeopardy" because "to do so would destroy the usefulness of the committee, quite aside from the fact that they might also embarrass the President." He felt that to contact graduates of the Civil Pilot Training Plan (CPTP) by mail and to inform them of Canada's need for aircrew would be an acceptable method, as long as great care was exercised in the letter's wording. Frederick King thought perhaps the Civil Aeronautics Authority (CAA) could spread, by word of mouth to CPTP graduates, the fact that Canada would welcome Americans into its air force. The legal adviser offered more hints as to how committee policy could be shaped. Given that foreign governments were not allowed to help Americans financially to make their way to other countries to enlist, the committee could not pay for the potential recruits' travel expenses. Nevertheless, Frederick King believed "there would not ... be any objection to the Canadian government making a reimbursement of travelling expenses, but in order to protect the Clayton Knight Committee from possible embarrassment, any grant made to the trainees by the Canadian government should not be called a travelling allowance."[26]

Armour's trip to Washington had been extremely successful. With a little imagination – and much caution – the committee's legal adviser and the CAA and CPTP officials all felt that American aircrew could be recruited without breaking the letter of US laws.[27] Confirmation also came from the highest level in the US military: Major General Arnold and Rear Admiral Towers approved of the committee's plan to approach CPTP graduates. Consequently, the Canadian government revised the Clayton Knight Committee's mandate in August 1941 to include recruiting Americans for aircrew training.[28] With this extended mandate, Homer Smith recommended to the air member for personnel that the Dominion Aeronautical Association and the Clayton Knight Committee be absorbed into one organization called the Canadian Aviation Bureau. In consultation with the minister of defence for air, the deputy minister approved the reorganization on 2 September 1941. All Canadian Aviation Bureau correspondence purposely made no reference to the RCAF and spoke only of Canadian aviation, so as to leave no paper trails of direct links between the bureau and the air force.[29]

Nonetheless, almost immediately after the Canadian government approved securing American aircrew trainees through the Canadian Aviation Bureau, the State Department faced a complaint about Canadians recruiting United States nationals. On 12 and 13 August 1941, US newspapers carried the story that Democratic representative Walter Pierce of Oregon had called for the US government to "investigate reports that persons posing as representatives of the Canadian Royal Air Force [*sic*] were seeking to enlist American flyers in Washington, Oregon, and Idaho."[30] On 15 August, Hume Wrong, chargé d'affaires at the Canadian Legation, contacted Prime Minister King in his second portfolio as the secretary of state for external affairs with more details about the complaint. Apparently, one Canadian Aviation Bureau representative had sent a letter on 9 August 1941 inviting Americans to enlist in the Canadian Coast Guard. The parents of one recipient complained to Representative Pierce, who then voiced his constituents' concerns to the State Department. The State Department immediately took Canada's side, even though they felt this particular committee representative had come very close to crossing the line of recruiting on US soil. The State Department told Pierce that "there is no legal barrier to the enrollment of civilian personnel in the United States," and that "Americans are free to go to Canada to join the armed forces if they so desire." The State Department even contacted the US Department of Justice and recommended that no further action be taken: "This was to forestall an attempt by Mr. Pierce to stimulate an investigation of the Clayton Knight Committee by the Department of Justice."[31] Once again, without hesitation, the State Department, presumably with the tacit approval of the Roosevelt administration, defended the existence of Canada's recruitment organization and excused and protected Canada's stretching of US laws.

Japan's attack on Pearl Harbor 7 December 1941 brought the United States into the war and swiftly ended the source of American air recruits. On 17 January 1942, the White House requested that Americans wanting to transfer from the Canadian armed forces into American services be allowed to do so. The next step was for the RCAF to determine the future of the Canadian Aviation Bureau's work. The air force decided that, effective 30 January 1942, American citizens "were no longer eligible for appointment or enlistment in the Royal Canadian Air Force."[32] Canadian Aviation Bureau offices in Canada closed in February 1942, and branch offices in the

United States closed in June 1942, although the headquarters in New York remained opened to write letters of apology to Americans still inquiring about enlisting in Canada's air force.[33]

By the end of the war, 8,864 US nationals had been members of the RCAF, and 5067 of them remained with Canada's air force until the end of hostilities. Forty-nine thousand American airmen contacted the Clayton Knight Committee (and its successors) for help, and over 2,600 volunteers were sent north to Canada. Of the 950 pilots directed to Canada by the Clayton Knight Committee, 763 were accepted to help with the BCATP. The Canadian Aviation Bureau sent 1,805 more Americans as possible aircrew trainees, and 1,455 were permitted to enlist and train in the RCAF.[34] These numbers – and the entire venture – would not have been possible without official American government support of Canada's persistence and the Clayton Knight Committee's quasi-illegal recruitment tactics.

Canadian officials – Clayton Knight and Wing Commander Homer Smith, the RCAF, civil servants, ministers of the government, and the prime minister himself – knew from the beginning of the war that securing American airmen for Canada's war effort would have to be done in a clandestine manner. The RCAF and the Canadian government knew that the United States had declared itself to be neutral and that laws existed prohibiting the recruitment of Americans for service in foreign armed services. Consequently, a fictitious separation was created between Canada's air force and the infrastructure to procure American pilots: the Clayton Knight Committee and its later variants such as the Dominion Aeronautical Association and the Canadian Aviation Bureau. This "private" agency was allowed to evolve into an organization that recruited American airmen as aircrew trainees for combat duty with the RCAF.

During World War II, the Canadian government skillfully took full advantage of the Roosevelt administration's undeclared sympathy for the Allied war effort. The US government tolerated Canada's clandestine activities because the Canadians had paid special attention to US concerns. The oath of allegiance was replaced with an oath of obedience so that Americans would not lose their citizenship if they joined the RCAF. The Clayton Knight Committee, the Dominion Aeronautical Association, and the Canadian Aviation Bureau obscured the Canadian government's role in aiding these non-governmental agencies to help Americans make their way to Canada. Committee officials emphasized their role in providing information about civilian jobs, so that attention would be drawn away from the reality of how easy it was for American fliers to be directed toward the RCAF once they were in Canada.[35] The committee and the Canadian government also heeded American legal advice and found less overt ways of advertising and providing travel funds to potential candidates.

Since the State Department protected the Clayton Knight Committee from prosecution, since American legal advisers suggested creative ways to bend American laws, and since the president expressed his support for the committee's activities and existence, one might ask, do borders matter in the relationship between Canada and the United States? This level of cooperation, determination, and tolerance occurred because both Canada and the United States felt secure in their sovereignty. The US administration did not feel threatened by Canada's surreptitious actions and disregard for US law. The Canadian government did not resist or resent State Department warnings and advice because Prime Minister King did not interpret this as an outside power dictating Canadian policy. King had spent his entire political career since the 1920s fighting for recognition of Canada as more than a British colony, fighting to protect the country's independence of decision making, fighting to avoid automatic commitments to any war. With the outbreak of World War II and with Canada's separate declaration of hostilities, the King government determined that the country's nationhood was secure. Hence, cooperation with the American administration – a gesture of respect for the border in order to further Canadian war aims and commitments – was not a sacrifice of Canadian sovereignty. Because of this emotional security, politicians were not obsessed with asserting independence of thought and action as token expressions of identity. Instead, King, Roosevelt, and their subordinates could focus on the greater goal of Nazi Germany's defeat.

NOTES

1 Britain and three of the five dominions (Canada, Australia, and New Zealand) signed the agreement. South Africa declined participation, and Eire remained neutral during the war. BCATP Agreement, 17 December 1939, Library and Archives Canada [LAC] RG 25, vol. 1858A, file 72-T-38.

2 W.A.B. Douglas et al., *The Official History of the Royal Canadian Air Force*, vol. 2, *The Creation of a National Air Force* (Toronto: University of Toronto Press 1986), 632–3; F.J. Hatch, *Aerodrome of Democracy: Canada and the British Commonwealth Air Training Plan, 1939–1945* (Ottawa: Canadian Government Publishing Centre 1983), 87; "Dominion Aeronautical Association Ltd: History and Statistics of Activities of the Clayton Knight Committee and its Successor the Canadian Aviation Bureau," Directorate of History and Heritage [DHH], file 181.003 (D3639); Clayton Knight, "Contribution to Victory, 1939–1942," DHH, file 80/68, part 2; Interview with Clayton Knight by Major Robert Hays (United States Air Force), 17 June 1965, DHH, file 80/68, part 3; Undated Press Release, DHH, file 80/68, part 46; Clayton Knight to Bogart Rogers, 30 June 1942, DHH, file 80/68, part 47; Beatrice Thomas (Secretary Clayton Knight Committee) to Robert Hinckley, 27 September 1944, DHH, file 80/68, part 45.

3 Douglas, *Creation of a National Air Force*, 633; "Recruiting in the United States of America," chap. 11 of RCAF *Personnel History, 10 September 1939–1945*, vol. 3, DHH, file 74/7 [hereinafter cited as "Recruiting in the USA"].

4 Douglas, *Creation of a National Air Force*, 633; quote from Knight, "Contribution to Victory, 1939–1942," DHH, file 80/68, part 2.

5 Douglas, *Creation of a National Air Force*, 633; Memorandum from W/C W.A. Curtis to Air Member for Personnel, 31 May 1940, LAC RG 24, vol. 5368, file 45-10-2.

6 Memorandum from A/C L.S. Breadner (Chief of the Air Staff) to J.S. Duncan (Deputy Minister of Defence for Air), 1 June 1940, LAC RG 24, vol. 5358, file 45-10-2.

7 Douglas, *Creation of a National Air Force*, 635; Hatch, *Aerodrome of Democracy*, 89; Interview with Knight, DHH, file 80/68, part 3; Clayton Knight Committee General Regulations, April 1941, DHH, file 80/68, part 28; Press Release, 27 May 1941, DHH, file 80/68 part 46; Newspaper Article "Seek Pilots Here to Fly Warplanes across Atlantic," *Tribune* [Minneapolis], 6 January 1941, DHH, file 80/68, part 50. Hollywood celebrated these ferry pilots in the movie *Captains of the Clouds*, which starred James Cagney as an American volunteer. See Dominique Brégent-Heald, *Big Spy Country*, chap. 5.

8 Douglas, *Creation of a National Air Force*, 634; Major-General H.H. Arnold to Clayton Knight, 19 March 1940, DHH, file 80/68, part 9; Knight, "Contribution to Victory, 1939–1942," DHH, file 80/68, part 2; Knight Interview, DHH, file 80/68, part 3.

9 Over the course of the Clayton Knight Committee's existence, many officials close to President Roosevelt would be involved in deciding its fate.
   John Hickerson was the assistant chief of the State Department's Division
   of European Affairs and secretary of the American Section of the Permanent Joint Board on Defence (an advisory body mandated to study maritime, land, and air problems relating to the defence of the Western
   Hemisphere's northern half). Harry Hopkins (personal representative and
   advisor to President Roosevelt) and Assistant Secretary of State Adolf A.
   Berle Jr were involved in discussions concerning the committee, but research in American primary sources shows that little was officially recorded concerning their opinions.
10 Douglas, *Creation of a National Air Force*, 634; Hatch, *Aerodrome of
   Democracy*, 87; Telegram from Loring Christie (Canadian Minister to
   the United States) to O.D. Skelton, 18 May 1940, LAC RG 24, vol. 5368,
   file 45-10-2.
11 Christie to Skelton, 4 November 1940, LAC RG 25, volume 779, file 379,
   Reel T-1794, 8–15.
12 Ibid.
13 Ibid.
14 Note from Legal Adviser to Prime Minister W.L.M. King, 12 November
   1940, Document 33, in David R. Murray, ed, *Documents on Canadian
   External Relations* [DCER], vol. 8, 1939–1941 (Ottawa: Department of
   External Affairs 1976), 52–3.
15 Extract of Cabinet War Committee Minutes, 19 November 1940,
   Document 34 in DCER 8, 53–5.
16 Memorandum by O.D. Skelton, 21 November 1940, LAC RG 25, vol. 779,
   file 379, reel T-1794, 29–32.
17 Extract of Cabinet War Committee Minutes, 22 November 1940,
   Document 36 in DCER 8, 57–8.
18 Skelton to M.M. Mahoney (Canadian Legation in Washington), 25
   November 1940, LAC RG 25, vol. 779, file 379, reel T-1794, 37–93.
19 Chargé d'Affaires to Skelton, 27 November 1940, LAC RG 25, volume 779,
   file 379, reel T-1794, 41–8.
20 Ibid.
21 Chargé d'Affaires to Skelton, 3 December 1940, LAC RG 25, vol. 779,
   file 379, reel T-1794, 5366.
22 Douglas, *Creation of a National Air Force*, 636–7; "Dominion
   Aeronautical Association Ltd," DHH, file 181.003 (D3639); April 1941
   Clayton Knight Committee General Regulations, DHH, file 80/68,
   part 28.

23 Stuart Armour (Managing Director DAA) to President and Directors of DAA, 22 July 1941, DHH, file 80/68, part 44; "Dominion Aeronautical Association Ltd," DHH, file 181.003 (D3639).

24 Armour to President and Directors of DAA, 18 June 1941, DHH, file 80/68, part 44; "Dominion Aeronautical Association Ltd," DHH, file 181.003 (D3639); "Recruiting in the USA," DHH, file 74/7; quote from Armour to President and Directors of DAA, 22 July 1941, DHH, file 80/68, part 44.

25 F.J. Hatch, "Recruiting Americans for the Royal Canadian Air Force, 1939–1942," in *Aerospace Historian* 18, no.1 (March 1971), 16; "Recruiting in the USA," DHH, file 74/7.

26 "Dominion Aeronautical Association Ltd," DHH, file 181.003 (D3639); first quote from "Recruiting in the USA," DHH, file 74/7; second quote from Armour to President and Directors of DAA, 22 July 1941, DHH, file 80/68, part 44.

27 "Dominion Aeronautical Association Ltd," DHH, file 181.003 (D3639); first quote from Armour to President and Directors of DAA, 22 July 1941, DHH, file 80/68, part 44; second quote from "Recruiting in the USA," DHH, file 74/7.

28 Douglas, *Creation of a National Air Force*, 638; Letter from Stuart Armour (Managing Director DAA) to President and Directors of DAA, 18 June 1941, DHH, file 80/68, part 44; Armour to President and Directors of DAA, 22 July 1941, DHH, file 80/68, part 44.

29 Hatch, *Aerodrome of Democracy*, 90, 92; "Dominion Aeronautical Association Ltd," DHH, file 181.003 (D3639); "Recruiting in the USA," DHH, file 74/7; Memorandum from w/c F.H. Smith to A/c H. Edwards (Air Member for Personnel), 22 July 1941, LAC RG 24, vol. 5368, file 45-10-3; Memorandum from A/c H. Edwards (Air Member for Personnel) to J.S. Duncan (Deputy Minister of National Defence for Air), LAC RG 24, vol. 5368, file 45-10-9; 27 August 1941, LAC RG 24 vol. 5368 File 45-10-9; Memorandum from Homer Smith to w/c Crabb (Director of Manning), 25 September 1941, LAC RG 24, vol. 5368, file 45-10-9.

30 "Says Canada Tries to Enlist US Flyers," *Sun* [New York], 12 August 1941; "Canadian Recruiting in US to be Probed," unnamed Washington, DC, newspaper, 13 August 1941; "US Will Probe Bogus Air Agents," *Daily Mirror* [New York], all in DHH, file 80/68, part 50.

31 H.H. Wrong (Chargé d'Affaires) to King, 15 August 1941, LAC RG 24, vol. 5368, file 45-10-5.

32 "Recruiting in the USA," DHH, file 74/7.

33 Douglas, *Creation of a National Air Force*, 640–1; Beatrice Thomas (Secretary Canadian Aviation Board) to Richard Landfear, 26 December 1942, DHH, file 80/68, part 30.
34 Douglas, *Creation of a National Air Force*, 640–1; "Recruiting in the USA," DHH, file 74/7; "Dominion Aeronautical Association Ltd," DHH, file 181.003 (D3639).
35 "Seek Pilots Here to Fly Warplanes across Atlantic," *Tribune* [Minneapolis], 6 January 1941; "Canada Wants US Fliers in Any Number, Says Envoy," *Oakland Tribune*, 28 January 1941; "Canada Seeks Aviators Here: Office Set Up in Boise to Give Information on Royal Air Force," *Boise Capital News*, 5 August 1941; "Hundreds of US Fliers Accept Canadian Posts," *Oregon Journal*, 16 August 1941, all in DHH, file 80/68, part 50; Beatrice Thomas to John Arthur Sage, 9 March 1944, DHH, file 80/68, part 30.

13

Nukes and Spooks

Canada-US Intelligence Sharing and Nuclear Consultations, 1950–1958

GREG DONAGHY

Major Charles F. Grove of the United States Air Force swore softly as he approached the St Lawrence River in the cold morning sunshine of 11 November 1950. His B-50 bomber, Inventory Number 46–038, had just lost its outside starboard engine. No sooner had Grove adjusted his bearings than the inside port engine started to backfire and was shut down. With only two engines left, 46–038 began to drop, and Grove ordered his crew to ditch their payload. Quickly, the bombardier, Major Newton Brown, set the fuse, hunched over his bombsight, and pressed the button. Slowly, and then faster, the Mark IV atomic bomb fell towards Rivière du Loup. Happily for the residents of this small Quebec town, the American weapon was without its nuclear core.[1]

Canadians rarely acknowledged the presence of American nuclear weapons in Canada during the early 1950s. For most of them, Canada has always been a step removed from the sordid and mad world of nuclear weapons – something that was best left to the Americans. Indeed, Canadians treasured their nuclear virginity until the 1960s when that oh-so-charming American president, John F. Kennedy, took unfair advantage of their decent homespun prime minister, John Diefenbaker, and foisted nuclear weapons on an unsuspecting Canada. But increasingly, as more and more documentation on the subject is declassified, historians learn that this mythical, pre-nuclear past never really existed and that Canada always participated in American nuclear activities. In its place, however, a new, equally inaccurate mythology threatens to rise. In this view, complicit and subservient politicians and bureaucrats hurried to fulfill peremptory American demands for help with its nuclear deterrent, secretly compromising Canada's sovereignty and placing Canadians in unwonted danger.[2]

But Canadian policy-makers during the early 1950s were always aware of the dangers involved and accepted them as a necessary consequence of the Cold War confrontation with the Soviet Union. As long as Moscow possessed nuclear weapons, the West too would need them. Moreover, as a leading member of the North Atlantic Treaty Organization (NATO), Canada felt obligated to contribute when it could to the American deterrent, on which Western security depended. Nevertheless, Ottawa was determined that its alliance with Washington should not drag it into an atomic war without adequate consultation. It mustered its few resources with some shrewdness and proved time and again that it was no pushover. Prime Minister Louis St Laurent and his secretary of state for external affairs, Lester B. "Mike" Pearson, knew exactly Canada's worth in American eyes. Washington depended on Canadian bases and airspace to operate its Strategic Air Command (SAC) and to defend North America against Soviet attack. Consequently, Ottawa set out in 1951 to use its geography to assert its right to be consulted in US decisions to employ nuclear weapons. Reconciling this right with the American view that Washington had an unfettered right to employ its nuclear weapons as it wished was not easy. Indeed, Canada's first efforts to have Washington acknowledge its obligation to consult its northern ally were inconclusive. Later efforts were more promising. Washington's growing reliance on its nuclear arsenal and the complete integration of the continental air defence system by the mid-1950s increased Canada's influence and made its cooperation more important. By the end of the decade, Ottawa had won the point, and Washington agreed in principle to consult Ottawa before taking any military measures that would lead directly to nuclear war – time permitting. It was admittedly a small step, but it was an important one, underpinning the subsequent history of Canadian-American nuclear relations.

The implications for Canada of NATO's strategy of nuclear deterrence came quickly into focus with the outbreak of the Korean War in June 1950. Convinced that the North Korean attack on its southern neighbour was the first phase in a Soviet assault on Western Europe and the North Atlantic, the United States escalated its military effort in July 1950. As American troops, in full retreat, were swept off the narrow Korean peninsula, dismayed and worried Pentagon officials ordered elements of the US Strategic Air Command to advance bases in Britain. On 18 August, the US Embassy in Ottawa approached the Department of External Affairs to request permission to deploy the USAF's 43rd Bomber Group to Goose Bay, Labrador, for what were euphemistically described as "training flights." At the same time, through more restricted service channels, the US Joint Chiefs of Staff asked the RCAF for permission to equip these bombers with atomic weapons. Brooke Claxton, the minister of national defence, and Louis St Laurent, the prime minister, told no one of the American request. Convinced that the Korean War was simply a prelude to a Communist attack in Europe, they quickly granted their permission. On 24 August, 1950, 65 B-29s and B-50s and 1,400 USAF personnel headed north to Goose Bay, carrying with them 11 atomic weapons with their nuclear cores removed. They remained there until driven south at the end of September by the cold.[3]

It was soon clear that the Americans wanted a more permanent arrangement for the base at Goose Bay. In early October, US officials hinted that the Pentagon was preparing proposals for the long-term operation of the base, which the Joint Chiefs of Staff thought would become "the principal Strategic Air Command assault base." Meanwhile, Washington wanted immediate permission to expand the base, adding atomic weapons storage facilities and barracks for four thousand airmen.[4] There was little doubt that the Canadian Cabinet would approve the American request. As the prime minister explained, Canada was "engaged in a collective effort [in which] the role of strategic bombing ... was one that could only be filled by the US"[5] Still, most ministers were disturbed by Washington's plans and worried about Canada's role in future SAC operations. While they nervously waited for Washington's formal proposals on the future of Goose Bay, both the domestic and the international dangers of the American nuclear deterrent became frighteningly clear.

In mid-November 1950, officials in the Department of External Affairs were horrified to discover that a SAC bomber had run into engine trouble over the St Lawrence and had been forced to jettison its atomic weapon into the river. Even without its nuclear core, the bomb carried enough explosives to terrify several nearby villages, grab headlines across Eastern Canada, and leave Ottawa with haunting nightmares of nuclear disaster.[6] More important, Canadian policy-makers were soon alarmed at Washington's apparent willingness – even haste – to resort to atomic weapons when the "going got tough." Relations between Ottawa and President Harry Truman's Democratic administration had been close and were marked by mutual confidence. Truman and St Laurent treated each other with considerable respect. Pearson was a close friend of Dean Acheson, the American secretary of state, whose appointment he greeted by quipping that he was "delighted personally, officially, internationally and alcoholically."[7] Acheson and Hume Wrong, Canada's ambassador in Washington, were also good friends, sharing a deep cynicism and a biting, sarcastic wit. Nevertheless, Pearson, Wrong, and other Canadian diplomats, who had learned their craft from British officials used to managing His Majesty's far-flung empire, had long suspected that the United States was not really up to leading the free world. Their fears were confirmed in late November 1950, when Chinese Communist troops suddenly appeared in North Korea, driving UN and American troops south in an astounding rout. The emotional and shrill reaction in the United States was deeply worrying. Responding to a reporter's question, Truman implied that the United States would use the atomic bomb in Korea if required. After all, he reportedly said, "it's one of our weapons."[8] "It seems to me," Canada's minister of trade and commerce, C.D. Howe (himself an American immigrant to Canada) wrote in December 1950, "that our friends in the United States are suffering from hysteria in a very advanced stage."[9]

Worried that the United States might use the atomic bomb against Beijing, Pearson and St Laurent insisted on Canada's right to be consulted before being dragged into a third world war. In a memorandum delivered to the State Department in early December, Pearson reminded Truman that the atomic bomb was not simply an ordinary weapon, but was "universally regarded as the ultimate weapon ... [and] should be treated as such." The memorandum recalled Canada's role in the development of the atomic bomb and argued that by virtue of its participation in the tripartite arrangements arising out of the 1943 Quebec Conference and its contribution of uranium to the American atomic weapons program, Canada would be especially implicated in any decision to use an atomic bomb. Therefore, Pearson concluded, "before a decision of such immense and awful consequence, for all of us, is taken, there should be consultation among the governments principally concerned."[10] The Americans tried to reassure their ally, but their confusing and uncertain response only added to Canadian worries. In private talks with British prime minister Clement Attlee, who had immediately flown to Washington on hearing Truman's remark, the president apparently promised to consult Britain before using the atomic bomb. But the public statement released after the meeting described their exchange in much more limited terms: "The President stated that it was his hope that world conditions would never call for the use of the atomic bomb. The President told the Prime Minister that it was also his desire to keep the Prime Minister at all times informed of developments which might bring about a change in this condition."

The State Department quickly assured Wrong that the president's commitment applied to Canada as well. But what exactly did Truman promise? Stopping in Ottawa on his way home, Attlee told St Laurent and Pearson that the president had promised to consult them all before using the bomb. But Wrong doubted this account. His discussions with the State Department and the British ambassador in Washington revealed disturbing differences in the US and British versions of the Truman-Attlee conversations. State Department officials reminded Wrong that the president could not undertake to consult other governments, since the US Joint Congressional Committee on Atomic Energy insisted that there should be no limits on the president's freedom to act. The president promised only to keep Canada and the United Kingdom informed of the conditions that might bring about nuclear war. It was, the undersecretary of state for external affairs, Arnold Heeney, explained to Prime Minister St Laurent, "an undertaking that could be interpreted very loosely."[11]

While Canadian officials wrestled with the implications of the American position on consultations, the US Joint Chiefs of Staff finally presented their proposals for Goose Bay in early January 1951. Their imperial arrogance stunned the Canadians. The Pentagon hoped to negotiate a general "canopy agreement" giving the United States unrestricted "prior approval" to deploy its strategic bombers and their atomic weapons at Goose Bay. The USAF also wanted advance permission to overfly Canadian territory on training missions and, in the event of war, to use Canada as a base for actual strikes. If Ottawa accepted the general principle of "prior approval," the United States undertook only to "notify" Canada through service channels of "such air movements, staging and strikes."[12]

St Laurent, Howe, Pearson, and Claxton considered the American proposal and dismissed it as inadequate. Ministers acknowledged the US desire to deploy SAC secretly and rapidly, and admitted in private that it was unlikely that Canada would ever deny the use of Goose Bay to the United States in an emergency. However, it seemed unwise to agree to "prior approval," surrendering in advance Ottawa's ability to use its geography and its bases to influence US decisions about the use of atomic weapons. Canadian decision makers could hardly present this argument to their American counterparts. Instead, Pearson instructed Wrong to explain that it would be "improper for Canada as a sovereign nation to permit unrestricted use in peacetime of facilities in Canadian territory for these operations." The government must be consulted at the highest level on all SAC operations involving fissionable weapons, including over-flights and actual strikes. Pearson added that routine training matters, the construction of storage facilities, the deployment of aircraft and even the movement and storage of bombs without their nuclear cores might be arranged on a service-to-service basis, provided there was advance notification.[13]

Washington was disappointed by Canada's response. Acheson suggested that the Canadian requirement for consultations might be met through a series of regular and frequent high-level discussions on the international situation. These would encourage a shared appreciation of the conditions that might lead the West "to accept a Soviet challenge of war." Ottawa cautiously welcomed the offer of consultations but continued to insist that the United States seek its permission for all SAC operations in or over Canada that involved "(a) possible strikes from bases in Canada; (b) storage of fissionable components on Canadian territory; (c) over-flights of Canadian territory by planes carrying fissionable components." The only exception, Pearson and Claxton agreed, would be "in the event of a major outright Soviet attack against continental North America."[14]

It was soon clear that Washington's determination to maintain its freedom to maneuver could not be reconciled with Ottawa's insistence on bilateral consultations before fissionable material was deployed into Canada. Indeed, Ottawa's offer to authorize the use of Canadian territory in the event of a major attack on North America merely underlined its refusal to approve other SAC operations in advance. In mid-May, US negotiators abandoned the "canopy agreement." They agreed to carry on the proposed "strategic consultations" in the hope that the two allies would develop a similar understanding of the likelihood of nuclear war in the event of a crisis. Pearson hoped so too, but just in case, he took the unusual step of asking Acheson to acknowledge formally the inconclusive result of the negotiations. In June 1951, the two foreign ministers agreed that the bilateral consultations left both countries free to act as they wished during any emergency and that the United States would continue to seek permission through the normal diplomatic channels before moving fissionable material into Canada.[15]

Consultations were held frequently during the next few years. Canadian officials soon treasured the opportunity these meetings provided to discuss in depth global strategy with American policymakers. They were especially reassured to learn during the first few encounters that the United States planned to use the atomic bomb only in the event of a direct, major confrontation with the Soviet Union. Washington too found the meetings helpful, as Acheson put it, "in proving that the US was not trigger happy." But trouble was on the horizon. A new, unfamiliar Republican administration, headed by President Dwight D. Eisenhower and his secretary of state, the virulent anti-communist, John Foster Dulles, assumed office in January 1953. Sharp differences in personality and policy quickly emerged. Eisenhower and St Laurent seemed to get along fine, but relations with the new secretary of state were difficult. Pearson thought Dulles a clumsy diplomat and once called him "stupid." Worse, the American was awkward and gauche. "Our dinner for the Dulles' was quite good," Canada's ambassador to the United States noted in his diary, "except for the Ds who are really without any of the social attributes."[16] For his part, Dulles resented Canada's constant demands for consultation. "You Canadians," he once sneered to Pearson, "are always complaining that we never consult you about our policies. 'Ike' as you know is a great golfer and, who knows, he may want [us] to play a few holes ... If we do and the score is all square on the 18th green, I'll wager that you'll intervene just as I am about to make the deciding putt to demand that I consult you about it first."[17]

Policy differences also divided the two North American allies. "The Eisenhower administration," Dulles explained to Pearson in February 1953, "was determined not to leave the initiative in the Cold War to the Soviet Union ... [and] to create situations which would worry the Kremlin."[18] In January 1954, the US secretary of state unveiled the administration's defence policy, which pundits dubbed the "New Look." Henceforth, the United States would depend on "a great capacity to retaliate, instantly, by means and at places of our choosing."[19] The speech signalled a shift in American thinking about the role of nuclear weapons, which would no longer be reserved for strategic purposes but might also be employed tactically, in local situations. Dulles confirmed the change when he told Pearson a few months later that the United States would not send troops to help the French in Vietnam but would rely on naval and air operations, armed "if necessary with atomic weapons."[20]

Eisenhower's new defence policy also included an accelerated program for continental air defence. Canada and the United States had acknowledged a shared responsibility for defending North America since the mid-1940s. In 1951, the two countries had agreed to build a system of radars, the Pinetree Line, extending from British Columbia to southern Ontario. This was followed in 1953 by a US proposal to construct a line further north, the Mid-Canada Line. In an early effort to come to grips with these developments, Pearson wanted to draft principles for defence cooperation in early 1953 but had been rebuffed by Dulles, who was anxious to keep a free hand.[21] Similarly, Eisenhower met St Laurent's worries about US activities in the North with a vague promise to "show full respect for Canadian sovereignty."[22] Now, however, the United States wanted more. Alarmed by growing Soviet nuclear capabilities, which were sufficiently powerful to strike North America, and spurred into action by Congressional pressure, Washington asked Canada in the summer of 1954 for permission to construct a third, more northern system, the Distant Early Warning Line. But this was only the first in a series of measures planned by Washington to bolster North American air defence, and in December 1954, officials in the Department of External Affairs warned Pearson and St Laurent that American plans, especially those calling for the introduction of interceptor aircraft equipped with tactical nuclear weapons, raised important problems of Canadian control over conventional and nuclear-armed military forces in its territory.[23]

The question of whose finger was on the nuclear trigger was also quickly coming to a head in another quarter. During the summer of 1954, Lieutenant General A.M. Grunenther, NATO's Supreme Allied Commander in Europe (SACEUR), had begun to examine his future defence requirements, factoring in the likely availability of US tactical nuclear weapons. By October, NATO military authorities had finished their studies. Their report, known as MC (48), after its reference number, concluded that NATO should base its defence plans on the assumption "that atomic weapons must be used in a major war by the Allies, without delay, and regardless of the Soviet use of such weapons."[24] It envisioned arming local NATO commands with tactical nuclear weapons for just that purpose. In November, MC (48) was turned over to NATO foreign ministers for final approval.

Not surprisingly, Lieutenant General Charles Foulkes, chairman of the Canadian Chiefs of Staff Committee and an active participant in the NATO study, urged the government to accept the report "in its entirety." Like many commanders, Foulkes was impatient with civilian efforts to meddle into military matters. In his view, MC (48) was only a planning document and did not authorize the use of atomic weapons. In any case, Foulkes insisted that the question of authorization was largely academic, since NATO had already approved the use of nuclear weapons for strategic bombing and the US president could launch an atomic assault without consulting NATO.

The Department of External Affairs and its minister were more cautious. NATO's earlier decision merely acknowledged what was generally known: Washington would respond to a major Soviet offensive with strategic atomic bombing. Moreover, it did not envisage supplying local forces with tactical nuclear weapons. As a historian, Pearson recalled the First World War, when the armies of Europe blindly marched off to war in accordance with pre-existing plans. "Policy," he warned Dulles, "is likely to become the victim of military plans, if great care is not taken."[25] The French and British were also concerned, emphasizing the danger that military preparations, including nuclear ones, might take on a life of their own once NATO forces were put on alert during an emergency. The British foreign secretary, Anthony Eden, suggested that the North Atlantic Council adopt a resolution noting SACEUR's planning assumptions but explicitly reserving for governments "the ultimate responsibility to take final decisions."[26]

The Americans were skeptical. Eisenhower, who had served as NATO's military commander in 1951–52, regarded SACEUR's report as simply a planning document, not authorization to act, and he wanted it adopted as it stood. The administration acknowledged the need to ensure political control over tactical nuclear weapons but made it clear that Washington would oppose efforts to set up a mechanism within NATO to exert political control over SACEUR. As Dulles pointed out to Pearson and Eden when they met a few weeks later in Paris, NATO could hardly wait for all fourteen of its members to agree on appropriate action in the event of a Soviet attack. The secretary of state suggested that the North Atlantic Council adopt the report as drafted, while the countries mainly concerned – the United States, Britain, and Canada – reached an informal understanding on "the political channels through which decisions would be conveyed to SACEUR." He cautioned "that any such arrangements should be kept very secret, and that NATO Council discussion of these matters, let alone public discussion, should be discouraged." Pearson and Eden agreed. And so NATO formally adopted tactical nuclear weapons in December 1954, while at the same time, Washington, London, and Ottawa began to consider how to control their use.[27]

It was clear to Eden and Pearson, who met privately before the NATO meeting adjourned, that at the heart of the problem was adequate access to the intelligence that would give rise to a military alert in the initial phase of an emergency. If Canada and Britain could secure access to the earliest American intelligence on Soviet or Communist activities indicating an increased likelihood of war, political leaders in London and Ottawa would be able to consult their Washington counterparts on the need for an alert in a timely manner, before the alliance was swept up in runaway military preparations. The two foreign ministers agreed to coordinate their work.

The initial Anglo-Canadian position was based on a paper prepared by Patrick Dean, Foreign Office spymaster and chairman of the British Joint Intelligence Committee. In Dean's scheme, when indicator intelligence arrived in any one of the three capitals, it would immediately and automatically be passed on to the other two for assessment and evaluation. The result would be passed up the chain of command, until it reached the political level, where it would form the basis for consultations between the heads of the three governments. If the president and the two prime ministers agreed that war could not be averted, their representatives would summon the North Atlantic Council, which would then declare a NATO alert and give SACEUR his orders.[28] In April 1955, after four months of back-and-forth discussions with the Foreign Office, Ottawa agreed that Dean's paper might form the basis for a tripartite agreement on intelligence sharing and political consultations. Later that month, the

British and Canadian ambassadors in Washington presented the paper to Dulles in parallel but separate representations.[29]

Washington hesitated. Unhappy with the prospect of sharing sensitive intelligence, the Pentagon dragged its feet and delayed responding. Military sources in Washington cited inter-agency complications and blamed the Central Intelligence Agency (CIA). More bad news was on the way. When Foulkes asked about the fate of the Anglo-Canadian paper in October 1955, Admiral A.W. Radforth, the chairman of the US Joint Chiefs of Staff, told him that while Washington might share tactical military intelligence with its allies, it wanted to restrict, not increase, the dissemination of strategic intelligence.[30]

Radforth's remarks, which struck at the very basis of the June 1951 Canada–United States agreement on strategic consultations, alarmed the Department of External Affairs. The US comments were especially upsetting in view of Washington's nuclear saber rattling during the Sino-American confrontation over Taiwan, Quemoy, and Matsu earlier that spring. The off-shore island crisis had worried Pearson, who was disturbed to discover that continental defences were already so integrated that Canada would be implicated in any American nuclear strike in the Far East, a region in which Canada had no significant interests. In preparing for action in Asia, the United States would certainly want to deploy SAC at Goose Bay and insist on placing the continental air defence system on a general alert in case Moscow intervened. Officials warned Pearson that these "precautionary measures ... might lead to a chain reaction of events which would tend to precipitate general war."[31] They urged him to abandon the British paper and seek a separate, bilateral arrangement that would ensure that Washington consulted with Canada before declaring a continental alert.[32]

Pearson agreed. Jules Leger, undersecretary of state for external affairs, Robert Bryce, clerk of the privy council, and General Foulkes met hastily in late November to draft a formula for consultations that might be passed to the Americans during a strategic consultation meeting slated for December 1955. Under its proposed terms, the two governments promised to share "invariably and immediately" any intelligence that might lead one of them "to conclude that there was a likelihood of hostilities occurring in which North America would likely be attacked." During a crisis, intelligence agencies in the two countries would also "automatically pass to one another all the relevant information, including the background necessary to understand the problem, and their respective assessments." This kind of intelligence sharing would equip Canadian ministers with the knowledge they required to arrive at "independent conclusions in an emergency."[33] The formula was duly presented to the Americans, who agreed to discuss the proposal early in 1956. At the same time, Ottawa informed Britain of its independent initiative, suggesting that London shelve its plans for a tripartite arrangement and follow the Canadian lead.

Progress was slow. Robert Amory, the CIA's experienced deputy director of intelligence, handled the American end. Amory was initially confused by the poorly drafted Canadian formula, which failed to detail the link between rapid intelligence sharing and political consultations. Convinced that Canada already had ample access to intelligence material through existing NATO and service channels, he was puzzled by the whole exercise. The explanations were left to George Glazebrook, minister at the Canadian Embassy in Washington, and Bill Crean, chairman of the Canadian Joint Intelligence Committee. A distinguished historian and a leading figure in Canada's wartime intelligence establishment, Glazebrook possessed a sharp mind and did not suffer fools gladly. Crean, who had spent the war working with the British secret service, was the closest thing Canada's small foreign service had to a real spy.[34] With barely disguised impatience, they explained that Canadian ministers could be consulted on a continental alert only if they had access to precisely the same intelligence assessments as their counterparts in Washington. Crean and Glazebrook hammered away at the CIA representative, before the American finally cut the Gordian knot by dividing the problem into two related parts: consultations and intelligence sharing.

Once divorced from the question of consultations, Amory thought that a mechanism could easily be worked out for sharing indicator intelligence on the terms set out in the Canadian formula. Since the two countries already shared intelligence, he considered this a simple "nuts and bolts" problem. By December 1956, a bilateral agreement had established direct communications links between Canada's Joint Intelligence Committee and the American inter-agency Intelligence Advisory Committee to share intelligence "automatically and by the most expeditious means."[35] Indeed, the arrangements proved so satisfactory that the terms employed were used again in early 1957 when Britain, Canada, and the United States resurrected the notion of a tripartite agreement to ensure intelligence sharing in a NATO context.

A bilateral agreement on consultations proved more difficult to negotiate. This raised an important question of principle for the administration, which Amory thought would be reluctant "to bind itself under any formula which required it to consult another government before taking any action itself."[36] Amory suggested that Ottawa take the matter up directly with the administration through the State Department. Ottawa opened the negotiations in May 1956 with a suggestion for a brief and straightforward exchange of letters in which the two governments "promise to consult" through their chiefs of staff and normal diplomatic channels if either government decided to declare a continental alert.[37]

The Canadian proposal met with a cool response. Although the US administration appreciated the desire for consultations, it argued that it was "difficult to visualize how prior consultation could be practicable under certain circumstances." Dulles insisted that the agreement take into consideration those "extreme circumstances" when Washington might have to act before it was possible to arrange an exchange of views between the two governments. He would accept the Canadian proposal provided it was amended in three important respects. First, it must explicitly permit either government to call an alert without consultations when an attack seemed "immediately probable or imminent." Second, it should permit consultations through either the "appropriate military or diplomatic channels." And third, the agreement must recognize each government's unfettered right to act in its own defence.[38]

The American reaction fell short of Canadian expectations. Officials in the Department of External Affairs were concerned that the United States draft failed to make "mandatory" government-to-government consultations occurring through the usual diplomatic channels. The department also suspected that the general US reference to using "appropriate military channels" would allow Washington to circumvent effective consultations at a senior, and more politically sensitive, level. Moreover, officials argued that the US definition of the "extreme circumstances" that might inhibit consultations was far too vague for Canadian purposes. They urged the government to insist on tightening up the terms of the agreement.[39]

The Cabinet Defence Committee agreed. In early March 1957, the undersecretary of state for external affairs again wrote to Dulles to insist that consultations must take place through the Chiefs of Staff *and* the usual diplomatic channels. In addition, the Canadian ambassador narrowed the US definition of "extreme circumstances" by emphasizing that consultations must precede the declaration of an alert, except when an attack on North America is "imminent or probable in a matter of hours rather than days."[40] A few days later, to underline the importance Ottawa attached to reaching an agreement quickly, R.M. Macdonnell, the deputy undersecretary, arranged to see the American ambassador, Livingston Merchant. Recalling recent US proposals to create an integrated North American air defence command, Macdonnell emphasized "that Canadian willingness to agree to joint operational control of the continental air defence forces should be met by a corresponding US recognition of the need for adequate consultation ... on matters which lead to the alerting of the air defence system."[41]

This was food for thought indeed, and a more forthcoming American reply, approved in draft by Dulles and Eisenhower, was delivered to the Canadian Embassy in late June 1957. In the meantime, John G. Diefenbaker's Progressive Conservative Party had defeated the Liberal government in the Canadian general election of 10 June 1957, though this change had no impact on the course of the negotiations. The new US position met most but not all of the Canadian desiderata. The United States agreed to Canada's demand for high-level consultations through the respective Chiefs of Staff and diplomatic channels. Washington also accepted Ottawa's more restrictive definition of the "extreme circumstances," when an alert might be declared without prior consultation.[42] There was only one new wrinkle. In order to reduce the number and frequency of the consultations, Washington suggested that they should occur only when an alert was "brought about by the declaration of a national emergency or a nation-wide civil defense emergency." Canada's diplomats wanted to omit the new paragraph but were persuaded by the Department of National Defence and the State Department that the United States wanted only to avoid consulting Ottawa every time an individual ship or airbase went on partial alert. After all, as Norman Robertson, perhaps Canada's most influential diplomat, argued from his new post as ambassador in Washington, whatever its limitations, the "proposed agreement provided for consultation at the final stages of a cumulative process of intelligence warnings, military alerts, and political decisions." Admittedly not perfect, the agreement was an important step forward and provided the basis for "further efforts to strengthen the consultative process at earlier stages."[43] This made sense, and although officials in the Department of External Affairs would have preferred not to define the kinds of alerts requiring consultations, they accepted the additional paragraph in the fall of 1957.

NOTES

Greg Donaghy is the Head of the Historical Section, Foreign Affairs and International Trade Canada. The views expressed in this article are the author's alone and do not represent the views and policies of the Government of Canada.

1 See Head of Defence Liaison Division to Under-Secretary of State for External Affairs [USSEA], 11 November 1950, and Canadian Ambassador in Washington to the Under-Secretary of State for External Affairs, 2 December 1950, reprinted in Greg Donaghy, ed., *Documents on Canadian External Relations [DCER]*, vol. 16, *1950* (Ottawa: Canada Communication Group, 1995), 1479–80, 1487. On the details of the flight, see John Clearwater, *US Nuclear Weapons in Canada* (Toronto: Dundurn 1999), 107–8.

2 This accusatory tone mars Clearwater's otherwise helpful study, *US Nuclear Weapons in Canada*. See, for examples, 11–13, 43, and 204.

3 Secretary of State for External Affairs (SSEA) to Canadian Ambassador in Washington, Despatch No. 2710, 13 September 1950, and Canadian Ambassador in Washington to USSEA, Letter No. 3088, 2 December 1950, reprinted in Donaghy, ed., *DCER*, vol 16, *1950*, 1466–7, 1487.

4 Memorandum by Defence Liaison Division, 6 October 1950, reprinted in Donaghy, ed., *DCER*, vol. 16, *1950*, 1467–8.

5 Cabinet Conclusions, 25 October 1950, reprinted in Donaghy, ed., *DCER*, vol. 16, *1950*, 1475–6.

6 Defence Liaison Division to USSEA, 11 November 1950, reprinted in Donaghy, ed., *DCER*, vol. 16, *1950*, 1479–80.

7 Cited in John English, *The Worldly Years: The Life of Lester B. Pearson*, vol. 2, *1949–72* (Toronto: Alfred A. Knopf 1992), 10.

8 Cited in Ian McGibbon, *New Zealand and the Korean War*, vol. 1, *Politics and Diplomacy* (New York: Oxford University Press 1992), 64–6.

9 Cited in Robert Bothwell, *Canada and the United States: The Politics of Partnership* (Toronto: University of Toronto Press 1992), 52.

10 Memorandum: Korea and the Atomic Bomb, 3 December 1950, reprinted in Donaghy, ed., *DCER*, vol. 16, *1950*, 254–5.

11 A.D.P. Heeney, Memorandum for the Prime Minister, 8 January 1951, reprinted in Greg Donaghy, ed., *DCER*, vol. 17, *1951* (Ottawa: Canada Communication Group 1996), 1302–3.

12 Canadian Ambassador in Washington to SSEA, Letter No. 19, 3 January 1951, reprinted in Donaghy, ed., *DCER*, vol. 17, *1951*, 1299–1302.

13 USSEA to Canadian Ambassador in Washington, Letter No. D-1407, 2 April 1951, reprinted in Donaghy, ed., *DCER*, vol. 17, *1951*, 1314–16.

14 USSEA to Canadian Ambassador in Washington, Letter No. D-189, 4 May 1951, reprinted in Donaghy, ed., *DCER*, vol. 17, *1951*, 1323.

15 Special Assistant to the SSEA to Canadian Ambassador in Washington, 19 June 1951 and enclosures, reprinted in Donaghy, ed., *DCER*, vol. 17, *1951*, 1356–65.

16 Cited in English, *The Worldly Years*, 121.

17 L.B. Pearson, *Mike: The Memoirs of the Rt. Hon. Lester B. Pearson,* vol. 2, *1948–1957* (Toronto: University of Toronto Press 1973), 69.

18 Memorandum of Conversation between Secretary of State of the United States and the Secretary of State for External Affairs, 15 February 1953, reprinted in Don Barry, ed., *DCER*, vol. 19, *1953* (Ottawa: Supply and Services Canada 1991), 981–9.

19 John Foster Dulles, "The Evolution of Foreign Policy, 11 US Department of State, *Bulletin*, vol. 30, no. 761, 25 January 1954, 107–10.

20 L.B. Pearson, "Memorandum of a Conversation with Mr. John Foster Dulles, Secretary of State of the United States, March 16, 1954," reprinted in Donaghy, ed., *DCER*, vol. 20, *1954*, 955.

21 "Memorandum of a Conversation between the Secretary of State of the US and the SSEA," 15 February 1953, reprinted in Barry, ed., *DCER*, vol. 19, *1953*, 981–9.

22 Canadian Ambassador in Washington to SSEA, Despatch No. 989, 13 May 1953, reprinted in Barry, ed., *DCER*, vol. 19, *1953*, 1005.

23 R.A. MacKay, "Memorandum for the SSEA" and attached "Memorandum by Defence Liaison (1) Division, 11, 8 December 1954, reprinted in Donaghy, ed., *DCER*, vol. 20, *1954*, 1055–60.

24 Benjamin Rogers, "Memorandum for the USSEA," 13 October 1954, reprinted in Donaghy, ed., *DCER*, vol. 20, *1954*, 728.

25 "Memorandum by SSEA, 11, 16 December 1954, reprinted in Donaghy, ed., *DCER*, vol. 21, *1955*, 771.

26 SSEA to Permanent Representative to the North Atlantic Treaty Organization (NATO), Tel 940, 6 December 1954, reprinted in Donaghy, ed., *DCER*, vol. 21, *1955*, 751–2.

27 "Memorandum by SSEA," 16 December 1954, reprinted in Donaghy, ed., *DCER*, vol. 21, *1955*, 771.

28 Patrick Dean, "Possible Stages of Action When Indications of Major Russian Aggression Are Received in Good Time," [December 1954], reprinted in Greg Donaghy, ed., *DCER*, vol. 21, *1955* (Ottawa: Canada Communication Group 1999), 331–3.

29 Ottawa to London, Tel No 574, 20 April 1955 and Ottawa to Washington, Tel EX-743, 21 April 1955, reprinted in Donaghy, ed., *DCER*, vol. 21, *1955*, 342–4.

30 A.D.P. Heeney to Jules Leger, 25 October 1955, and George Ignatieff, Memorandum for the USSEA, 28 October 1955, reprinted in Donaghy, ed., *DCER*, vol. 21, *1955*, 344–6.

31 R.A. MacKay, "Memorandum for the Minister," 21 February 1955, reprinted in Donaghy, ed., *DCER*, vol. 21, *1955*, 1527–31.

32 George Ignatieff, Memorandum for the USSEA, 21 November 1955, and Jules Leger, Memorandum for the Minister, 30 November 1955, reprinted in Donaghy, ed., *DCER*, vol. 21, *1955*, 345–7 and 670–3.

33 Attachments to Jules Leger, Memorandum for the Minister, 30 November 1955, reprinted in Donaghy, ed., *DCER*, vol. 21, *1955*, 673–4.

34 John Starnes, *Closely Guarded: A Life in Canadian Security and Intelligence* (Toronto: University of Toronto Press 1998), 69–70, 84–5.

35 Robert Murphy to A.D.P. Heeney, 4 December 1956, Library and Archives Canada (LAC) RG 24, vol. 21370, file 1795-1.

36 Confidential Source.

37 A.D.P. Heeney to John F. Dulles, 14 May 1957, LAC, RG 24, vol. 21370, file 1795-1.

38 Robert Murphy to A.D.P. Heeney, 4 December 1956, LAC RG 24, vol. 21370, file 1795-1.

39 Memorandum to Cabinet Defence Committee, 22 January 1957, reprinted in Donaghy, ed., *DCER*, vol. 23, *1956–57, Part II*, (Ottawa: Canadian Government Publishing 2002).

40 A.D.P. Heeney to John F. Dulles, 1 March 1957, reprinted in Donaghy, ed., *DCER*, vol. 23, *1956–57, Part II*. Emphasis added.

41 USSEA to Canadian Ambassador in Washington, Letter No. G-251, 6 March 1957, reprinted in Donaghy, ed., *DCER*, vol. 23, *1956–57, Part II*.

42 Washington to Ottawa, Tel No 1426, 21 June 1957, LAC RG 25, file 50030-AB-4-40, vol. 7967.

43 Washington to Ottawa, Tel No 2130, 4 October 1957, LAC RG 24, vol. 21370, file 1795-1.

PART FIVE

Future Imperfect

14

O.D. Skelton and the Rise
of North Americanism

NORMAN HILLMER

Nineteen thirty-five was a good year for the Canadian-American connection. Prime Minister R.B. Bennett began the negotiation of a trade agreement with the United States in the spring. Another leader, Mackenzie King, finished the job in time to celebrate his success on Armistice Day, the 11th of November, from his perspective the appropriate occasion to contrast the cooperative peoples of North America with those of a barbaric Europe.[1] O.D. Skelton, King's chief foreign policy adviser, as he had been Bennett's, was delighted by the substance of freer trade, but even more by its potential for the shaping of a "North American mind."[2] That would distance the country from the trap of British imperialism and European militarism.

The first four decades of the twentieth century, the period of Skelton's academic and public service career, witnessed the rise of a North Americanism that went to the core of his thought. North Americanism was not an organized impulse, nor was it the dominant force driving attitudes and policy in Canada or the United States. But it was on a rising trajectory during Skelton's adult life. North Americanism came from many directions: from the growth of United States power and ambition and the dimming of the British Empire's light and authority; from the resolution of the Canadian-American disputes that had dogged the late nineteenth and early twentieth century; from the sense that a superior North American diplomatic structure was taking shape, with the International Joint Commission (IJC) as both symbol and evidence of an ability to resolve knotty problems co-operatively; and from continental publicists such as J.T. Shotwell and J.W. Dafoe. It came, too, from intensifying links of economics and culture and from the merchants, doctors, engineers, lawyers, bankers, unionists, bureaucrats, academics, entertainers, and athletes who moved effortlessly and increasingly across the border.

When Americans and Canadians turned away from the world in the years between the two world wars, North Americanism took a tighter hold. Sir Robert Falconer, the president of the University of Toronto, wrote in 1925 that North America was the hope of the world: "Fear of force is unknown, vessels of war are not seen on the lakes nor fortifications on the frontier, and such rivalries which exist spring not from incompatible racial ambitions but from legitimate trade between two peoples of mutual affinity and respect." How sad, by comparison, was "the plight of Europe: country set against country, race against race, frontiers watched by suspicious guardians, enclaves and fragments of peoples only tolerated by necessity."[3] Canadians regularly travelled to the League of Nations to read what became known, and not in a complimentary way, as the "Canadian speech," prescribing the IJC's methodologies of investigation, reason, and discussion as a remedy for the world's ills. Canadians, Mackenzie King told the League in 1928, lived "in perfect harmony ... with their neighbour to the south."[4]

From 1935 into the Second World War, the Carnegie Endowment for International Peace, St Lawrence University, and Queen's University convened large and buoyant Canadian-American relations conferences, alternating between Canadian and US sites and drawing on a wide range of expertise from both countries. In 1936 J.T. Shotwell launched Carnegie's series of scholarly examinations of the relationship, which eventually reached twenty-five sober blue volumes. At the first of the Canada–United States meetings, held in upstate New York, J.W. Dafoe, the celebrated editor of the *Winnipeg Free Press*, argued that Canada and the United States constituted a cultural, intellectual, and moral unity, "North American in character and range."[5] That summarized a broad intellectual trend.[6]

By the later 1930s, according to the US Chamber of Commerce, there were eleven non-governmental organizations in the United States pushing for close Canadian-American relations. The Good Neighbor League, organized in 1936, claimed thirty thousand members two years later. US chapters of the Kiwanis Club joined in, arranging an annual Canada–United States Goodwill Week each April. Kiwanis headquarters encouraged the State Department to commemorate officially the signing of the 1817 Rush-Bagot Agreement for the limitation of naval armaments on the Great

Lakes, another of the emblems of continental concord, regularly trotted out by every rhetorician of the Canadian-American relationship on both sides of the border.[7] President Franklin Roosevelt, who admittedly leaned towards such politesse, said that Americans were as one with Canadians as friends and neighbours. They were anything but foreigners.[8]

O.D. Skelton was the exemplar of North Americanism, convinced that Canada and the United States were bound inextricably by economics, ideas, and interests. Adam Shortt, a political economist who became a mentor, promoter, and friend, taught Skelton the North American creed at turn-of-the-twentieth-century Queen's University. For Shortt, the continent was the crucial fact of Canadian economic life. The boundary line between the two countries was imaginary, separating two communities that had far more in common than the people of Ontario and Quebec. Yet that did not mean that Canada was an impossibility. Shortt believed quite the opposite: "the very affinity of Canada and the United States showed that Canada had a separate but equal potential as an economic as well as political entity."[9]

Skelton's practice accompanied Shortt's theory. As a young man, Skelton came to know the United States at first hand as a teenager in Cornwall, on the Canadian-American border, and twice as a graduate student at the University of Chicago, periods separated by a stint as a magazine editor in Philadelphia, in his view the quintessential US city.[10] From his earliest conjectures on Canadian politics, Skelton argued that the United States could not be ignored as a factor in his country's future. Writing to Shortt from the United States in 1902, the twenty-four-year-old reacted angrily to the "Britisher" rhetoric that had captured the Canadian discourse and went against the grain of his North American experience. Deeply concerned that the British Empire's emotional tide could sweep away all the solid nation-building work that had been achieved since Confederation, he was already talking, at a time when it was a long way off, about "Canadian independence" as "the ideal I've always cherished." That fierce and instinctive nationalism was set firmly in the context of what Skelton characterized as the North American "current of destiny." The continent was where Canada's "lasting community of interest" lay, not with "Australia or Timbuctoo, or whatever other part of the map a Jingoistic spree may chance to paint red."[11]

Skelton returned to Queen's University in 1907 and remained there as a political economist and administrator until the early 1920s, taking on the role of a public intellectual who wrote fluidly, wittily, and critically about politics, the economy, and international affairs. The analysis of the United States that emerged from Skelton's commentaries was mixed.[12] He admired the drive, spirit, and optimism of Americans and the widespread and earnest reforming zeal that could throw up Jane Addams, "the world's foremost woman." But the US economic system was unfair, its capitalism the most ruthless and unbridled in existence. Skelton liked the political structure no more. The US Constitution was too rigid, the courts too powerful, the politicians too easily corrupted. He rejoiced in Canada's inheritance from Britain of Cabinet responsibility as the sheet anchor of democracy, where the close connection between executive and Parliament brought efficiency, liberty, and responsiveness. Canadians had another immense political advantage. They displayed a more "slow-going temperament" than Americans, with "greater immunity from waves of '100 per cent' emotionalism."

Skelton was an early enthusiast of the Canada-US Boundary Waters Treaty of 1909 and of the International Joint Commission, which was the accord's centrepiece. The treaty negotiations, involving an equal number of Canadian and American officials, with only a hint of British assistance, had been fair and businesslike. The Americans had tempered their competitive instincts. Agreement had been unanimous. The IJC had investigative and reporting powers and a means to break deadlocks. There was even a clause that allowed the two countries to refer any issue at all to the IJC. "Serious friction between the two democracies which halve the continent," Skelton concluded, "will henceforth be almost as inconceivable as a clash in arms between Alberta and Saskatchewan or New York and New Jersey." North America had given Europe an example of common sense in international relations.

The Canadian public's rejection of the Laurier government's 1911 reciprocity agreement with the United States was a much less happy episode for Skelton, a Liberal Party sympathizer who acted as an advisor to labour minister Mackenzie King on the issue. There were, he asserted, ninety million prosperous English-speaking customers at Canada's doors. Better access to that market, and the competition that accompanied it, would push Canadians to diversify their industrial base and become, perhaps, a greater manufacturing centre than the United States itself. North America was an economic unit, but not a political unit. In fact, freer trade would make for much more of the political unity the nation needed. Nervous distrust of the United States, with Canada's history and scanty numbers, was understandable enough, but a trade agreement was just that and nothing more. When a Canadian farmer sold a bag of potatoes to a New Yorker, he did not throw his country into the bargain.

Nervous distrust, assiduously cultivated, won the day. Skelton lamented that big money and big talk had been able to convince a gullible public that freer trade amounted to national suicide and the end of the British connection. Canadians, it transpired, were not as self-reliant and self-confident as he had hoped and predicted. He kept his sense of humour. He and his anti-imperialist friends had indulged in the gentle art of twisting the British lion's tail, and that had formed a model for the practice of plucking the American eagle's feathers in the great reciprocity debate of 1911.

Skelton was a supporter of Canada's participation in the First World War, but he was not among the critics of the US decision to remain neutral until 1917. He complimented the flexibly opportunistic leadership of President Woodrow Wilson, which brought Americans to the Allied side long before it brought them into the war. US interests and politics, Skelton deduced, kept it out of the conflict, along with "the ideas that drive men on." Those ideas were North American: pacific, co-operative, untainted by power politics or an unsavoury history. Skelton thought the former Republican president, Theodore Roosevelt, an incurable egotist, "prone to demagogic violence," but agreed with him that the continent had its fundamentals in order. Canada and the United States had been fortunate, it was true. The New World did not have the prepossessions and prejudices of the Old, where "specially unfavourable" thinking had taken root. North Americans had similar interests and ideologies that did not compete.

Skelton had no wish to merge the Canadian identity in a political union with the United States. He acknowledged the force of annexationist arguments about the community of North American interests, as well as the undeniable economic and security advantages of union. Yet no material gain could outweigh the powerful urge for autonomy and the "aggressive confidence in our ability ourselves to play whatever role fate may assign." Each country, moreover, was already as large as could be controlled from a single metropolis with efficiency and local freedom. Two experiments in democracy north of the Rio Grande would do the world more good than just one. There was so much to respect in the United States, Skelton concluded in 1920, but it had problems that "we are not over-anxious to share. We wish to work with our neighbors, we must work with them; but we do not think it necessary to sacrifice our nationhood to do so."

The Great War, Skelton could see, gave nationalism a new fire and explosiveness all over the British Empire. In Canada, national feeling could take many forms, one of them inspiring those who wished to remake the British Empire in English Canada's image. Skelton was as disdainful of anglophilia as he was of annexationism. Canadians, he insisted, had "become convinced, rightly or wrongly, some modestly, some bumptiously, that in war or in peace we can hold our own with the men of any other land." A passionate patriotism was on the move, and Canadians ought to separate themselves from Britain with a charter of freedom and nationhood. Independence would deliver what a colony or a fraction of a centralized empire could not possess: a clear-cut and intelligible status in the world and a sense of national responsibility in foreign affairs. Above all, it would unify the country. "We can never have a united country so long as we retain political ties with a country from which only half our people are derived." Only Canada's independence could take the hyphen out of French-Canadian, Irish-Canadian, or Scotch-Canadian.[13]

Mackenzie King engaged Skelton as a foreign policy adviser for the Imperial Conference of 1923 and two years later hired him as deputy minister of the fledgling Department of External Affairs. As disciples of the British Liberal leader, William Ewart Gladstone, the beau ideal of liberal democracy in late-nineteenth and early-twentieth-century Anglo-North American politics, King and Skelton shared the same vision of international affairs. The Gladstonian mission was to eliminate the symbols and substance of inferior colonial status. It was to end imperial domination and to achieve real self-government. It was to move toward a more compassionate and cooperative international community.[14] When Skelton wrote that the British had "a repute for fair play, for devotion to liberty, and for ordered progress that any country may well seek to share,"[15] he was evoking Gladstone's Britain.

There was, even so, a fundamental difference between the leader and his deputy that was never resolved. Mackenzie King at bottom

conceived of Canada as the Britain of the West, a proud outreach of
the best traditions and values of the British homeland. He believed
that a strong and continuing British connection protected Canadians
against influences that could turn the country into the forty-ninth
state of the United States. Declarations of independence were what
Americans did. The vast majority of Canadians were content on
the autonomous middle ground between sovereignty and a British
Empire controlled from the centre. Skelton thought very differently.
Independence was a requirement if Canadians were not to become,
as they had in 1914, the cat's paw of British imperialism. A resolute
North Americanism would ensure against another slide into colonialism. Britain was part of Europe, he insisted, separated from Canada
"by three thousand miles of sea and incalculable differences in culture, in problems, in outlook. We are British North America; Britain
is British West Europe."[16]

In one of his first position papers for King, Skelton strenuously
argued that Canada already had achieved autonomy in its relationship with the United States. Foreign policy was the extension of domestic affairs, the course a country chose in its day-to-day dealings
with other nations, consisting largely of economic questions and
dominated by what one neighbour said or did to another. The country's intimate relationship with the United States was the most natural thing in the world, and over the past fifty years, the Canadian
Parliament and government had consistently widened the range of
Canadian-American issues under their control. Trade, tariffs, immigration, and boundary disputes over power, navigation, and fisheries were matters that half a century ago were considered beyond
Canadian jurisdiction but were no longer so. Although he privately
admitted that the International Joint Commission ought not to be
extolled as a remedy for all the ills of other countries, he cited it as
an example of Canada's "wide measure of control" in its bilateral
relationship with the United States.[17]

It was convenient to contend, given Skelton's predilections, that
Canada was independent where it counted and that the United States
filled most of the Canadian external affairs quotient. That contention masked the reality. Canada, as Skelton knew well and bitterly
regretted, continued to be tied tightly to the mother country. Britain
still mattered most in Canadian foreign policy. His departmental
memoranda over the years reflected this fact. The undersecretary of
state for external affairs was preoccupied by Britain, which remained

the essential fact of Canada's external life until the 1940s. The United States received next to no attention in Skelton's official writings. It was, after all, a good neighbour and, in the larger scheme of things, no threat at all. Skelton administered the Department of External Affairs from 1925 until his death in January 1941. During those sixteen years, he put his dream to one side. He understood that Canadians would not hear of independence quite yet, and he quickly found that the politicians would not either. Instead, he campaigned for a foreign policy grounded in Canadian interests, which began at home and stayed nearby, on the North American continent.

Simple survival stood first on the list of national interests. Canada was a fragile adolescent, Skelton thought, struggling to build an economy, create a distinctive national life, and unify a vast territory. It was a tremendous undertaking: ten million people trying to shape half a continent, with its vast distances, varied economic interests, and mixed racial composition. Canada stretched over an area as large as all of Europe, with problems of communication, social order, development, and regional-cultural difference as difficult to confront as many of the problems the ancient continent had to face. Canada, indeed, had too much geography and complexities from which older, developed, and smaller countries were relatively exempt. Canadians would be lucky if they could complete their own nation-building job without listening to the shout of imperial grandeur or undertaking to do other peoples' work in faraway countries. They did not have the power or knowledge to settle the destinies of countries thousands of miles away. They had no surplus of statesmanship or good fortune to expend elsewhere.[18]

Canada asked nothing, demanded nothing, and owed nothing. It did not have old grudges or new envies. Crusade and conquest were not part of its vocabulary or experience. Nor, except perhaps from the United States, would Canadians get any help from outsiders in meeting their own challenges and difficulties. "We are staggering," Skelton wrote in 1926 when the opportunity arose to sign onto a European security agreement, "under burdens assumed in a war to settle European quarrels, a war in which we sought no gain and found none. Is it not now Europe's part to look after itself? Canada lies side by side for three thousand miles with a neighbour fifteen times as powerful. She is not asking Europe to join in a pact for her security. She knows that not a country on the Continent of Europe would lift its little finger to help if the United States were to attack her. Her security lies in her own reasonableness, the decency of her neighbour, and the steady development of friendly intercourse, common standards of conduct, and common points of view. Why not let Europe do likewise?"[19]

The United States was "a neighbour that any free country in the continent of Europe or elsewhere would thank its stars to have." Within memory great friction had existed, but negative feelings were evaporating. In their place, and on both sides of the border, "there is a realization of common ideals and common interests, a genuine friendliness and increasing understanding, which facilitate agreement on most issues that arise and make it no serious calamity if for the moment agreement is not reached on others."[20] Yet the United States was a competitor as well as a friendly neighbour. Its prosperity and proximity acted as a magnet, pulling Canadians southwards. The American aloofness to Europe was appealing to many people. To be different, to impose on Canadians burdens and commitments arising out of the League of Nations or the British connection, was to risk invidious comparison to the United States. Canada's imperative was to build up a still unfinished country, "with this power of attraction ever present at her side."[21]

The 1930s challenged Skelton's North Americanism. Mackenzie King was defeated in the federal election of 1930, and until 1935 Skelton was employed by R.B. Bennett, a passionate anglophile who believed that Britain's sophisticated diplomats knew best. In the beginning, Bennett wanted no part of Skelton, a celebrated Liberal partisan and independentist, although that quickly changed when the prime minister discovered that his inherited employee was too useful to cast aside. In the second half of the decade, Mackenzie King came back, politically stronger than ever and determined in the final analysis to stand by the mother country. For Skelton, that meant the prospect of another entanglement in Europe, the wrong place for the wrong reasons.

In the Bennett years, Skelton did not stop trying to North Americanize Canadian external policy. During the crisis precipitated by Japan's move against the Chinese province of Manchuria in the autumn of 1931, he sought to align Canada with the tough stance against the Japanese advocated by the United States, while fending off a prime minister who tilted towards the conciliatory approach of the British. This was chaotic enough, but it became publicly so when Bennett's representative at the League of Nations delivered the

Canadian view a year into the Manchurian affair. Unauthorized by Ottawa, the speech had three parts, the first favouring the prime minister's position, the second pouring scorn on the Chinese, and the third reproducing a text provided by Skelton, which warned Japan of the possible consequences of its actions. The deputy minister joked about what the Herbert Hoover administration must be thinking, after having been informed by the Canadian minister in Washington that their northern neighbour was a staunch ally in condemning Japanese aggression. Had the Americans not known, wrote Skelton, "that we Canadians are simple folk, unversed in the ways of diplomatic intrigue, they would have thought we had double-crossed them."[22]

Encouraged by the election of Franklin Roosevelt to the American presidency in 1932, Skelton was soon quietly encouraging a trade deal with the United States. In July 1933, he sent his son Sandy, an expert on Canada-US trade, as an emissary to Secretary of State Cordell Hull. Speaking "personally and unofficially for his father," the young Skelton urged, in the words of a Hull assistant, "the importance of concluding at an early date some form of reciprocal tariff agreement with Canada."[23] When the Canada-US negotiations really got going, too close to the 1935 election for success to be likely, Skelton nevertheless pressed the Americans hard. He repeatedly made the point that they would be far better off reaching an agreement with the Conservatives than the King Liberals, because the high-tariff folk in the Canadian Manufacturers' Association would not be critical of a deal reached by their Tory allies in government. In early October, Skelton expressed his "extreme discouragement" to the American minister in Ottawa, Norman Armour, when the Washington government had been unwilling to consider many of the central demands made by Canada. Armour reported home that Skelton "deeply regretted the trend events had taken as he really felt that the list of concessions his Government had been prepared to make to us, had we been able on our part to present a more 'effective' list, would have resulted in a really constructive and worth-while agreement."[24] There is no indication that Skelton was holding back, knowing that his Liberals would soon be in power and able to reap the rewards of an undoubted political coup.

As soon as the election results were in, and Mackenzie King returned as prime minister, Skelton continued the quest. He did not wait for King's approval to assume the role of his spokesman. In a meeting on 17 October with Armour, Skelton said that the Liberals, always a low-tariff party, would surely want to pick up the negotiations where the previous government had left off. Canada and the United States had reached a "very important crossroads in our relations." If they were able to conclude a commercial agreement sufficiently broad to effect real improvement in the two economies, "then all would be well." If not, how regrettable that would be, particularly at a time when the international order was threatened by Italian aggression against the powerless African country of Ethiopia. Canada would be forced back into the arms of the British, who were ready with commercial offers of their own. Canadians would have no choice but to fall in line with the narrow British plan for "a world-wide British economic Empire whose interests, as progressively developed from London, might soon diverge seriously" from those of the United States. Canada would become a British colony once again, with its economic interests dominated by London and important secondary industries falling by the wayside. As Armour summarized the conversation, Skelton thought it essential to move towards a closer North American political community "and that this would be difficult if the doors to the United States were closed and Canada was told, to all intents and purposes, that we were not interested or at any rate not able to meet them half way and they better throw in their lot with the British."[25] All in all, "it's a fine job," Skelton wrote to his wife from Washington once an agreement was safely in place.[26]

As the world tumbled towards a big war in the later 1930s, Skelton liked to remind King that Canada's foreign policy ought to be as influenced by geography as that of any other country – as much as Britain's, for example. Canadians lived a long way from Europe and Asia, and very close to the United States. North America was a comfortable place. Canada was fortunate in her neighbours – and in her lack of neighbours. America's friendliness and its healthy devotion to its own safety were the most important and most enduring factors in Canadian defence thinking, and the influence of American isolationist sentiment on opinion to the north had to be factored into the strategic equation as well. Even putting the United States aside, any danger of attack on Canada was minor in degree and second-hand both in origin and extent. The rumours of foreign plans to invade Canada and to seize the country's tempting resources were infantile and absurd. The strategic and transportation difficulties of transoceanic invasion were too formidable, and "every potential aggressor has not only potential objects of its ambition many thousands of miles nearer which would be the object of any attack, but potential and actual rivals near at hand whom it could not disregard by launching fantastic expeditions across half the world." But self-defence could not be ignored. It was needed "in appropriate measure, and in self-respecting cooperation with the United States."[27]

These arguments were part of Skelton's rationale for North America and against Europe. He admitted that the world was interdependent and that Canadians could not cut themselves off from contact with events beyond their border. Canada was a trading nation and a democratic one. War, and even preparations for war, put these characteristics in jeopardy.[28] Yet, were Canadians forced to fight Europe's battles again, it would not be for Canadian reasons, for trade or democracy, but for imperial "sentiment and sentimentality, profit and propaganda, old memories and old loyalties."[29] "Canada is supposed never to think of her own interests in foreign policy," he said sarcastically in January 1939.[30]

The gap between Mackenzie King and his deputy widened in the late 1930s. Prompted by Skelton, King sometimes repeated publicly what Skelton wrote privately, and angrily, with its emphasis on what Canada could not be expected to do or might unreasonably be asked to do. But Skelton seemed to King an increasingly negative force, lacking a broader vision of world affairs, a US-style "republican" serving a prime minister who was a proud British monarchist.[31] For the leader, Crown and Country were inseparable. King had always promised himself (and occasionally others) that Canada would support Britain if the call of duty came. When that call came in September 1939 and King unhesitatingly took Canada to war at Britain's side, Skelton reacted with disillusionment and anger. It was doubtful, he claimed in a bitter memorandum that apparently never left his office, that a majority of the people favoured the government's action. There was "a widespread feeling that this is not our war, that the British Government which blundered into it, should have been allowed to blunder out, that it is fantastic and insane for Canadians to allow themselves to be maneuvered and cajoled every quarter century into bleeding and bankrupting this young country because of the age-long quarrels of European hotheads and the futility of British statesmen." At the end of the First World War, Canada had been driving inexorably towards independence. Now, twenty years later, it had been consigned to the imperial display window. Canadians were the "prize exhibit" of the continuing power of the British Empire.[32]

Canadians had tossed their North American heritage to one side, but Skelton was convinced that the setback would be short-lived. He foresaw resentment at first against a neutral United States and more resentment when that country's economy boomed on the backs of those who were doing the fighting. The war, however, would damage Canada, bringing debt and death and division, and the British Empire would fracture further. With Canada weakened, and the British weakened, Canadians would turn towards the United States. "Canada," Skelton confidently predicted, "will definitely become more North American."[33]

Whatever his initial reservations, he committed himself fully to the war effort. Watching with satisfaction as US President Roosevelt tilted his nation in a pronouncedly Allied direction, Skelton wanted more. "True," he wrote at the end of April 1940, "the United States is already giving in many respects as much help as if it were in the war, but its further diplomatic and financial and naval and perhaps air support are powerful potentialities. Our task is twofold: to make effective our own share and to speed in every practical and discreet way the cooperation of the United States."[34]

On 10 May, Germany let loose a sudden strike on France, Belgium, and the Netherlands. Mackenzie King noted in his diary that Skelton's reaction, with an invasion of Britain a distinct possibility, was to demand an all-out effort to assist the British. "He now sees that the real place to defend our land is from across the seas. He did not want the Americans to undertake the protection of our coasts, lest they might not do as much for Britain."[35] Three months later, when King and Roosevelt entered into a Canada-US military alliance at Ogdensburg, Skelton reflected on the North American bonds that had been formed during his time in External Affairs but also on the survival of the world beyond the continent. Ogdensburg, he told the prime minister, "was certainly the best day's work done for many a year. It did not come by chance, but as the inevitable sequence of public policies and personal relationships, based upon the realization of the imperative necessity of close understanding between the English-speaking peoples."[36] "It amuses me a little," King mused, "to see how completely some men swing to opposite extremes. No one could have been more strongly for everything being done for Canada, as against Britain, than Skelton was up to a very short time ago."[37]

Skelton's journey to Britain's side, as it stood on the very edge of its existence, is not really so surprising. He had consistently argued over the years that the world needed both Britain and the United States and good relations between those great powers. He was, moreover, an intellectual citizen of the North Atlantic. "We have many a lesson to learn from England and from the United States," he wrote as a young professor. "We are heirs to the memory of Lincoln, just as the men of Massachusetts may share with Britain and with us Milton and Cromwell."[38] Skelton took his ideas and inspirations where he found them. He was a Wilsonian liberal and a Gladstonian liberal. He despised, on the other hand, professional imperialism, whether it originated in London or Washington.

In purely practical terms, the United States was a more useful example for Canada to follow than Mother Britain, because Americans' "problems and their stage of advance are more nearly ours."[39] More than that, the United States was a partner that shared essentially the same spirit, traditions, and interests, and one that had made a mighty contribution to world peace, internationalism, and "the development of practical good neighborliness" in its North American policies.[40] European states did not enjoy the same good luck in their neighbours as Canada. "It may be that this fortunate position is not due to any special virtue on our part," Skelton speculated before the war, "that it is an accident of geography and of history, but one has only to be in any European country a day to realize how relatively fortunate a position it is, and what folly it would be to throw it away."[41]

The great cause of Skelton's life was Canada's independence from the British Empire, which he judged an impediment to an autonomous national existence. North Americanism aided in the cause. The influence of neighbourhood was an immunization against the effects of blood and tradition, a poisonous combination when cynically exploited by followers of empire, either in Britain or in Canada. For Skelton, Mackenzie King's decision to enter the Second World War at Britain's side was a victory for imperialism and a repudiation of North Americanism. But it was only a temporary check on an irresistibly rising force. The dynamics of the conflict, he rightly predicted but did not live to see, would combine to make Canada more North American.

Skelton was a post-colonial in a colonialist age. Intensely aware of the importance of the United States but of Britain too, influenced mightily by each, a critic and admirer of both, he did not believe that Canada was incomplete without them. In a 1931 comment on an American professor's question, "Does the future of Canada lie with the United States or the United Kingdom?" Skelton replied bluntly: "It does not seem to have occurred to the gentleman ... that the future of Canada might perhaps lie with Canada."[42]

NOTES

This chapter was originally published in the *International Journal* 40, 1 (winter 2004–5) and is reprinted with gracious permission of the *Journal*. The author is grateful to Susan B. Whitney, H. B. Neatby, Robert Bothwell, Stephen Azzi, Philippe Lagassé, and Michael Ryan.

1 Library and Archives Canada (LAC), W.L.M. King fonds, MG 26, King Diary, 30 October 1935.
2 Franklin Delano Roosevelt Presidential Library, Hyde Park, New York, F.D. Roosevelt Papers, PSF, Canada, 1933–1941, Norman Armour to William Phillips, 22 October 1935; United States National Archives, Washington, Department of State Records 611.4231/1273, Armour to secretary of state, 17 October 1935, with memorandum of same date, and Phillips to Roosevelt, 7 November 1935.
3 Sir Robert Falconer, *The United States as a Neighbour from a Canadian Point of View* (London: Cambridge University Press 1925), 242.
4 Norman Hillmer, "The Canadian Diplomatic Tradition," in Andrew Fenton Cooper, ed., *Canadian Culture: International Dimensions* (Toronto and Waterloo, ON: Canadian Institute of International Affairs/Centre on Foreign Policy and Federalism, University of Waterloo 1985), 53; Donald M. Page, "Canada as the Exponent of North American Idealism," *American Review of Canadian Studies*, 3, no. 2 (autumn 1973), 38.
5 J.W. Dafoe, "Final Luncheon," in Walter W. McLaren, Albert B. Corey, and Reginald G. Trotter, eds., *Conference on Canadian-American Affairs Held at The St. Lawrence University, Canton, New York, June 17–22, 1935* (Boston and New York: Ginn and Company 1936), 282–3.
6 Carl Berger, *The Writing of Canadian History: Aspects of English-Canadian Historical Writing, 1900–1970* (Toronto: University of Toronto Press 1976), chap. 6; Allan Smith, "Doing the Continental: Conceptualizations of the Canadian-American Relationship in the Long Twentieth Century," Canadian-American Public Policy Occasional Paper No. 44 (Orono: The Canadian-American Center, The University of Maine 2000), 5–6.

7 Gordon T. Stewart, *The American Response to Canada since 1776* (East Lansing: Michigan State University Press 1992), 182.

8 Smith, 4; J.L. Granatstein and Norman Hillmer, *For Better or For Worse: Canada and the United States to the 1990s* (Toronto: Copp Clark Pitman 1991), 103.

9 Barry Ferguson, *Remaking Liberalism: The Intellectual Legacy of Adam Shortt, O. D. Skelton, W.C. Clark and W.A. Macintosh, 1890–1925* (Montreal and Kingston: McGill-Queen's University Press 1993), 72. See also Berger, *Writing of Canadian History,* 142.

10 O.D. Skelton, "Current Events," *Queen's Quarterly* 15, no. 1 (July–September 1907), 78.

11 Quoted in Norman Hillmer, "The Anglo-Canadian Neurosis: The Case of O.D. Skelton," in Peter Lyon, ed., *Britain and Canada: Survey of a Changing Relationship* (London: Frank Cass 1976), 65.

12 Unless otherwise noted, the material in the six paragraphs that follow is drawn from Skelton's frequent writings in the *Queen's Quarterly* from 1907 to 1921.

13 O.D. Skelton, "Canada, the Empire, and the League," 1, *Grain Growers' Guide,* 25 February 1920, 7, 71–3.

14 Robert Kelley, *The Transatlantic Persuasion: The Liberal-Democratic Mind in the Age of Gladstone* (New York: Alfred Knopf 1969), chaps. 5 and 6, and 416.

15 "Current Events," *Queen's Quarterly,* 17, no. 1 (July–September 1919), 113.

16 LAC, Department of External Affairs fonds, RG 25, A 4, vol. 3419, file 1-1926/22, 17, "The Locarno Treaties," 1 January 1926.

17 "Canada and the Control of Foreign Policy," 1923, King fonds, J 4, vol. 81, file 641, microfilm, reel C-2695, C62245-69.

18 O.D. Skelton, "Imperial Conference 1937," 15 April 1937, King fonds, J 4, vol. 174, file 1631, microfilm, reel C-4264, 123278–85; O.D. Skelton, "Note re Canada's Foreign Policy, Particularly in Relation to the United Kingdom," 1938, ibid., vol. 167, file 1541, microfilm, reel C-4262, C119691-702.

19 "The Locarno Treaties."

20 O.D. Skelton, "Canada and Foreign Policy," 30 March 1938, Department of External Affairs fonds, A 2, vol. 715, file 4, microfilm, reel T-1745, 270–82.

21 O.D. Skelton, "Preliminary Review," 1923, King fonds, J 4, vol. 81, file 641, microfilm, reel C-2695, C62377-87.

22 Norman Hillmer and J.L. Granatstein, *Empire to Umpire: Canada and the World to the 1990s* (Toronto: Copp Clark Longman 1994), 118–22.

23 HSC to file, 8 July 1933, and letter of introduction from Canadian high commissioner to Britain to Hull, 29 January 1933, Department of State Records 611.4231/826.

24 Armour to Hull, 4 October 1935, ibid., 611.4231/1264; see also chargé d'affaires to Hull, 23 September 1935, ibid., 611.4231/1257.

25 Armour to Phillips, 22 October 1935, Roosevelt Papers, PSF, Canada, 1933–41; Armour to Hull, 17 October 1935, with memorandum of same date, and Phillips to Roosevelt, 7 November 1935, Department of State Records 611.4231/1273.

26 LAC, O.D. Skelton fonds, MG 30 D 33, vol. 4, file 23, Skelton to Isabel Skelton, 16 November 1935.

27 Skelton, "Note re Canada's Foreign Policy" and "Imperial Conference 1937"; O.D. Skelton, "Canadian Defence," 14 November 1938, Department of External Affairs fonds, A 2, vol. 754, file 235, microfilm, reel T-1763, 159–63.

28 O.D. Skelton, "Foreign Policy Discussions in London 1935," 15 April 1935, ibid., A 2, vol. 761, file 263, microfilm, reel T-1766, 1–30; speech of Mackenzie King (drafted by Skelton), House of Commons *Debates*, 18 June 1936, in R.A. MacKay and E.B. Rogers, *Canada Looks Abroad* (London: Oxford University Press 1938), 357.

29 Quoted in Norman Hillmer, "The Pursuit of Peace: Mackenzie King and the 1937 Imperial Conference," in John English and J.O. Stubbs, eds., *Mackenzie King: Widening the Debate* (Toronto: Macmillan, 1978), 153.

30 O.D. Skelton, "Recent Developments in Sino-Japanese Conflict," 7 January 1939, King fonds, J 4, vol. 211, file 2011, microfilm, reel C-4281, C144802.

31 King Diary, 13 November 1938; see also 16 December 1936.

32 O.D. Skelton, "Confidential," 10 September 1939, Department of External Affairs fonds, A 2, vol. 726, file 74, microfilm, reel T-1750, 561–73.

33 Ibid.

34 O.D. Skelton, "The Present Outlook," 30 April 1940, Department of External Affairs fonds, A 2, vol. 774, file 353, microfilm, reel T-1791, 1–12.

35 King Diary, 24 May 1940.

36 Skelton Papers, vol. 5, file 4, note of 18 August 1940.

37 King Diary, 24 May 1940.

38 "Current Events," *Queen's Quarterly*, 17, no. 1 (July-September 1909), 79–80.

39 Ibid.
40 O.D. Skelton, *Our Generation: Its Gains and Losses* (Chicago: University of Chicago Press 1938), 50–1.
41 MacKay and Rogers, *Canada Looks Abroad*, 357.
42 Quoted in J.L. Granatstein, *The Ottawa Men: The Civil Service Mandarins, 1935–1957* (Toronto: Oxford University Press 1982), 30.

15

Great Expectations

America's Approach to Canada

STEPHEN J. RANDALL

Geography has made us neighbors. History has made us friends.
Economics has made us partners. And necessity has made us allies.
President John F. Kennedy

The title of this chapter implies that since World War II the United States has had a concrete policy toward Canada that has been general, consistent, and coherent, as distinct from an ad hoc series of policies generated by circumstances as they have arisen.[1] The challenge in attempting to address this question is in part methodological and in part conceptual. Does there need to be consistency and coherence in all facets of foreign policy – politics, economics, defense, and culture – for us to reach a conclusion? Do we need to include all levels of policy and decision making from the president through the operational levels of the Departments of State, Defense, Energy, Agriculture, Labor, Treasury, and Commerce, to note the most important? Or is it sufficient to consider only the presidential level? Where does Congress fit in? Given the importance of several interest groups in the private sector, what is their impact on policy?

It is essential in approaching these and possibly other questions to avoid setting Canada outside the larger context of United States foreign policy. Although the literature, as well as public statements, has over the years been replete with references to a "special" relationship between Canada and the United States, it is misleading to place too much emphasis on a notion that implies uniqueness. US officials have equally identified Great Britain and Mexico as having a "special" relationship with the United States, and Australia has claimed a similar pride of place. Thus, to understand US policy toward Canada, it is critical to delineate and to understand the general nature and direction of US foreign policy since World War II and, in fact, earlier. Although there may well be too many "schools" of thought on US foreign policy, several are instructive. One is the "open-door" school associated with William A. Williams and Walter LaFeber and their students and disciples. Immanuel Wallerstein's world systems theory is a variation on this approach because of his focus on the expansion of the capitalist world system, although he is more explicit about the relationship between the metropolis and the periphery in the system than is either Williams or LaFeber.[2] The open-door school places primacy on economic factors driving policy, although LaFeber posits a critical synthesis among economic, strategic, and ideological forces as they came together to produce an aggressive expansionism in the late nineteenth century. An additional variation on the open-door interpretation is the work of Gabriel Kolko, more explicitly Marxist in its underlying assumption that policy-makers are the product of the capitalist system, the capitalist class, and capitalist values.[3] The most influential interpretation in historical and political science analysis of US foreign policy over the past fifty years has likely been that of the realists, an interpretation associated most closely with Hans Morgenthau and George Kennan.[4] A third group is the more recent "corporatist" school associated with Michael Hogan and Melvyn Leffler. Although Hogan emphasizes economic issues and Leffler national security, both perceive policy to be the product of an integration of public and private power and interest.[5]

Leffler's analysis is especially instructive, since he has sought to provide a bridge between traditional realist, or balance-of-power, analysts and those who contend that domestic economic forces and social structures are the primary factors explaining policy. To Leffler, the national security approach "acknowledges that power plays a key role in the behavior of nations and the functioning of the international system ... It recognizes that an overarching synthesis must integrate questions of political economy, military policy, and defense strategy. It assumes that fears of foreign threats are a consequence of both real dangers in the external environment and ideological precepts, cultural symbols, and mistaken image."[6]

If one accepts this approach and recognizes that there have been fundamental differences between Canadian and US perceptions of

the dangers in the external environment, in the "ideological precepts," and in the "cultural symbols" between the two countries, it
would have been surprising, indeed, had there not been some tension
between the two nations over the past half century and a mixture
of bewilderment and irritation with varying degrees of empathy in
Washington when Canadian policy appeared to digress from expected and desired directions.

The main periodization and primary challenges of US foreign
policy since World War II may also be instructive in understanding
US policy toward Canada. From 1945, through the collapse of the
USSR and the fall of the Berlin Wall, the main preoccupation of US
foreign and defense policy pertained to East-West relations and the
Cold War and their global implications. Insofar as Canada's relationship with the United States can be placed in that Cold War
framework, US officials assumed and worked actively to encourage
Canada's cooperation. That engagement was forthcoming, even if
with some reservations and a varied vision of Cold War challenges:
NATO, the Korean War, NORAD, the continued Canadian-American
military-industrial collaboration, and integration. Those factors all
clearly illustrated the Canadian buy-in to shared values and assumptions about the challenges posed by the Cold War, especially in
its first two decades. Canadian policy toward Castro's Cuba, the
Vietnam War, recognition of the People's Republic of China, and the
Central American crises in the 1980s provided a variation on bilateral solidarity in subsequent decades. Without minimizing the importance of these divergent approaches, it might nonetheless be
suggested that the differences were over means rather than ends, and
this distinction to some extent helps us explain why the differences
were not more contentious. In addition, it is essential to recognize
that the relationship between the two countries over the past half
century has been one managed most effectively at the operational
level: military to military, bureaucracy to bureaucracy, and to a
large extent outside government through the private sector. Jack
Granatstein and Robert Bothwell phrased this most succinctly in
their analysis of Pierre Trudeau's foreign policy: "Canadian-American
relations transcended what presidents and prime ministers, and their
minions, said and did … The private side of Canadian-American
relations largely determined what the public side would discuss."[7]
The bilateral relationship has to some degree been analogous to an
opera, with the political leadership singing the arias, frequently

off-key (the Ronald Reagan-Brian Mulroney duet of "Irish Eyes" comes to mind), and the chorus doing the real work.

US policy toward Canada can most appropriately be characterized as a policy of expectation within the broader contours of US foreign policy. US policy-makers, from the president through the bureaucracy, have consistently and appropriately sought to advance the national interest in bilateral and international relations, whether dealing with Western Europe, the Soviet Union, Asian countries or Canada. US policy-makers throughout the post-1945 era have had as their goal an international order in which the United States held pre-eminent power. Multilateralism and collective security have been sought when they served US goals, the national interest, and American values. If there is any consensus among historians of US foreign policy, it is that policy has been a shifting blend of realism and moralism, a dichotomy that was drawn, much too sharply, early in the history of the republic between George Washington and Thomas Jefferson and in the twentieth century between Theodore Roosevelt and Woodrow Wilson. For US policy-makers to have consciously pursued goals considered inconsistent with the national interest would have been curious indeed. This is not to judge those goals but merely to observe their origins and inherent logic within the American system.

US officials understandably assumed that Canada, as the main trading partner of the United States, its physical neighbour, and the nation perceived rightly or wrongly as the most like it politically, economically, and culturally, would collaborate on the critical foreign policy and defense challenges that faced the Western world after 1945. There was also clearly an expectation that Canada's approach to such issues as trade and foreign investment would coincide with US goals and values. To the extent that Canada has not fulfilled US expectations, those differences have at times reflected conflicting personalities and egos at the presidential and prime ministerial levels, as for instance in the case of John Diefenbaker and John Kennedy, Pierre Trudeau and Richard Nixon, or Jean Chrétien and George W. Bush. At times even underlying clashes of ego, tensions over policy directions have reflected a divergence of perceived national interests and values. Such was the case with the debate over nuclear weapons in the early 1960s, with foreign investment controls in the 1970s and 1980s (including the ill-conceived and ill-fated National Energy Policy), with the Third Option foreign policy,

with cultural protectionism during the US-Canada free trade negotiations in the late 1980s, and in the Liberal Government's decision
in 2003 not to support the US-led coalition in its war on Saddam
Hussein. Canada also adopted a policy toward Castro's Cuba that
was fundamentally distinct from that of the United States, although,
except for the controversy that swirled around the Helms-Burton
legislation, Canada's policy on Cuba evoked little real concern in
Washington, in part because Canadian officials provided the United
States with a window into Cuban affairs.

In general there has been appreciation in Washington that Canada's
foreign policy will from time to time, even on fundamental issues,
differ from that of its southern neighbour. Henry Kissinger captures
that understanding and tolerance in his memoirs on his years in the
Nixon and Gerald Ford administrations as National Security Advisor
and Secretary of State. Kissinger and other senior US officials in the
Nixon administration gave little consideration to Canada. Why
should they have, given the much larger issues of grand policy that
concerned them, including détente, China, the Soviet Union, Vietnam,
and even Chile? Nonetheless, Kissinger and Trudeau clearly shared
mutual intellectual respect, and Kissinger evinced both respect and
understanding of Canada in his memoirs.[8] Kissinger observed with
respect to NATO, for instance, that Canada's "somewhat aloof position combined with the high quality of its leadership gave it an influence out of proportion to its military contribution." On Canadian
foreign and domestic policies more generally, Kissinger commented:
"Canada, in fact, was beset by ambivalences which, while different
from those of Europe, created their own complexities. It required
both close economic relations with the United States and an occasional gesture of strident independence ... Its instinct in favor of a
common defense conflicted with the temptation to stay above the
battle as a kind of international arbiter. Convinced of the necessity
of cooperation, impelled by domestic imperatives toward confrontation, Canadian leaders had a narrow margin for maneuver that they
utilized with extraordinary skill." Alluding particularly to the relationship between Trudeau and Nixon on NATO, anti-ballistic missile
defense issues, and economic relations, Kissinger argued that "United
States-Canadian relations demonstrated that the national interest
can be made to transcend personal sympathies."[9]

What US officials at various levels have said about American
policy toward Canada on specific issues reinforces the accuracy of

Kissinger's assessment. A few examples may suffice. From the early Cold War through the articulation of the Liberal Government's notion of soft power in the 1990s, US officials have generally taken the perspective that, while appreciated, Canada's military capacity and its contribution have been far too insignificant and that a strand of anti-militarism in Canadian politics and political culture has weakened Canadian commitments to international security during and after the Cold War.[10] Such concerns of US officials bracketed the half century after World War II. Former US ambassador Stanley Woodward lamented in 1953, at the time of his retirement, that Canadian nationalism was an impediment to the full realization of bilateral defense cooperation.[11] At the end of the twentieth century and shortly before leaving office, then deputy secretary of defense John Hamre informed a University of Calgary audience in a critical observation on soft power that the "Canadian" notion was meaningless, that the only important power was "boots on the ground." Hamre told an audience at the Calgary Chamber of Commerce during the same visit that in terms of defense capability, "We look to Canada, frankly, with a bit of alarm. We don't see a bottoming out of the sentiment on what needs to be sustained in the defense community ... We are the only country in the world that wants a stronger military power on its border."[12] US frustration with Canada's policy on military cooperation in the early Cold War was evident in the discussion over NATO. US and Canadian postwar aims both converged and diverged in the establishment of the North Atlantic Treaty Organization: the Canadian Liberal governments in the early Cold War were concerned about the broader political and economic development of Europe, and the Truman administration focused on the military containment of the USSR and Communism. Truman's secretary of state, Dean Acheson, thought Canadian policy-makers "incurably inclined toward moralizing in foreign policy and utterly naïve about international power politics" and pushed NATO and Canada toward a purely military, collective security role for NATO.[13]

Further illustration of US concern over Canada's military capacity and commitment were the comments of Deputy Secretary of Defense Rudy de Leon in Ottawa in late September 2000. While complimenting the Canadian contribution to the efforts in Bosnia and Kosovo, de Leon, quoting Secretary of Defense William Cohen, stressed that the disparity in capabilities among the NATO members "if not corrected could in fact threaten the unity of this Alliance." De

Leon noted that the disparity was one reason why NATO launched the Defense Capabilities Initiative at the Washington Summit in 1999, but there was little progress in its aftermath, although US officials were "encouraged by the modest increases in Canada's investment in national security ... and hope that it is the start of a more pronounced trend." He added, "When Canada invests in its military, its foreign and security policy is strengthened, bringing with it a stronger NATO, a stronger security alliance between our nations, and a stronger independent voice for Canada."[14]

A US policy of expectation was clearly evident in the case of Korea and the Korean War. Truman administration officials pressed the initially reluctant Canadian government of William Lyon Mackenzie King as early as 1948 to become involved in the region, first as a member of the UN supervisory commission and then as a partner in the UN coalition, which followed US military intervention after the North Korean invasion of the South in June 1950.[15] What was true of the US desire for Canadian involvement in Korea was equally applicable to the larger notion of continental defense against the Soviet Union, specifically in the US government's insistence on the establishment of the Distant Early Warning system in the Canadian Arctic, with US troops and equipment based on Canadian territory, or the establishment of the US Strategic Air Command airbase at Goose Bay, Newfoundland.[16]

Few if any issues created more tension and, at one stage, outright anger in the White House than the waffling of the Diefenbaker and Lester Pearson governments on the adoption of nuclear weapons, the placement of US-controlled nuclear weapons on Canadian territory, or the failure of the Diefenbaker government to respond immediately and positively to the Kennedy administration's confrontation with the USSR over the placement of Soviet nuclear weapons in Cuba in 1962. The bilateral relationship in the late 1950s and early 1960s was replete with ironies and contradictions. On the one hand, Diefenbaker and Dwight Eisenhower appeared to work together effectively. If anything Diefenbaker was as much a hard-line Cold Warrior and anti-Communist as Eisenhower and the members of his administration, and he strongly supported a range of US policies in the late 1950s. He seems not to have shared the disquiet of some Canadian diplomats over the US focus on a defense policy of massive retaliation, nor was he sympathetic to Fidel Castro and the Cuban Revolution. When Eisenhower administration

officials, in particular Christian Herter, who succeeded John Foster
Dulles as secretary of state, perceived a shift in Canadian policy
away from the adoption of nuclear weapons, they worked hard in an
effort to ensure continued bilateral cooperation on Cold War de-
fenses. They failed, however, to have Diefenbaker's government live
up to its initial commitment on nuclear weapons or even to proceed
with a planned joint air defense exercise. The CIA, in a report on its
intelligence estimate at this stage, "Trends in Canadian Foreign
Policy," captured the level of anxiety in Washington over the direction of Canadian policies. The report fretted that the Diefenbaker
government might take Canada in a direction inconsistent with US
policy goals, focusing more on disarmament, a nuclear test ban,
arms control, and support for the integration of the People's Republic
of China into the United Nations. As I have suggested elsewhere,
"Kennedy and his senior advisers saw the Diefenbaker government,
Howard Green in particular, as willfully oblivious to the threat
posed by Nikita Khrushchev's expansionist Soviet regime."[17]

Relations reached a low point, however, during the Missile Crisis.
The differences between Kennedy and Diefenbaker were in part personal. More importantly, they derived from the Kennedy administration's frustration with the failure of Canadian officials to take a
harder line against Castro in the course of 1961, to impose economic
sanctions and break off diplomatic relations. Since Diefenbaker was
as hostile to Castro as Kennedy was, the differences between the two
governments were more over means than ends. Nonetheless, the ac-
tivist Cold Warriors of the Kennedy administration had no patience
for such subtleties. As National Security Advisor Walt Rostow indicated in his crumpled note carelessly left behind in a wastebasket
after the second Kennedy-Diefenbaker meeting in 1961, the objective of US policy and of the meeting was to "push" the Canadians to
adopt policies toward Asia and Latin America that coincided with
American policy.[18] Even if US officials had been more tolerant of the
desire of the Diefenbaker government to follow a seemingly contradictory policy line, its failure to rally immediately to the US side, as
other US allies had done when confronted by the Soviet military
buildup in Cuba in 1962, would still have been the last straw for
Kennedy. When Kennedy telephoned Diefenbaker early in the crisis
with the request that Canadian NORAD forces be placed on Defcon
3 alert and that Canada support the US position at the United
Nations, Diefenbaker was defensive, uncooperative, and angry, in

particular over the absence of prior consultation.[19] It was the end of any Kennedy administration tolerance for the Diefenbaker government and of US hopes for improved bilateral relations on such issues as nuclear weapons and a stronger Canadian commitment to NATO. Kennedy shifted to Lester Pearson and the Liberals.

There is little if any evidence that the efforts of the Pearson government to promote a negotiated settlement of the Vietnam conflict during the Lyndon Johnson administration were well received in Washington. Former secretary of defense Robert McNamara effectively captures the perspective of the US administration in his memoirs. Commenting on the Christmas bombing pause at the end of 1965, which was perceived to have resulted in increased US casualties, President Johnson was increasingly skeptical about other concessions to Hanoi. McNamara notes that "much to his [Johnson's] annoyance he confronted another such attempt just two months later. This time it originated ... with Canadian Prime Minister Lester Pearson. In March, retired Canadian diplomat and old Far Eastern hand Chester A. Ronning traveled to Hanoi and brought back a message from North Vietnamese premier Pham Van Dong that, if the Americans stopped the bombing 'for good and unconditionally, we will talk.'" McNamara stressed that "many in Washington" distrusted the intent of the message, as well as "Pearson's and Ronning's prior open criticism of Washington's Vietnam policy." McNamara conceded in retrospect that "we were mistaken in not having Ronning at least probe the meaning of Pham's words more deeply."[20]

US trade and foreign investment policy internationally and toward Canada has been consistent throughout the post-World War II years. The goal has been to maximize US access to markets, to encourage other nations to establish and maintain liberal trade and foreign investment regimes, and to work actively to undermine statist economic policies. The US approach was clear in 1947–48, when the governments of Mackenzie King and Harry Truman conducted what were ultimately unsuccessful and initially highly private discussions of a free trade agreement. The draft agreement would have abolished all bilateral tariffs. One State Department memo described what would certainly have been a historic agreement as a "unique opportunity of ... knitting the two countries together – an objective of United States foreign policy since the founding of the Republic."[21] It is within that policy framework that one needs to view the bilateral and then trilateral free trade debates in the late 1980s and

1990s, as well as the current but largely stalled Free Trade Agreement of the Americas initiative. US trade policy has been consistent as well as persistent in seeking to create hemispheric cooperation and solidarity in trade and investment regimes, beginning with a focus on Canadian-American solidarity from the 1930s discussion of reciprocal trade agreements, then expanding that to include Mexico and later the rest of the hemisphere.

No two initiatives of the Trudeau Liberal governments evoked more concern in official as well as private-sector circles than the Foreign Investment Review Agency and the National Energy Policy, although Trudeau's notion of a Third Option foreign policy was also negatively perceived. The underlying objection by US officials was to the evident discriminatory treatment of foreign capital under the regulations. Immediately following the announcement of the NEP by Allan MacEachen in the fall of 1980, officials from President Jimmy Carter's administration flew to Ottawa to express their concern and opposition to the investment and price control provisions in the legislation. The strong concerns expressed by the Carter administration became far more strident under the Reagan presidency a few months later, with official protests presented by Reagan's first secretary of state, Alexander Haig, in early March of 1981 and by US officials during and immediately following President Reagan's meeting with Prime Minister Trudeau in Ottawa that same month. The US position hardened in the course of the year until the Trudeau government backed away from its initiative.[22] Regardless of whether or not there were merits in the NEP, the episode effectively illustrates the consistency of the official US commitment in the post-World War II years to open trade and investment policies and a willingness to play hardball when a country is seen to be deviating from that ideal. The US government perspective that Canada does not take its military commitments sufficiently seriously has been more sharply expressed since the terrorist attacks of 9/11 on New York and Washington. In the aftermath of 9/11 and in view of the ongoing concern over international terrorism, US ambassador to Canada Paul Cellucci was outspoken and persistent in advancing the US government's perspective that Canada was just as much at risk as the United States, that an attack against the United States could have a significant impact on Canadian border cities, and, echoing both Hamre's earlier comments and Canadian critics of Canada's military strength, he stressed that Canada needed an enhanced military capability. "We cannot defend ourselves without Canada's help," he recently informed an audience at the University of Western Ontario. He also observed that although the Canadian government had made a positive contribution to peacemaking in Afghanistan and a financial contribution to rebuilding Iraq, Canadian citizens "do not appear to understand" the need for enhanced security.[23]

The events of 9/11 have sharpened the expectations US officials have concerning Canada's military contribution, and the ambassador's comments notwithstanding, there has been a high level of collaboration between Canadian and US police, intelligence, and military forces. One example was the conclusion in 2002 of the Joint Strike Fighter program between the Pentagon and the Department of National Defense. At the time of the signing of the agreement at the Pentagon, Undersecretary of Defense Peter Aldridge praised the level of bilateral cooperation: "We in the United States government," he observed, "treasure our relationship with our neighbor to the north. This is yet another example of our cooperation across so many different programs. Our cooperation effort on Joint Strike Fighter will reinforce a longstanding and close relationship between our two countries and will serve to strengthen the interoperability of our industrial base."[24]

That is the past. As for the future, any crystal ball is cloudy and mechanically unsound. Any observations can return to haunt the observer if subsequently proved unfounded. At the same time, to understand the future one needs only to look to the past, both distant and more recent. The broad contours of United States foreign policy have been strikingly consistent over the past century, at least since the nation acquired the military and economic capacity to assert its will internationally and the confidence to do so. There have admittedly been shifts between periods of, on the one hand, aggressive international interventionism driven by both messianic zeal and considerations of realpolitik and, on the other hand, briefer periods of retrenchment, apparent isolationism, economic protectionism, even insecurity.

Unless there is a resurgence of Russian capacity internationally or until China achieves the status of a superpower, which it may well do, the United States will continue to be the only nation with the unilateral capacity to impose its will on the rest of the world. That capacity, as Vietnam demonstrated earlier and Iraq and Afghanistan underline now, is largely military and severely constrained by domestic politics in the United States and the cultural, economic, and military realities that prevail in those areas where it seeks hegemony. Europe is also a serious contender once again as a counterbalance to US hegemony. China may well emerge as another contender, and Russia should not be readily discounted. The continued expansion of the European Union, the strength of the European economies, and the general unpopularity of US policies internationally may further constrain the capacity of the United States to act unilaterally or to build the coalitions it needs to achieve its international goals.

In all of this Canada is a minor player and has by all accounts become even less important, given the decline in its military capacity to reinforce its claims to moral superiority. The establishment of the European Union and the clear commitment of Great Britain to Europe have left Canada with little choice except to be a nation of the Americas, something that the Conservative governments of both Mulroney and Stephen Harper appear to have understood. The terrorist attacks on Washington and New York on 9/11 made, and will continue to make for the foreseeable future, security the primary focus of US domestic and international policies, regardless of who occupies the White House. The less well-loved US policy becomes internationally, the stronger will be US pressure on Canada for support in tangible as well as symbolic ways, and the less tolerant the United States will be of Canada's aspirations to assert its differences.[25]

As well, several factors have undermined the capacity of the United States to claim omnipotence internationally. One is the contrast between the overwhelming ability of the United States to wage successful war and the difficulty it has had in crafting the postwar peace, as evidenced in Afghanistan and Iraq, although it is also debatable that there has been military success in Afghanistan. A second factor is the frustration the United States, and indeed other nations, have experienced in containing terrorism at home and abroad. The country has the capacity to bring an iron fist down on a nation like Iraq, but it is rife with uncertainty and anxiety over where the next terrorist attack on American territory will occur. The US and Canadian economies, including their electric energy grids and their supply of oil and natural gas, are so closely integrated that US and Canadian national interests require their protection against internal and external threats. Past and current pressures to harmonize the two economies

and to design compatible immigration and refugee policies and produce effective integration of defense forces and effective border
regulation will almost certainly intensify. The weaker Canada is on
the international stage in peacemaking and peacekeeping, the weaker will be its leverage in dealing with its bilateral relationship with
the United States.

We will see continued integration and collaboration at both the
policy and the operational levels between Canadian and US military
officials. One step the US government has taken to improve the balance in defense capabilities among its allies, including Canada, has
been to continue to facilitate industrial cooperation on defense, for
instance through the liberalization of the US system for sharing technology. The Defense Trade Security Initiative was the first major re-
form to the US export control system since the Cold War. It was
designed to remove a number of US licensing requirements, in order
to permit military technology to be shared more easily and to
strengthen the collective protection of that technology.

The Canadian rejection of formal involvement in the National
Missile Defense System was one of the most recent Canadian decisions that bewildered American policy-makers. President Clinton
deferred a deployment decision on the system until George W. Bush
took office, but by the end of Bush's first term Canada had opted
out. Regardless of the merits of the missile initiative and its implications for the Anti-Ballistic Missile Treaty, the perspective of senior
US officials on the reluctance of Canada to make a commitment at
an early stage of the program has meant that Canada was "deprived
... of influence on the system's design and architecture especially as
it may or could affect the defense of Canada."[26]

US expectations toward Canada will remain as they have been in
the past. President Bush commented in a press conference at the
January 2004 Special Summit of the Americas in Monterrey, Mexico,
following his meeting with Prime Minister Paul Martin, that he
"understood why people disagreed with the decision" he took to
invade Iraq.[27] The fact that Canada was one of the decisive non-
participants in that adventure, a decision that was premised on what
were seen to be Canadian values, combined with the evident personal chill between the two leaders, left the two nations by the end
of 2008 at one of the lowest points in their bilateral relationship.
Canadians appear to have marched in relief to cast their symbolic
ballots for Barack Obama in November 2008, evidently believing

that his values were somehow representative of Canadian values as well. One year into the administration of the new Democratic President, it remains to be seen if that premise was well-founded. Kissinger's analysis of relations during the Nixon and Trudeau era have as much resonance for the present and future as they did for his own political generation. US policy-makers, whether Democratic or Republican, will have expectations of Canada as a close neighbour and a close ally with highly integrated economies. Some US leaders may even take Canadian foreign policy seriously. The more subtle among them will also understand what Kissinger understood, that Canada is "beset by ambivalences," that its leaders will be "convinced of the necessity of cooperation" even if domestic politics, fueled by perceived differences over local, regional, and national interests from softwood lumber and salmon fisheries to continental missile defense systems, will continue to contribute to bilateral disputes. As in the past, the more meaningful aspects of the bilateral relationship are more likely to be invisible on the national news channels or the front pages of the print media, with the constancy of the relationship on both sides continuing to be driven largely by the bureaucracies and the private sector.

NOTES

The author would like to express appreciation to Ms Jillian Dowding, Masters in Strategic Studies, for her collection of data and for her insights offered during the preparation of this chapter.

1 There are few scholarly efforts to explore the broad sweep of US policy toward Canada with the focus specifically on the United States: see especially Gordon T. Stewart, *The American Response to Canada since 1776* (East Lansing: Michigan State University Press 1992); Adelgard Mahant and Graeme S. Mount, *Invisible and Inaudible in Washington: American Policies toward Canada* (Vancouver: University of British Columbia Press 1999); more focused is Lawrence Aronsen, *American National Security and Economic Relations with Canada, 1945–1954* (Westport: Praeger 1997). There is, nonetheless, a misconception among many scholars that the historical and political-science literature in Canadian-American relations does not address sufficiently the nature of US policy. Various studies by, among others, Jack Granatstein, Robert Bothwell, R.D. Cuff, David Bercuson, Aronsen (cited above), and John H. Thompson and Stephen

Randall deal specifically and extensively with US policy and draw on US
archival sources. Where there is unquestionably a deficiency in the treatment of US policy toward Canada is in the US foreign policy literature
written by US scholars. Except for analyses of such specific events as the
Alaska Boundary Dispute, one would search in vain in most of the standard foreign policy literature for references to, let alone sustained analysis
of, the US relationship with its major world trading partner, Cold War
ally, and sharer of the world's longest undefended, but now "smart," border. See, for instance, Walter LaFeber, *The American Age* (New York:
Norton 1989); Alexander DeConde, *A History of American Foreign
Policy*, 2d ed. (New York: Scribner's 1971); Thomas McCormick,
America's Half-Century: United States Foreign Policy in the Cold War
(Baltimore: Johns Hopkins 1989).

2 William A. Williams, *The Tragedy of American Diplomacy*, 2d ed., rev.
(New York: Dell 1972); Walter LaFeber, *The New Empire* (Ithaca: Cornell
University Press 1962); Immanuel Wallerstein, *The Modern World System*
(New York and London: Academic Press 1974); *The Capitalist World
Economy* (Cambridge: Cambridge University Press 1979).

3 Gabriel Kolko (with Joyce Kolko), *The Limits of Power: The World and
United States Foreign Policy, 1945–1954* (New York: Harper 1972).

4 Hans Morgenthau, *Politics among Nations: The Struggle for Power and
Peace*, 5th ed. (New York: Knopff 1978); George Kennan, *American
Diplomacy 1900–1950*, rev. ed. (Chicago: University of Chicago Press
1984).

5 Michael J. Hogan, *The Marshall Plan*; "Corporatism," in Michael J.
Hogan and Thomas Paterson, eds., *Explaining the History of American
Foreign Relations* (Cambridge 1991); Melvyn Leffler, *A Preponderance of
Power: National Security, The Truman Administration and the Cold War*
(Stanford: Stanford University Press 1992).

6 Leffler, "National Security," in Michael J. Hogan and Thomas Paterson,
eds., *Explaining the History of American Foreign Relations* (New York:
Cambridge University Press 1991), 203.

7 J.L. Granatstein and Robert Bothwell, *Pirouette: Pierre Trudeau and
Canadian Foreign Policy* (Toronto: University of Toronto Press 1991), 48–9.

8 Granatstein and Bothwell capture this relationship most effectively in
Pirouette. See, in particular, 48–9.

9 Henry Kissinger, *White House Years* (Boston, Toronto: Little Brown
1979), 383.

10 The most sustained critique of Canadian military policy, however, is provided by Canadian historian J.L. Granatstein in a number of publications,

including, among others, *Who Killed the Canadian Military?* (Toronto: Phyllis Bruce Books 2004); "The Importance of Being Less Earnest: Promoting Canada's National Interests through Tighter Ties with the US" (C.D. Howe Institute, 21 October 2003).

11 Woodward to Dean Acheson, 13 January 1953, Woodward papers, Truman Presidential Library.

12 US Department of Defense, Speeches, Deputy Secretary of Defense, John J. Hamre, Calgary Chamber of Commerce, 18 February 2000, located at http://www.defenselink.mil/speeches (12 April 2004).

13 John H.Thompson and Stephen Randall, *Ambivalent Allies,* 3d ed. (Athens: University of Georgia Press 2002), 193.

14 US Department of Defense, Rudy de Leon address in Ottawa, 28 September 2000, located at www.defenselink.mil (1 April 2004).

15 Ibid., 193.

16 Ibid., 198–9.

17 Ibid., 217.

18 Ibid., 221.

19 Knowlton Nash, *Kennedy and Diefenbaker: Fear and Loathing across the Undefended Border* (Toronto: McClelland and Stewart 1990), 194–5.

20 Robert S. McNamara, *In Retrospect: The Tragedy and Lessons of Vietnam* (New York: Random House 1995), 247–8.

21 Cited in Robert Cuff and J.L. Granatstein, "The Rise and Fall of Canadian-American Free Trade, 1947–48," *Canadian Historical Review* 57, no. 4 (1977): 469, 473.

22 Stephen Clarkson provides a colourful version of these events in *Canada and the Reagan Challenge: Crisis and Adjustment, 1981–85* (Toronto: James Lorimer 1985).

23 18 March 2004, *CBC News,* www.cbc.ca.

24 American Forces Information Services, "Canada Joins Strike Fighter Effort," 7 February 2002.

25 Former foreign minister and prime minister the Right Honourable Joe Clark expressed a similar assessment in his closing remarks to the annual meeting of the Canadian Institute of International Affairs, Calgary, 28 March 2004.

26 Cited in Granatstein, "The Importance of Being Less Earnest," 23.

27 US Office of the Press Secretary, 13 January 2004. Interestingly, the photographs accompanying the press release show President Bush not with Prime Minister Martin but with the president of Argentina, the Argentinian flag prominently hanging adjacent to the Stars and Stripes behind the presidents.

Contributors

MICHAEL BEHIELS is professor of Canadian history at the University of Ottawa and holder of the University Research Chair: Canadian Federalism and Constitutional Studies. He is a writer, public affairs commentator, and consultant on contemporary Canadian political, ideological, and constitutional developments. Professor Behiels has authored several books, including the seminal *La Francophonie canadienne, renouveau constitutionel et gouvernance scolaire* (Ottawa University Press 2005); *Canada's Francophone Minority Communities: Constitutional Renewal and the Winning of School Governance* (MQUP 2004); and *Prelude to Quebec's Quiet Revolution: Liberalism versus Neo-Nationalism, 1945–1960* (MQUP 1985). He has authored dozens of chapters in books and is currently working on "History of Canada's Charter of Rights and Freedoms, 1960–1982."

RUTH COMPTON BROUWER is professor of history Emerita, King's University College, and adjunct research professor, Department of History, University of Western Ontario. She has published two books: *Modern Women Modernizing Men: The Changing Missions of Three Professional Women in Asia and Africa, 1902–69*, and *New Women for God: Canadian Presbyterian Women and India Missions, 1876–1914*, as well as numerous articles on women and missions. Her current research deals with CUSO, the first Canadian NGO to undertake development work from a secular stance and in postcolonial contexts.

GREG DONAGHY is head of the Historical Section and deputy director, Policy Research Division, Foreign Affairs and International Trade Canada. He is general editor of the series *Documents on Canadian External Relations*, as well as editor of six volumes in this series. Most recently, he has edited *Contradictory Impulses: Canada and Japan in the 20th Century* (with Patricia Roy; UBC 2008) and *Architects and Innovators: Building the Department of Foreign and International Trade, 1909–2009* (with Kim Richard Nossal; MQUP 2009). His publications also include *Tolerant Allies: Canada and the United States, 1963–1968* (MQUP 2002).

ROBIN FISHER is provost and vice-president academic at Mount Royal University in Calgary, Alberta. His scholarly interests are in the history of Native people in British Columbia and in comparisons with the United States, New Zealand, and Australia. He has also written on early European exploration of the Northwest Coast and the political history of British Columbia. His first book, *Contact and Conflict: Indian European Relations in British Columbia, 1774–1890*, won the John A. Macdonald prize for Canadian History, and *Duff Pattullo of British Columbia*, the Dafoe prize for writing contributing to Canadian history. In his current administrative position he writes more memos than history, but his next project will be a biography of the anthropologist Wilson Duff.

RACHEL LEA HEIDE, an air force historian, has spoken and published on the subjects of air force organization, training, leadership, morale, accident investigation, professionalization, civil-military relations, and government policy between World War I and the early Cold War period. She has also written on topics of present-day defence policy, peacekeeping intelligence, expeditionary air forces, counterinsurgency, and terrorism and counter-terrorism. She earned a PHD in history from Carleton University, where her dissertation was entitled "The Creation of a Professional Canadian Air Force, 1916–1946." Heide is a defence scientist/strategic analyst with Defence Research and Development Canada's Centre for Operational Research and Analysis.

NORMAN HILLMER is professor of history and international affairs at Carleton University. Most recently, he is the author of *Canada's International Policies: Agendas, Alternatives, and Politics* (with Brian W. Tomlin and Fen Osler Hampson) and *Empire to Umpire: Canada and the World into the Twenty-First Century* (with J.L. Granatstein). He has won several teaching, publishing, and research prizes, including the Canada-Japan Prime Minister's Award and, twice, the Marston LaFrance Research Fellowship. He was the 2008 O.D. Skelton Memorial Lecturer of the Department of Foreign Affairs and International Trade Canada. Professor Hillmer is completing a biography of Dr Skelton.

JENNIFER MACLENNAN holds the D.K. Seaman Chair in the College of Engineering, University of Saskatchewan. She has written several standard texts in communications and many papers on professional communication. Much of her career has been devoted to developing the communication skills of professional engineers through teaching, workshops, and textbooks, as well as professional papers. Her principal research interests include the rhetoric of cultural identity, the theories of Northrop Frye, and teaching as rhetorical practice. She is also a past president of the Canadian Society for the Study of Rhetoric.

BRUCE MUIRHEAD is professor in the Department of History at the University of Waterloo and associate dean of Arts, Graduate Studies and Research. As well, he is a senior fellow at the Centre for International Governance Innovation in Waterloo, Ontario. He has written extensively on Canadian trade negotiations since World War II, as well as Canadian politics, diplomacy, and economic development. Muirhead is currently working on several projects focusing on Canadian development assistance, including an SSHRC-funded history of Canadian official development assistance from 1945 to 1984. Along with Ron Harpelle, he is the author of *The International Development Research Centre: Forty Years of Research for Development* (2010). He is also the co-editor, with Ron Harpelle, of *Long-Term Solutions for a Short-Term World: Canada and Research Development* (2010).

TAMMY NEMETH is an independent historian living in the south of France. Her dissertation manuscript, "Continental Drift: Canada-US Oil and Gas Relations," is being considered for publication by Texas A&M University Press. Dr Nemeth is the author of several articles on Canadian-American oil and gas policy, including a forthcoming article for the hundredth anniversary of DFAIT titled "Conflicting Visions? Pierre Trudeau, External Affairs, and Energy Policy," eds. Greg Donaghy and Michael Carroll (Calgary: University of Calgary Press 2010); and "Duel of the Decade," in *Alberta Formed, Alberta Transformed*, eds. Michael Payne, Donald Wetherell, and Catherine Cavanaugh (Calgary: University of Calgary Press 2007). She has twice won the Petroleum History Society's Article of the Year Award, in 2002 and 2006. While raising two young children, Dr Nemeth is currently writing an article on the energy policy-making processes of Presidents Richard Nixon and Gerald Ford and also planning a book on the energy policies of the Trudeau government.

ROGER L. NICHOLS, a Wisconsin native, received his PHD in American history from the University of Wisconsin. Currently he is professor of history and affiliate professor in American Indian stud-ies at the University of Arizona. His scholarship focuses mainly on frontier and Western America, and comparative Indian affairs in the United States and Canada. Past president of the Pacific Coast Branch, American Historical Association, his most recent books include *Indians in the United States and Canada: A Comparative History* (Nebraska 1998); *American Indians in US History* (Oklahoma 2003); *Indian: Past and Present* (Oklahoma 2008); and *Natives and Strangers* (Oxford: Dinnerstein & Reimers 2010).

GALEN ROGER PERRAS, PHD (University of Waterloo), is as-sociate professor of History at the University of Ottawa. He spe-cializes in US diplomatic and military history and US-Canada relations. His major publications include the monographs *Franklin Roosevelt and the Origins of the Canadian-American Security Alliance, 1933–1945* (Praeger), and *Stepping Stones to Nowhere: The Aleutians Islands, Alaska, and American Military Strategy, 1867–1945* (UBC Press). His current project deals with salmon wars in the North Pacific and international efforts to restrain Japan prior to World War II.

STEPHEN J. RANDALL is professor of history at the University of Calgary and a fellow with the Canadian International Council, with the Canadian Defense and Foreign Affairs Institute, and with the Centre for Military and Strategic Studies at the University of Calgary.

An elected member of the Royal Society of Canada, Professor Randall held the Imperial Oil-Lincoln McKay chair in American Studies (1989–97) and served as dean, Faculty of Social Sciences, at the University of Calgary (1994–2006). He held previous appointments at McGill University (1974–89) and the University of Toronto (1971–74). He was awarded the Grand Cross Order of Merit by the Presidency of Colombia (2000) for his academic contributions to understanding inter-American relations and Colombian foreign policy. He held the Fulbright Chair in North American Studies at American University in 2007. He is the author of a number of books, among them *The Diplomacy of Modernization: The United States and Colombia 1920–1940* (1977); *United States Foreign Oil Policy: For Profit and Security* (1985); *United States Foreign Oil Policy since World War I* (2005) and *Hegemony and Interdependence: Colombia and the United States* (1992), both of which have also been published in Spanish; and *An International History of the Caribbean Basin* (1997, with Graeme S. Mount). His most recent books are *Canada and the United States: Ambivalent Allies* (4th edition 2008), with John H. Thompson, and the authorized biography of former Colombian president Alfonso López Michelsen: *Su Vida, Su Epoca* (Bogotá 2007).

STÉPHANE ROUSSEL is currently an associate professor in the Department of Political Science at the Université du Québec à Montréal (UQAM) and Canada Research Chair in Canadian Foreign and Defence Policy. His most recent publications include *Politique internationale et défense au Canada et au Québec* (Presses de l'Université de Montréal 2007; with Kim Richard Nossal and Stéphane Paquin); *Culture stratégique et politique de défense; l'expérience canadienne* (Athéna 2007), and *L'aide canadienne au développement* (Presses de l'Université de Montréal 2008; with François Audet and Marie-Eve Desrosiers).

PHILIP V. SCARPINO is professor of history at Indiana University/ Purdue University, Indianapolis; director of the Graduate Program in Public History, and director of Oral History at Indiana University's Tobias Center for Leadership Excellence. His areas of expertise are historic preservation, oral history, public history, and environmental history, and his related publications are *Great River: An Environmental History of the Upper Mississippi River, 1890–1950*

(University of Missouri Press 1985); "Large Floodplain Rivers as Human Artifacts: A Historical Perspective on Ecological Integrity" (US Geological Survey, Special Refereed Report, 1997); "Environmental Diplomacy: The Great Lakes Water Quality Agreement of 1972," in *Environment Atlas* (Routledge 2003); "Interpreting Environmental Themes in Exhibit Format," in Martin Melosi and Philip Scarpino, editors, *Public and Environmental History* (Krieger Press 2004); "Great Lakes Fisheries: International Response to the Decline of the Fisheries and the Lamprey/Alewife Invasion," in Terje Tvedt and Richard Coopey, editors, *A History of Water, volume 2, The Political Economy of Water* (I.B. Tauris 2006). Gray literature: "Cultural Resources on Isle Royale National Park (Lake Superior): An Historic Context," funded through a grant from the United States National Park Service (2010). Work in Progress: *An Environmental History of the Great Lakes: A Comparison of Canadian and US Perspectives*, a book-length study that will focus on the late nineteenth century to the present; an article for a special issue of the *George Wright Forum*, based on a cultural resources study of Isle Royale National Park.

REGINALD C. STUART is professor of history and political and Canadian studies (and former dean of Arts and Science) at Mount Saint Vincent University in Halifax, Nova Scotia. He has taught and published widely and comments regularly in the media on US and Canadian- American history and affairs. In 2004 he held a Canada-US Fulbright Fellowship at the Canada Institute, Woodrow Wilson International Center for Scholars, in Washington, DC He is the author of several books, including *Civil-Military Relations during the War of 1812* (2009); *Dispersed Relations: Americans and Canadians in Upper North America* (2007); *United States Expansionism and British North America, 1775–1871* (winner of the 1990 Albert C. Corey prize); *War and American Thought: From the Revolution to the Monroe Doctrine* (1982); and *The Half-way Pacifist: Thomas Jefferson's View of War* (1978).

Index